COMPLIANT BEHAVIOR

COMPLIANT BEHAVIOR

Beyond Obedience to Authority

Edited by
Max Rosenbaum, Ph.D.
*Co-director, American Short-Term
Therapy Center
New York City*

HUMAN SCIENCES PRESS, INC.
72 FIFTH AVENUE,
NEW YORK, N.Y. 10011

Copyright © 1983 by Human Sciences Press, Inc.
72 Fifth Avenue, New York, New York 10011

All rights reserved. No part of this work may be reproduced or utilized in any form or by any means, electronic or mechanical, including photocopying, microfilm and recording, or by any information storage and retrieval system without permission in writing from the publisher.

Printed in the United States of America
3456789 987654321

Library of Congress Cataloging in Publication Data
Main entry under title:

Compliant behavior.

   Includes bibliographies and index.
   1. Conformity—Addresses, essays, lectures. 2. Compromise (Ethics)—Addresses, essays, lectures. 3. Authority—Addresses, essays, lectures. 4. Obedience—Addresses, essays, lectures. 5. Repression (Psychology)—Addresses, essays, lectures. 6. Autonomy (Psychology)—Addresses, essays, lectures. I. Rosenbaum, Max, 1923–
HM291.C625 1983   303.3'6   LC 82-21158
ISBN 0–89885–115–7

To my mother—

Who tragically lost her hearing, but taught me to listen to other languages.

The only thing necessary for the triumph
of evil is for good men to do nothing

The people never give up their liberties
but under some delusion

Edmund Burke

CONTENTS

Introduction by Max Rosenbaum   11
Contributors   23

1. COMPLIANCE   25

    Max Rosenbaum

    References   47
    Suggested Readings   49

2. COMPLIANCE AND CONFORMITY IN AN AGE OF SINCERITY   50

    Kurt W. Back

    Ethics, Politics, and the Psychology of
        Compliance   50
    Sincerity and Individualism   53
    The Religion and Politics of Sincerity   55
    The Language of Sincerity   58
    The Role of Rhetoric   59
    Persuasion   63
    Social-Psychological Theories   64
    Compliance in the Laboratory   71

	Psychotherapy	72
	Conclusion	73
	References	74
3.	COMPLIANCE? BETWEEN FREEDOM AND COMPULSION	77

Raymond Battegay

The Conflict of Norms	77
The Necessity for a Continuously Renewed Decision	78
A New Kind of Superego	79
Compliance to a Group	81
The Longer Arm of a Lever	82
The Educational System	84
The Protecting Group	85
Compulsion and Freedom	86
The Point of View of Psychoanalysis	87
Dependence on Neurophysiological Conditions	88
The Influence of the Past	88
Freedom by Reason and Consciousness	89
Chance or Necessity	90
The Human Responsibility Towards the Law	91
Freedom and Compulsion in Education	92
Compulsion and School Systems	93
From Outside Motility to Inner Motion	94
Restriction of Freedom and Aggression	95
Freedom in Games	97
Psychotropic Drugs: A Help?	98
The Freedom of the Mentally Ill Patient	99
Obedience	100
Security and Free Creativity	101
Conclusion	103
References	104

4.	RELIGION AND COMPLIANCE	107

E. Mansell Pattison

Historical Perspectives	107
The Definition of Religion	114

	Religion and Cultural Compliance	115
	Religion and Social Network Compliance	118
	Religious Compliance and the Family	126
	Religious Compliance and the Individual	131
	Conclusion	134
	References	134
5.	THE HEALTHY SIDE OF COMPLIANCE	137

Joseph A. Braun

External and Internal Compliance	138
The Extrinsic and Intrinsic Institution	139
A Basis for Unhealthy Compliance	142
Compliance in Service of Fidelity and Love	143
Compliance in Service of Priorities and Creativity	145
Conclusion	147
References	147

6. DEMONIC POSSESSION: A SOCIAL PSYCHOLOGICAL ANALYSIS — 149

Nicholas P. Spanos

Characteristics of the Demonically Possessed	149
Psychiatric Interpretations	154
A Social Psychological Interpretation	162
Implications	183
References	188
Footnotes	195

7. THE CONTROL OF CONDUCT: AUTHORITY VS. AUTONOMY — 199

Thomas S. Szasz

Control	200
Power	202
Principles for Regulating Social Relations	204
Footnotes	205

8. SUMMARY OF REMARKS BY JOHN DEAN OCTOBER 29, 1977, WALDORF-ASTORIA HOTEL, NEW YORK CITY — 206

Max Rosenbaum

9. COMPLIANCE OR SELF-FULFILLMENT? THE CASE OF
   ALBERT SPEER   213

   Michael I. Selzer

   Footnotes   227

10. THE GUYANA INCIDENT: SOME GROUP DYNAMIC
    CONSIDERATIONS   229

    Hugo J. Zee

    References   241

    EPILOGUE   243

    Max Rosenbaum

    References   244

Index   245

INTRODUCTION

Max Rosenbaum

It is the decade of the 1980's, and we are all closer to George Orwell's *1984*. The political climate of the United States is moving toward conservatism, and many parts of the world are in ferment. Moslem fundamentalism for example, has come to the fore with an intensity that would have been deemed inconceivable just 5 years ago. The idealistic dreams of post-World War II have been rudely interrupted by a resurgence of far-right political activity in many parts of the world. Terrorism is the order of the day.

This is a time during which people seem to be looking for easy answers, or at least answers that will give them immediate relief to pressing problems. In spite of intermittent spurts of concern, there is a sense of apathy in the American population, and perhaps this is a warning-sign that people appear all too ready to leave major decisions to others.

What paradigm should we use in attempting to understand why people comply to others and give up their individuality? Shall we use the paradigm of terror and power? Orwell, in his book, *1984*, sees the totalitarian need to control as the need for *power:*

> ... At those moments his secret loathing of Big Brother changed into adoration, and Big Brother seemed to tower up, an invincible, fearless protector, standing like a rock against the hordes of Asia. (Orwell, 1949, p. 16)
>
> ... the face of Big Brother, black-haired, black mustachio'd, full of power and mysterious calm. (Orwell, 1949, p. 17)
>
> ... Power is not a means; it is an end. One does not establish a dictatorship in order to safeguard a revolution; one makes the revolution in order to establish the dictatorship. The object of persecution is persecution. The object of torture is torture. The object of power is power. (Orwell, 1949, pp. 266–267)

It is worth noting that Henry Ford, one of the major figures in the industrialization of America, was ruthless in his treatment of his employees. He considered himself a completely moral man, and therefore justified his definition of virtue: Temperance and clean living (as he defined it). He sent private investigators into the homes of his employees to check on their lifestyles. The not too subtle warning was that his employees were to live "morally" or they would be fired from the Ford Motor Company. Henry Ford followed the principle of John Calvin: He was the leader and carried out his definition of God's mandate. His concept of the Ford automobile, the same color, size, and design, while praised by industrial engineers as the epitome of American industrialization, bears an uncanny resemblance to the automobile that Hitler later ordered to be designed for the German people—the Volkswagen (people's wagon), all the same color, size, and design. But Ford's story is not unique: the history of American industry details the story of industrial leaders who were completely totalitarian in their treatment of employees.

In an effort to understand compliance to such totalitarianism, perhaps we could use Hannah Arendt's theories about authority and compliance and power

> Power is what keeps the public realm, the potential space of appearance between acting and speaking men, in existence. . . . While strength is the natural quality of an individual seen

in isolation, power springs up between men when they act together and vanishes the moment they disperse. (Arendt, 1958, p. 200)

... The only indispensable material factor in the generation of power is the living together of people (Arendt, 1958, p. 201)

Or shall we use the paradigm of *a need to belong*? It was in 1978 that the mass poisoning occurred in Jim Jones' commune in Guyana, along with the airstrip murder of Congressman Leo Ryan, and yet it all seems so long ago. The transcript of the recording of the final 43 minutes of mass deaths at Jonestown, Guyana, on November 18, 1978 begins with Jones saying to his followers: "I've tried my best to give you a good life." It appears that he was sincere in what he said, but the fact is that mass deaths did occur following his remarks. Can Pattison's chapter help us shed light on the need to belong and the religious manifestations of this need?

When I first conceived of this book, my major concern was with the *negative* impact of compliance. The horrors of World War II and Hitler's impact on the world were much on my mind. The brutalities that later occurred in Vietnam seemed to confirm my concerns about blind obedience and compliance. But as I thought about the problem more and more, I began to wonder about those people who comply thoughtfully—even with a degree of perceptiveness and compromise. The major groups that came to my mind were the military and the religious. The military commitment to obedience and compliance has been well documented, and I decided to invite a student of the "religious," who in his practice of psychodynamic psychotherapy with clergy, observes both the unhealthy and healthy aspects of compliance to contribute here. Thus, Braun's chapter is concerned with this problem and touches upon Pattison's work and observations.

Arendt, in her studies of the totalitarian state (1966), noted that:

"The chief qualification of a mass leader has become unending infallibility; he can never admit an error." (pp. 348–349)

> Mass leaders in power have one concern which overrules all utilitarian considerations: to make their predictions come true. The Nazis did not hesitate to use at the end of the war the concentrated force of their still intact organization to bring about as complete a destruction of Germany as possible in order to make true their prediction that the German people would be ruined in case of defeat. (p. 349)
>
> The propaganda effect of infallibility, the striking success of posing as a mere interpreting agent of predictable forces, has encouraged in totalitarian dictators the habit of announcing their political intentions in the form of prophecy. (p. 349)

When we consider what happens to a group of people in a totalitarian society, it is pertinent to note Arendt's comment about the importance of total terror as a vehicle for social control in totalitarianism. Arendt states:

> But total terror leaves no arbitrary lawlessness behind it and does not rage for the sake of some arbitrary will . . . It substitutes for the boundaries and channels of communication between individual men a band of iron which holds them so tightly together that it is as though their plurality has disappeared into One Man of gigantic dimensions. (pp. 465–466)

Recently, I took part in a property owners' meeting at which some ecological problems and treatment of lake water were being discussed. Almost the entire group kept insisting that they wanted a definite answer regarding the problem from the individual who was responsible for treating certain weed growth in the lake water. Although it was obvious that no definite answer could be given, the stress was upon an *authoritative answer*. The people were ready to give up *their* decision-making authority, if only the expert would give *the answer*.

Daniel Lang interviewed a group of Germans concerning their attitudes toward Adolph Hitler and reported on his interviews in the *New Yorker* magazine in 1977. His interviews were later incorporated in his book, *Germans Remember* (1980). Lang observed that most of the Germans he interviewed professed ignorance of the crimes that were committed during the period that Hitler was in power, even to the extent of denial of the barbarism that occurred in the concentration camps. Many of the Germans interviewed reasoned that violence was endemic to all humankind and that the saturation bombings of German cities could be equated to the mass murders in the concentration camps. There was no apparent recognition of the fact that the bombings of German cities was preceded by saturation bombings of England, and particularly London. Or, that the Allied High Command decided to bomb German cities so that the impact of war could be brought home to the German people so that German air defenses would be shifted from the coast of France, where the Allied invasion was to be staged, to the defense of German cities. But this is mere military logistics—Lang's book is especially horrifying as he describes how the German veterans of World War II recall their military service as a time of idealism and heroism. The brutalities that the German military exercised against conquered nations are ignored. This denial of what happened in Germany is part of the mechanism of repression which enables people to live with memories of unbearable events. Therefore, people will search for any information which supports the repression mechanism.

A British historian, David Irving, has stated in his book, *Hitler's War* (1977), that no evidence exists that Hitler knew of Henrich Himmler's *final solution*—the extermination of millions of Jews, Slavs, gypsies, and other "inferior peoples."

> ... When his closest crony of all these years, SS General Josef ("Sepp") Dietrich, was asked by the American Seventh Army for an opinion of Hitler on June 1, 1945, he replied, "He knew even less than the rest. He allowed himself to be taken for a sucker by everyone." (1977, p. xiv, Introduction)

While it appears incredible to any student of history, there are many who deny that the Holocaust ever existed and maintain that it is a product of propaganda. Today, there are more and more people who want to push away the barbarism of Hitler's Germany and use every rationalization to explain the behavior (see Seltzer's chapter). Hannah Arendt, in her book about Adolph Eichmann, writes about "the banality of evil" (1964) and observed that Eichmann, the mass murderer, could be "every man."

> Eichmann stated: "With the killing of Jews I had nothing to do. I never killed a Jew, or a non-Jew, for that manner—I never killed any human being..." ... he left no doubt that he would have killed his own father if he had received an order to that effect. (1964, p. 19)

Recently, a friend, while visiting Hungary, found that Eichmann had systematically collected material concerning Jews so that he could develop archives for historical purposes. As he systematically annihilated people, he maintained a history of the people he murdered.

When man becomes part of a mass, he has no "social ego," a term first used by Arendt (1958). Social ego is an extension of what psychoanalysts speak of when they speak of the individual ego. The individual in the larger society agrees to postpone immediate, impulsive satisfactions because in that way he or she ensures a future that will be rewarding and much more gratifying. The society which has no social ego and which refuses to look to the larger problems of life, begins to exercise arbitrary control over minor areas. Thus, the Mexican police will insist that people have short haircuts while ignoring the poverty of the peasants and their nondemocratic state. So people look for simple answers—if only the streets were clean, life would be better. If only our young people were more well mannered, life would be simpler. The fact that the air, sky, water, and seas are polluted is ignored. Becker has detailed this "fetishistic approach" where people look to control, an oversimplification of life's problems (1969).

One of the most amazing stories of World War II was detailed by Joseph Borkin (1978), an attorney who was chief of the patent and cartel section of the Antitrust Division of the Department of Justice and who is presently in private practice of law in Washington, D.C. Borkin, in his masterfully detailed book, presents the unholy alliance of I. G. *Farbenindustrie,* the giant German chemical complex, with the Nazi party and Nazi morality.

Hitler plundered Europe and I. G. Farben played the jackal. It finally reached the point that the slave labor of the concentration camps, labor that was free to I. G. Farben and unlimited to the extent that Hitler and the Germans were able to enslave more and more people, serviced the enormous industrial complex of I. G. Farben. Huge profits accrued to this infamous corporate structure. Nowhere was there any recognition of the Nazi morality, and if it was recognized, it was embraced with fervor. The outstanding fact is that the monstrous barbarism that reduced human beings to numbers for a chemical complex had existed from *World War I*—and might even happen again. The supposedly civilized and cultured executives of I. G. Farben simply ignored the evil of which they were a part.

How many readers of this book remember that it was December 1978 when the horror of mass suicide was reported from Guyana—a horror story replete with transcripts of mass poisoning and tapes of Reverend Jim Jones exhorting his followers to kill themselves? So the phenomenon of compliance appears to be a much deeper problem that can be attributed to the violence of the twentieth century. There has been mass murder since time immemorial, but never on the scale of the Holocaust. Yet, the question continues to haunt behavioral scientists: Why do people comply and obey orders that are barbaric? The question will not go away.

Maurice Walsh, a psychiatrist on the staff of the Mayo Clinic in Rochester, Minnesota and a consultant to the United States Surgeon General, and during World War II to two air forces, examined 25 leaders in politics, industry, the military, medicine, organized labor, and religion "who were psychiatrically extremely healthy." He found patterns of marked callousness for human life and human rights, a marked tendency to distort the truth to further self-interest, and that the "pathologically charismatic leader demonstrates . . . an intense narcissism of self-centeredness," so that personal suffering is the only measure of anyone else's suffering and "mass atrocities and murders" are carried out without any guilt (1980)! This is the same behavior as that of Rudolph Hess, the Nazi who flew to England from Germany during World War II in order to establish a liaison with the Allies.

While there are "psychiatric" explanations, they appear to focus on individual behavior (see the Battegay and Zee chapters). That is why I asked students of social psychology and sociology to express their views. Back, in his chapter, approaches compliance as a social psychologist. Spanos in his detailed statement of demonic possession ventures opinions from *his* view as a social psychologist and points out the thin line that separates normal and abnormal behavior.

Milgram (1963) originally reported a study which was called a behavioral study of obedience. His report was later expanded to a book illustrating why people obey. Harvey, Harris, and Barnes, some years later (1975), varied Milgram's study, which is one approach to obedience. They induced some subjects to play the role of teachers and to administer severe electric shocks while other subjects believed that they were only administering mild electric shocks. The subjects who were playing the role of teachers accepted less responsibility for the student-learners' apparent distress when the shocks appeared as severe rather than mild. Third-person observers described the teacher-subjects as more responsible for the student-learners' severe distress than did the teacher-subjects. Apparently, one of the ways that the teacher-subjects could cope with administering severe electric shock was to deny responsibility. This is akin to those Nazi guards in the German concentration camps who disclaimed knowledge of what was going on.

As has been pointed out by many observers, the Milgram experiments, when seen against the passage of time, provoke at least as many questions as they answer. Do subjects in an experiment respond to what they believe that the experimenter wants? Are there nonverbal cues at work? In psychotherapy it is conceivable that patients respond to please the therapist. Is this what happened in Milgram's experiments?

Mixon (1972) showed that in the Milgram obedience study the compliance of subjects could range from 0 to 100 percent. This depended upon what interpretation of the situation was *mutually* agreed upon by the subject and the experimenter. When we use experiments that simulate reality, there is the concept of the *negotiated definition of reality*. The subject can always say to the experimenter, "I thought that was what you wanted."

Gergen (1973), in evaluating Milgram's study of obedience, illustrated that Milgram's results were dependent on contemporary attitudes toward authority. Therefore, every time period would show another response to authority. For example, compliance to authority in 1943 (during World War II) would not be the same as in peacetime in 1983. But this interpretation may overlook the subtle nuances—the same basic urge or desire to comply may cut across *all* time periods.

The problems with experiments on compliance are many, but a primary difficulty with these attempts to simulate reality is that there is something unique about an experimenter-subject relationship and there is a limit on how much one can generalize from an experiment in a psychological laboratory. Studies indicate that in the laboratory an experimenter can capriciously elicit behavior that subjects had never engaged in before. The volunteer subject may be overhelpful and compliant out of a desire to please the experimenter, and the results of the experiment may be distorted. Sometimes there is an ironic twist as the subject keeps cooperating in an effort to find out the experimenter's "real" purpose or hypothesis (Orne, 1962).

This may be too kind an explanation. McGuire (1969) has expressed deep skepticism about the external validity of any laboratory experimentation in social psychology since there is often a nonverbal contract between experimenter and subject that contaminates the results. Why would people hurt others when commanded to, or in order to please others in positions of authority? Is it all hopeless? Is there a glimmer of hope?

Even if people are stimulated to violence, many of us have ways of moving beyond the hostility. A dramatic example of this was demonstrated by Sherif, Harvey, White, Hood, and Sherif (1961) in their classic *robber's cave* experiment. In this field experiment, the investigators encouraged intergroup competition between two teams of boys at a summer camp. This created fertile ground for anger and hostility even in previously benign, noncompetitive circumstances such as movie-watching. Positive relationships between the groups were ultimately achieved only after both groups were required to work cooperatively to solve a common problem—the water in their camp was shut off.

Milgram states: "The most far reaching consequence . . . is

that a man feels responsibility *to* the authority directing him but feels no responsibility *for* the content of the actions that the authority prescribes..." (Milgram, 1974, p. 146). The psychological literature on responsibility has roots in cognitive psychology and Gestalt psychology approaches to perception. Heider (1958) proposed developmental stages of responsibility. Heider's stages (1958, p. 113) were five in number:

1. Association: A person is "... held responsible for each effect that is in any way connected with him or that seems in any way to belong to him."
2. Commission: Anything "... caused by a person(p) is ascribed to him ... the person is judged not according to his intention but according to the actual results of what he does."
3. Foreseeability: "... Person(p) is considered responsible, directly or indirectly, for any after effect he may have foreseen even though it was not part of his own goal."
4. Intention: "... Only what person(p) intended is perceived as having its source in him."
5. Justification: "... Even the person's (p's) own motives are not entirely ascribed to him but are seen as having their source in the environment ... responsibility for the act is at least shared by the environment."

While it is not our intention to go into the legal aspects of responsibility, the five stages may be grouped as follows: association–legal responsibility; commission–liability; foreseeability–negligence; intention–criminal responsibility; justification–legal excuses. However, the concept of responsibility has many different meanings. Thus, Shaver (1975) pointed out that people can be responsible in the sense of having caused, without accepting liability. Someone can occupy a certain position or role and perform duties, but not accept liability. Shaver delineated between *moral* and *legal* liability (responsibilities). We are clearly in the area of social roles—what the community expects of the individual and the person's development of conscience as internalizing the community's demands and expectations (Freud, 1974; Mead, 1934).

This same differentiation between moral and legal was the basis of Eichmann's defense when he was tried in Jerusalem for the mass murder of the people in the concentration camps. The same type of problem surfaced in the trial of Lt. Calley when he was called to account for the My Lai massacre in Vietnam. Surveys of the American community clearly established that there were those who believed that he should be tried as an individual who was responsible for the consequences of his actions, and there were those who felt that he was only obeying orders in a military setting (Kelman & Lawrence, 1972).

Probably the most significant information to emerge from the Kelman-Lawrence survey report is that opinions about Lt. Calley were related to education, occupation, and social class. People from lower-class backgrounds were more apt to follow orders. This appears related to their perception of how they fit into the societal structure. It may also explain the willingness of members of Rev. Jim Jones' commune to follow orders or comply. He offered these unhappy people a structured setting where they held a clear role and status, and they followed orders—even when it meant suicide.

In the chapters that follow, these are possible explanations for why people comply. The reader is encouraged to synthesize his or her own answers.

REFERENCES

Arendt, H. *Eichmann in Jersualem: A report on the banality of evil.* New York: Viking Press, 1964.
———. *The human condition.* Chicago: University of Chicago Press, 1958.
———. *The origins of totalitarianism* (3rd ed.). New York: Harcourt, Brace and World, 1966.
Becker, E. *The structure of evil.* New York: Free Press, 1969.
Borkin, J. *The crime and punishment of I. G. Farben.* New York: Free Press, 1978.
Freud, S. *The standard edition of the complete psychological works of Sigmund Freud.* London: Hogarth Press, 1953–1974.
Gergen, K. J. Social psychology as history. *Journal of Personality and Social Psychology,* 1973, 26:309–320.

Harvey, J. H., Harris, B., & Barnes, R. D. Actor-observer differences in the perceptions of responsibility and freedom. *Journal of Personality and Social Psychology*, 1975, *32*:22–28.

Heider, F. *The psychology of interpersonal relations*. New York: Wiley, 1958.

Irving, D. *Hitler's war*. New York: Viking Press, 1977.

Kelman, H. C., & Lawrence, L. H. Assignment of responsibility in the case of Lt. Calley: Preliminary report on a national survey. *Journal of Social Issues*, 1972, *28*(1):177–212.

Lang, D. *Germans remember*. New York: Farrar, Straus & Giroux, 1980.

McGuire, W. Some impending reorientations in social psychology: Some thoughts provoked by Kenneth Ring. *Journal of Experimental Psychology*, 1969, *3*:124–139.

Mead, G. H. *Mind, self and society*. Chicago: University of Chicago Press, 1934.

Milgram, S. Behavioral study of obedience. *Journal of Abnormal and Social Psychology*, 1963, *67*:371–378.

———. *Obedience to authority*. New York: Harper and Row, 1974.

Mixon, D. Instead of deception. *Journal for the Theory of Social Behavior*, 1972, *2*:146–177.

Orne, M. On the social psychology of the psychological experiment: with particular references to demand characteristics and their implications. *American Psychologist*, 1962, *17*:776–783.

Orwell, G. *1984*. New York: Harcourt, Brace, 1949.

Shaver, K. G. *An introduction to attribution processes*. Cambridge, Mass.: Winthrop, 1975.

Sherif, M., Harvey, O. J., White, J., Hood, W., & Sherif, C. *Intergroup conflict and cooperation: The robber's cave experiment*. Norman, Okla.: University of Oklahoma Institute of Intergroup Relations, 1961.

Walsh, M. *Symposium on Political Uses of Psychiatry*. Report delivered at the 133rd annual meeting of the American Psychiatric Association, May 1–9, 1980, San Francisco, Calif.

CONTRIBUTORS

Kurt Back, Ph.D., James B. Duke Professor of Sociology, University, Department of Sociology, Durham, North Carolina.
Ramon Battegay, M.D., Professor of Psychiatry, Kantonspital, Petersgraben 4, Basel, Switzerland.
Joseph Braun, Ph.D., Private practice, faculty member at the New Jersey Institute for Training in Psychoanalysis, Park Ridge, New Jersey.
E. Mansell Pattison, M.D., Professor and Chairman, Department of Psychiatry, Medical College of Georgia, Augusta, Georgia.
Nicholas P. Spanos, Ph.D., Professor of Psychology, Carleton University, Ottawa, Ontario, Canada.
Michael Seltzer, Ph.D., Montclair, New Jersey.
Thomas S. Szasz, M.D., Professor, Department of Psychiatry, Upstate Medical Center, Syracuse, New York.
Hugo J. Zee, M.D., Assistant Clinical Professor of Psychiatry, Emory University Medical School, Atlanta, Georgia.

Chapter 1

COMPLIANCE

Max Rosenbaum

All the good of which humanity is capable is comprised in obedience. (J. S. Mill, *On Liberty*)

Obedience, Bane of all genius, virtue, freedom, truth,
Makes slaves of men, and of the human frame,
A mechanized automaton. (Shelley, "Queen Mab")

A synonym for compliance is obedient. The definition is "(1) act or practice of complying; yielding, as to a desire, demand or proposal; (2) a disposition to yield to others (Webster's Collegiate Dictionary, 1945). Obedience is defined as the (1) act or fact of obeying, or state of being obedient.

Men and women tend to obey authority. There is nothing new about this statement; it expresses an idea known for millenia, and utilized by every leader from the primitive tribal chieftain to the contemporary corporation president. We are taught from infancy to obey authority figures, at home and in school; taught that obedience is necessary to function in society and that it is indispensable for the existence of civilization. Why then, as we near the second millennium, as increasingly interdependent and related members of social groups, do we still debate and question the merits of obedience to authority?

Even more frightening is the ready disposition to yield to others. Therefore, it appears to be more than simple obedience but rather compliance. A recent instance of mass compliance was the mass poisoning of the followers of Rev. Jim Jones at the commune in Guyana. Newspaper and magazine accounts referred to the people surrounding Rev. Jones as a cult, and yet Jones and his followers were praised as public-spirited and devoted citizens. Indeed, state, local, and federal politicians stumbled over one another as they attempted to court favor with Rev. Jones. Since then, evidence of secret bank accounts in Switzerland and Panama, has come to light, as has evidence of "hit squads," organized to assassinate people who Jones believed to be unfriendly to him or his ideas.

There are tape recordings of the bizarre happenings at the Jonestown commune and recordings of Rev. Jones calling out: "Mothers, you must keep your children under control. They must die with dignity." While it is now clear that both suicide and murder occurred in the last hours of the Jonestown commune, the majority of people there were all too willing to comply. What would motivate mothers to kill their children? There is so much literature describing mother love, and stories of wildlife are replete with vignettes of the mother animal fighting to defend her young. The extraordinary degree of psychological submission such leaders as Rev. Jones and Adolf Hitler received from followers had to do with a promise of transcendence that they offered their disciples. A disciple who attaches himself to such a leader— and to a simple, all-clarifying (that is, totalistic) theology—is able to feel a part of something larger than himself. He feels a part of something that will never die and will never permit him to die. This kind of relationship requires cultivation and maintenance— thought reform or brainwashing. Messianic leaders use three major principles of thought control:

> Control of all communication in the environment. If the cult is in an environment where borders can be sealed off, it makes it that much simpler (the Jonestown massacre and Nazi Germany offer good examples).
> Stimulation and manipulation of individual guilt feelings. The pattern of evil thoughts is set up so that inner doubts

are attributed to the influence of the devil. The devil may be seen as school, society, or even one's own parents. The guilt is reinforced by small group meetings. Criticism, self-criticism, and confessions are all part of the program of guilt. Sometimes there are public denouncements or public confessions. Every totalitarian movement has emphasized guilt as a way of enforcing compliance. (See later, the *demonic* principle.)

The distinction is sharply drawn between God's children and the outsiders—the sinners. There is only one way to heaven—the messianic leader defines this—and those who do not follow the "light" are in league with the devil and may be persecuted in every way.

The egalitarian prophets and flagellants of Europe during the Middle Ages, the Handsome Lake and Ghost Dance cults of the nineteenth century American Indians, the Melanesian Cargo cults of the 1940's, the Vietnam Cao movement of the 1950 and 1960 decades, and the People's Temple of Rev. Jim Jones, circa the decade of 1970—all these cults came into being during periods of social upheaval, when people were experiencing major social and economic dislocation. These people all felt left out of the mainstream of life, left out of jobs and what they saw as the "good life" of others. The peasant and artisan of the Middle Ages followed visionaries who promised them everything they longed for. The followers of Jim Jones joined his People's Temple to find meaning and purpose in a society where they felt powerless and alienated.

All of the leaders of messianic movements promise their followers relief from uncertainty. All these leaders appeal to an early religious communism that is described in the New Testament: "All that believed were together and had all things in common" (Acts 2:44).

It may be said that every generation must reexamine the validity of authority and the idea of obedience (Kelman & Lawrence, 1972). Certainly, in the 1940's, in the wake of World War II and the disclosures of Auschwitz and Dachau, men thought long and hard about obedience, authority, compliance, and the capacity of individuals to relinquish all traces of moral responsibility.

But since that time, especially in the United States, these questions have lain dormant. It was not until the events of the past two decades—news of American atrocities in Indochina, the resistance to American involvement, the revelations of Watergate and CIA activities—that America really began to grapple with her own attitude toward obedience and authority and why people comply. Events of recent years have demonstrated that the relinquishment of personal standards of morality and the concomitant acceptance of authoritarian rule are the province of no one nation or society: It can happen here.

In 1971, at the end of a decade marked by the conflict between conformity and dissent, Milgram (see Introduction) performed experiments on obedience to authority. In each case, two people took part in what they believed would be an experiment on learning and memory. One person was designated as a *learner* and the other as *teacher*. The learner was strapped to a chair, and electrodes were placed on his wrists. He was told to memorize a list of word pairs; for every mistake he made, he would be punished by electric shocks. The teacher was then placed before a shock generator console in an adjacent room. He was told to start at the lowest shock level (15 volts) and increase the voltage in 15-volt increments each time the learner erred.

Unknown to the teacher, the learner was actually an actor who received no shock at all. The screams of pain and protest which the teacher heard when he increased the voltage were feigned by the actor. The real focus of the experiment was the teacher: How far would he continue, under orders by the experimenter, to inflict pain on another individual?

The results of this experiment, repeated in different areas of the country with people of various educational, ethnic, and socioeconomic backgrounds, generated shock, dismay, and controversy. Two-thirds of the subjects obeyed the experimenter's commands, and continued to inflict what they believed were severe electric shocks, despite the protests of their victims. Clearly, then, this phenomenon could not be dismissed as the aberrant behavior of a small, sadistic fringe element. How can one interpret the behavior of these individuals? More importantly, what light does this shed on the larger question of obedience to authority in real-world situations? Why did people comply?

Milgram showed that a high percentage of experimental subjects carried out acts which in real-life settings would be considered harmful and destructive to others. (Amusingly enough, the American Psychological Association's *Code of Ethics on Experimental Research* (1981) would not permit a replication of Milgram's experiments, since the experiments involve deception of the experimental subject,—a code violation.) He has stated that the acts were presumably carried out in compliance with the authority's orders.

Few cross-cultural studies have been reported which replicate Milgram's experiments. In Germany (Mantell, 1971) and Australia (Kilham & Mann, 1974) there was a similar incidence of compliance and overobedience to authority. The studies have used young to middle-aged adults, and were carried out in American or European cultures.

Shanab and Yahya (1977) extended Milgram's original study of obedience to a new culture (Jordan in the Middle East) and younger age groups (six to eight, ten to twelve, fourteen to sixteen years). The Jordanian psychologists were not only interested in replicating Milgram's experiments but also ascertaining whether his findings would hold in a Middle Eastern culture. The Jordanian subjects were given freedom of choice to give or not give electric shock as punishment. Three hypotheses were tested. First, that the experimental subjects would administer punishment as they complied with the authority's requests. Second, more females than males would comply with orders to inflict punishment. Third, that obedience and compliance is an increasing function of age, since psychologists who believe in the learning theory approach believe that obedience and compliance is a learned response.

The 192 Jordanian subjects, 96 male and 96 female, were exposed to Milgram's original test of obedience. The first hypothesis was confirmed. The subjects followed orders. However, the second hypothesis, sex difference, and the third hypothesis, age difference, were not confirmed. Mantell (1971) found a higher obedience rate among his German subjects, but the differences cross-culturally are not statistically significant. The findings about sex differences in compliance and obedience are inconclusive and await further research. However, it does seem that obedience and compliance to authority exist in many cultures. It is interesting that the results of sex differences and compliance remain inconclusive. Sheridan and King (1972) worked with teenagers in their study and found that significantly more American females than males complied with instructions to give shock. Kilham and Mann (1974) reported that Australian females were less obedient than Australian men.

Milgram, in his book *Obedience to Authority* (1974), offers his own observations and insights. He notes certain behavioral patterns common to many of the subjects studied. First, he observes an increased interest in the narrow technical aspects of the procedure, along with a corresponding loss of concern for moral issues. The teachers became absorbed in the accurate use of the generator. They came to value their proficiency and tried to perform competently. They seemed to view themselves as technicians and functionaries, and transferred any ethical responsibility and judgment to the experimenter. Many subjects also came to view the experiment as an entity unto itself, divorced from human control—a characteristic which Milgram terms *counteranthropomorphism*. This psychological tendency to view inanimate objects or systems as human is reminiscent of a more primitive mind. It is manifested here as the tendency to see human creation as above or outside of human control. As Milgram writes, subjects tend to concur when the experimenter states, "The experiment requires that you continue." Milgram also notes a tendency to devalue the learner as a consequence of the teacher's action against him. He notes such comments as "He was so stupid and stubborn he deserved to be shocked." Instead of beginning with a bias or antagonism toward the learner, the teachers seemed to develop this attitude as a result of the procedure. This can be seen as an unconscious attempt to rationalize distasteful personal conduct.

But these observations do not tell us why individuals react as they do to figures of authority. Why would ordinary people continue to obey injunctions that contradict their own moral values, both in the microcosm of this experiment and in the real-world situation?

The first explanation that Milgram postulates can be termed the *evolutionary explanation*. Accepting the evolutionary theory, that behavioral traits tend to continue through generations only if they have some survival value, Milgram postulates the survival value of obedience. Men are not solitary animals; they tend to function in hierarchical groups because, the evolutionist contends, the individual has the greatest chance of survival as a member of a group. Such groupings demand obedience to certain authorities and acceptance of one's role in the hierarchy. Might not this be the basis for human obedience? Is this why people comply?

A second, related explanation Milgram offers for obedience to authority is based upon the cybernetic model of human behavior, e.g., the self-regulatory, biological mechanisms, such as thirst and hunger, which help an organism maintain a homeostatic state. One may argue that the same type of behavioral mechanisms exist in group behavior. Somehow, the argument goes, members of social groups are imbued with certain biological and social traits which contribute to the survival of the group. Such mechanisms, for example, might be instinctual curbs against devouring other members of an animal's species. In man, this control mechanism might be conscience or superego.

If we may assume that most human groups are hierarchical, such personal control mechanisms as conscience would tend to become subordinate to the controls of superiors. Milgram uses this theory to explain the modification from autonomous to systematic functioning which an individual undergoes when he enters a group. The individual ceases to view himself as responsible for his own actions, and instead sees himself as the agent of another; this Milgram terms the *agentic state*.

While it is unknown at the time whether there are actual neurological or chemical alterations associated with this behavioral alteration, certain phenomenological characteristics are evident. The behavior manifested by many of the subjects in Milgram's experiment is characteristic of agentic behavior:

1. Concentration on narrow technical details instead of larger implications—the tendency to see the trees and not the forest.
2. Concentration on the desires of the authority figure.
3. Acceptance of the authority's definition of the situation.

4. Abdication of responsibility for one's actions—the movement from an individual code of conduct to loyalty.

An individual's shift from an autonomous to an agentic state is predicated, of course, by a host of antecedent conditions. For the subjects in Milgram's experiment, as for most Americans, the idea that obedience to authority will lead to some reward was learned in the family, at school, and at work. Obedience was one aspect of the social order internalized by individuals.

In Milgram's experiment, certain immediate antecedent conditions also contributed to the subjects' compliance:

> The perception of an authority figure: The subjects expected someone to be in charge of the experiment, to serve as an authority figure from virtue of his position, not necessarily his personal character. The experimenter's trappings of authority—in this case, his lab coat, air of competence, status as a scientist—all helped fulfill that expectation. In addition, there was the marked absence of any competing or dissenting figure.
>
> The voluntary nature of the experiment: None of the subjects were forced to take part in the experiment. The knowledge that they chose to be there led to a greater sense of commitment to the experiment.
>
> The perceived logic of the orders: Although the experimenter's injunctions tested strained the subjects' ethical systems, they seemed logically consistent. In a learning experiment, the subjects were only punished when they erred, not simply at random.
>
> The accepted legitimacy of the institution: The awareness that this was a scientific experiment, and the legitimacy and regard for science in our society, also contributed to the subjects' compliance.

An examination of the *binding factors* is an important aspect of the Milgram experiment. Once they began to obey orders, what caused them to continue? One obvious reason is anxiety—

the fear the individual experiences at challenging an authority figure. But other, less apparent factors are also at work. The *sequential nature* of the experimental procedure tends to keep the subjects in *compliance*; to stop at any point would be to admit the wrongness of prior acts. Another important binding factor may be called *situational etiquette*. Many subjects expressed embarrassment at contradicting the experimenters' demands, lest they appear arrogant or hurt the experimenter's feelings. While at first glance this may seem an insignificant reason for obeying a command, it plays an important role in many social relations with authority figures.

The experimental result of such widespread obedience to authority raises the subsequent question: Why did some subjects disobey? Milgram terms the act of disobedience, "the ultimate means whereby strain is brought to the end." For some subjects, the inner doubt of the validity of their actions produces such an extreme psychological tension that they must find some recourse. Unlike the majority of subjects, the usual avoidance measures of denial, minimal compliance, or blaming the victim cannot reduce their inner conflict to a tolerable level. In all cases of dissent, the path from doubt to actual disobedience is a long, difficult, and anxiety-provoking one. Even after a choice has been made to disobey, the subject is left with a feeling of failure and faithlessness.

Elegant and impressive laboratory experiments in the social sciences can tell us much about human behavior. They remain no more than parlor games, however, if they fail the acid test of scientific validity—their application to events in the real world. It is the tragedy of our age that we need not look far to find real-world corollaries for Milgram's experimental results: the history of our century is one of heinous acts committed by men obeying authority. The social philosopher and historian Hannah Arendt analyzed the most extreme and abhorrent crimes against humanity—the genocide of European Jewry by the Nazis—in her book, *Eichmann in Jerusalem* (1964).

In this study, Arendt coined the phrase, "the banality of evil," to describe the actions of Eichmann and other Nazis who committed abhorrent crimes in the pursuit of obedience to authority. The central point of Arendt's study is that Eichmann and his cohorts lacked any uniqueness as individuals. Most of the Nazis expressed no great cruelty or vengeance in their personal lives, nor were they monstrous psychopaths, totally removed from the social fabric of modern civilization. As a group, they were rather faceless, petty bureaucrats, with no particular intelligence or talents, whose banal concerns were responsible for the destruction of a continent.

Eichmann's well-known explanation of his actions—that he was only following orders—rationalized his actions and his abdication of personal responsibilities. At his trial, Eichmann spoke of his own feelings of guiltlessness following the 1942 Wannsee Conference, where the plans were laid for the final solution to European Jewry:

> Here now, during this conference, the most prominent people had spoken, the Popes of the Third Reich .... At this moment, I sensed a kind of Pontius Pilate feeling, for I felt free of all guilt.

Some theologians have shared with me the following observation. At the time of the trial of Jesus Christ, Pontius Pilate was in residence at Caesarea, a lovely seaside setting on the Mediterranean Sea, not far from the modern city of Tel Aviv. But the trial forced him to go to Jerusalem. Pilate complained bitterly about the heat and crowded conditions of Jerusalem and was very eager to return to his seaside palace. His creature comforts took precedence over Jesus' trial, since he viewed the entire proceeding as a political squabble. Eichmann, like Pontius Pilate, was living very luxuriously, and could he justify anything as long as his creature comforts were taken care of?

The major figures of legitimate authority in Eichmann's life—the high civil servants, government ministers, party officials, educated men of high social standing—were deciding a course of action. There was no dissent at Wannsee, but rather discussions of such technical matters as legal clauses and the optimum methods of mass slaughter. For Eichmann, a man of low rank and social standing, but a fervent believer in the "good society" and the success ethic, this was his first chance to mingle socially with prominent and successful people. One can imagine what he must have felt at the apex of his career, intoxicated by his proximity to power, honored to be considered important enough to join in the discussion. As Arendt writes, the importance of Eichmann's belief in the success ethic and the social hierarchy cannot be underestimated:

> What he fervently believed in up to the end was success, the chief standard of "good society" as he knew it. Typical of his last word on the subject of Hitler: "Hitler," he said, "may have been wrong all down the line, but one thing is beyond dispute: the man was able to work his way up from lance corporal in the German Army to Fuhrer of a people of almost eighty million.... His success alone proved to me that I should subordinate myself to this man...." Eichmann did not have to "close his ears to the voice of conscience," as the judgment has it, not because he had none, but because his conscience spoke with a "respectable voice," with the voice of respectable society around him. (1964, p. 1)

It is critical to realize that Eichmann's conduct was based upon more than a sense of duty, upon obedience to German law. During the Third Reich, the legal system of Germany was based upon Hitler's words; in short, whatever the Fuhrer said became, de facto, the law of the land. Eichmann combined this obedience to law with a code of conduct odd to us, but according to Arendt, common in Germany:

> ... To be law abiding means not merely to obey the law, but to act as though one were the legislator of the laws that one obeys. Hence, the conviction that nothing else less than going beyond the call of duty will do. (1964, p. 1)

After the Wannsee Conference in January 1942, Eichmann had no apparent need to justify his conduct. He quickly became totally involved in the coordination of the final solution—the administration of the movement of Jews across Europe to death camps. His time was consumed with a vast amount of paperwork and administrative detail, as well as political intrigue and jockeying for rank and position. Eichmann was in the role he knew best: neither leader nor theorist, but a competent administrator. The picture Arendt presents of Eichmann, then, is of an individual undistinguished by either intelligence or imagination, but obedient to figures of authority. As such, his behavior bears some striking resemblances to that of Milgram's experimental subjects: the abdication of personal responsibility, an increased attention to technical and procedural concerns, and the acceptance of an authority's definition of the situation—in short, the picture of an individual in an agentic state. The necessary preconditions for this behavior were also met: the expectation of an authority figure; the acknowledged legitimacy of institutions (the German government, the German law, etc.); the perceived logic, however barbaric, of the demands (the genocide of European Jewry followed an involved rationalization for this act); and the perception of human institutions as apart from, and transcending, human control (the Fuhrer's words, the German state, etc.). Arendt's words are most telling when she speaks of the difficulty in trying Eichmann for his crimes:

> They (the judges) knew, of course, that it would have been very comforting indeed to believe that Eichmann was a monster.... The trouble with Eichmann was precisely that so many were like him, and that the many were neither perverted nor sadistic, that they were, and still are, terribly and terrifyingly normal. (1964)

Yet, Arendt seems to miss something, and perhaps students of the *Holocaust* have found the reason why so many Germans complied with orders to commit barbaric acts. In a lecture (April 1973) delivered at a symposium held at Yad Vashem, the memorial to the 6 million martyrs located at the outskirts of Jerusalem, Israel, Nathan Rotenstreich, a philosopher, pointed out the uniqueness of Nazi (National Socialism) antisemitism. He relates this to a predisposition in the German nation and the community perception of Christianity. Earlier, in the same symposium, Jacob L. Talmon, an historian, wondered how people could deviate from the hallowed injunction "Thou shalt not kill" to the point at which the innocent and defenseless could be slain without benefit of proper trial. Further, how was cooperation obtained—the compliance of the "mass of executioners"? The conclusions in the symposium stem partly from Freud's observations of murder within the family and from cultural anthropologists who observed that murder in the family occurred because of incest. The instincts of aggression are overtly carried out as acts of murder, resulting in feelings of guilt and culminating in conscience as the final act. But even this would not explain the psychological strain to which the "mass of executioners" would be exposed.

Rotenstreich (1974) notes that Christianity was the heir to Judaism, and theologians who followed what St. Augustine preached believed that those who did not accept the Messiah (Christ) were in league with the devil and could be assigned a demonic status. Very subtly, St. Augustine's teachings were warped to a new percept: the Jews did not accept the Messiah, were in league with the devil, and indeed were demonic. Here, the twisted brilliance of Nazism took over. The Nazis placed Jews outside of the human race since they, the Jews, were demonic and in league with the devil. Indeed, since they were demonic, they were not part of the human race and could be destroyed like any other organic material. In short, the Nazis used the idea of demonism without getting involved in any of the Christian theology and historic controversies regarding the coming of the Messiah. It was a convenient "out" for those Germans who wanted to obey and comply with the barbarism of the Wannsee Conference.

Carl Jung attempted to explain the appeal of National Socialism (nazism) from his point of view—in terms of the ancient German god, Wotan (1970). He was apparently aware that economic and political forces were at work, but maintained that the German soul was repossessed by Wotan. This pre-Christian god of the Germans, actually the tribes of the forest, was described as a restless wanderer who lusted for battle and could unleash passions—a god of storm and frenzy. He also described Wotan as having a manic, ecstatic side which would surface. Jung traced the German Faith movement, whose members were urged to believe that Wotan, and not Jesus Christ, is the true god of the German nation. Hitler was seen as an agent of Wotan who infected the

German people. In Jung's view, then, the Germans are *victims* of evil rather than active *agents* of evil.

Jung also claimed that Europe had produced Germany and as a consequence should share the German guilt concerning nazism. He based this evaluation on the German predisposition to feelings of inferiority, exacerbated by raging inflation, unemployment, and urbanization. According to Jung, this predisposition to inferiority was compensated for by the grandiosity and pathology symbolized in the personality and behavior of Adolph Hitler. Thus, Hitler is the incarnation of the average German and represents their collective hysteria. Jung defines *hysteria* as opposites, which are in every person, being further apart than normal. In hysteria this results in inner disharmony and tension. Thus, Jung cites Goethe's story of Faust's pact with the devil as Germany's abandonment of the spiritual for the material.

Since Nietzsche, a German, proclaimed God to be dead, the German people had to search for a God. Possibly, this search was symbolized in Adolf Hitler. Thus, Jung absolves Germany and sees Europe as responsible for the problem of collective guilt.

Jung elaborated upon these themes in two papers in his collected writings. In one, *The Fight with the Shadow* (1970), he saw Hitler as the symbolic representation from everyone's unconscious—the inferior part of everyone's personality. In the second, epilogue to *Essays on Contemporary Events* (1970), drawing on earlier papers and lectures, Jung traced the behavior of Germany from the end of World War I, 1918, and the breakdown of all optimism to what he called the *mass psychosis* of the National Socialist movements of the early 1930's. Apparently, Jung was still looking for something positive in the collective unconscious of National Socialism, and he maintained that the beneficial characteristics of nazism were not realized. This may in turn reflect Jung's defensiveness since he was criticized strongly for not speaking out against National Socialism. However, Jung maintained that his job was not to condemn, but to help people understand the nture of the process they were experiencing. This may in the long run prove to be Jung's own denial, since he earlier described the influence of Wotan, the god of lust for battle, as the pre-Christian god of the German people. Certainly, Wotan was *never* a kindly or benign god.

Thomas Szasz, psychiatrist and author of *The Myth of Mental Illness* (1961), is known primarily as a critic of conventional psychiatric practices. He is also an astute analyst and theorist of human behavior whose studies of personal conduct shed light upon the issue of compliance and obedience. Szasz takes issue with the traditional definitions of behavior used in psychology, which he says emphasize entities, such as personality, rather than processes and activities. He compares the difference between *entity* and *process* views of psychology with the difference between modern and classical physics. Szasz also takes issue with what he believes to be the historicism basic to psychiatry and psychoanalysis—the idea that certain historical factors, whether instincts or childhood experience, necessarily cause subsequent factors. Instead of this psychological causality, Szasz postulates a theory of behavior based upon functioning rather than being—what he terms a *role-playing* theory of behavior. The role-playing theory has been extensively explored by social psychologists such as George Herbert Mead (1934) [Strauss, 1956], Charles Cooley (1956), and contemporary psychiatrists, e.g., Jacob L. Moreno (1946), the founder of psychodrama, and Eric L. Berne (1966), the founder of transactional analysis.

According to the role-playing theory, it is not necessary to know an individual's personal history in order to foresee his actions; it is enough to understand the *role* he is playing, and the parameters of that role. Since one plays according to certain accepted rules, a modification of those rules can lead to an alteration of personal conduct and values; behavior becomes a mutable series of learning experiences derived from the social environment.

Since behavior, for Szasz (1961), does not exist in an inflexible causal framework, an examination of the rules which govern ones behavior is essential; ethics, thus, become inextricably linked with psychology. Man is not an instinctually driven animal; he learns how to act from his society: "Social life," writes Szasz, "is never a matter of survival, it is a matter of surviving in a certain way."

Szasz identifies a number of rules inherent in our cultural tradition. Among the most prominent is a pattern of activity "characterized by the helplessness of one member and the helpfulness of another." He blames Judeo-Christian teachings and parent-child relationships for this learned helplessness where, he says, disability is rewarded:

> ... Social life—through the combined impact of ubiquitous childhood experience of dependence and religious teachings—is so structured that it contains endless exhortations commanding man to behave childishly, stupidly, and irresponsibly. (1961).

Added to these unspoken rules, writes Szasz, are the unspoken threats implicit in every society—that personal survival is dependent upon obedience and compliance. Where men once feared that rebellion would incur the wrath of God and result in the physical destruction of the universe, they now believe that disobedience would mean the collapse of society and civilization. It is this silent fear that gives greater power to authority figures.

The combination of all these factors discussed—learned helplessness, fear of dissent, social conditioning—are ideal preconditions for what Milgram (1974) would term the *transformation to the agentic state*. To Szasz, it is no surprise that men would so quickly relinquish personal autonomy in the face of authoritarian injunctions.

The analyses of obedience situations with resultant compliance posed by Milgram, Arendt, and Szasz, are all based, to some degree, on examinations of large-scale interpersonal relationships—social environments, cultural conditioning, etc. There are those, however, who would explain obedience to authority and compliance differently, more in terms of intrapersonal, instinctual drives, or the psychological influences of single individuals.

Freud and subsequent orthodox psychoanalysts would explain instances of obedience and compliance at the expense of morality as a manifestation of man's instinctive aggressiveness. They would argue that all men have basic aggressive and destructive tendencies, that these tendencies are curbed by ego functions, but that man constantly seeks release in acts of violence and destructiveness.

Both Milgram and Arendt mention and dispute this theory.

First, Milgram argues, the behavior of obedient subjects was not self-instigated; it was carried out under pressure of duty to authority. Second, there were no expressions of truly aggressive or sadistic emotions. If the subjects had wanted, they could have immediately turned the shock generator dial to its highest voltage and maintained that level for as long as possible. Instead, most of the teachers only continued to raise the voltage under pressure from the experimenter, and concomitant extreme emotional duress. It seemed obvious that the infliction of pain was a difficult and unpleasant act.

There is one more theory of obedience and compliance behavior, increasingly discussed in recent years, which merits consideration. This is an explanation that says many cases of obedience and compliance behavior are based upon some form of hypnosis; individuals abdicate personal responsibility because they are brainwashed. The phenomenon of hypnosis has been observed, if not understood, for years. In the last few decades, hypnosis, or brainwashing, has been discussed in connection with the behavior of various political and social groups, and deviant individuals. Some theorists explain Hitler's methods in terms of mass hypnosis, the mass political rallies at night, under blinding lights directed at the crowd, along with the rhythmic chants and cries of acclaim. The term *brainwashing* was widely used to discuss the methods of both the north Koreans and the Chinese Communists in the 1950's. Recently, the appeal of various domestic religious and politicosocial cults has been attributed to hypnosis and brainwashing techniques. Certainly, Rev. Jones used brainwashing and Rev. Moon has been accused of this.

A study of a basic textbook on hypnosis evokes many comparisons with the techniques and results of Milgram's experiment (1974). Many of the preconditions for effective hypnosis have striking similarities with Milgram's experimental techniques:

1. A state of fixation or concentration of attention
2. An induced monotony (the repetition of commands and procedures)
3. Limitations of voluntary movement
4. Limitation of the field of consciousness (confinement in the laboratory; lack of competing authority)

The textbook examples of typical behavior under hypnosis also correspond well with experimental results. There is the progressive involvement in the desired behavior until "... they seem to submerge completely in it." There is the same compulsion to carry out the suggestions:

> When hypnotized, many individuals appear to experience some sort of compulsion to carry out the suggestions. When the response is prevented from taking place, the subject usually develops tension which can be reduced only by acting out or removal of the suggestion.

Experienced hypnotists claim that no individual is absolutely insusceptible to hypnosis—the hypnotist needs only to find the way to tap this potential. Some theorists believe that this ubiquitous susceptibility to suggestion is psychoanalytically based: the subject experiences transference towards the hypnotist, accepts him as a superego, and regresses to an infantile state of submissiveness, loss of critical facility, and feelings of acceptance and security. There is a large body of literature with arguments pro and con the transference hypothesis (Freud, 1974).

Thus, we have seen various explanations of the same phenomenon of obedience to authority and compliance explanations which emphasize evolution, instinct, role playing, behavior regulation, and societal conditioning. Each analysis has its merits; perhaps none are complete. The definitive reasons for compliance remain to be found, but a central question can still be answered: Why should we care? Eric Fromm, in his classic book, *Escape From Freedom* (1941), argued that unless we know man's propensity to comply, democracy is imperiled.

In the late 1920's and early 1930's, a group of sociologists and behavioral scientists at the University of Frankfurt, Frankfurt am Main, Germany, conducted research which involved the propensity of people to look for strong leaders to follow unquestioningly. They predicted accurately that the German labor unions would search for a strong leader who would resolve the problems of the working class—that leader turned out to be Adolf Hitler. Unfortunately, their prediction came true. The same labor unions that were the spawning grounds of great liberalism also bred nazism. While it is not pertinent here to follow the activities of one person, it is relevant to note patterns that may shed light on why some people do *not* comply. In October 1934, Wolfgang Kohler, one of the important figures in the development of Gestalt psychology in Germany, delivered the William James Lectures at Harvard. These lectures were later published in a book, *The Place of Value in a World of Facts* (1938). Kohler was for the most part concerned with the philosophical aspects of the correspondences that his version of Gestalt psychology postulate exist between the physical world, experience, and the operations of the brain. He believed that values *do* have a place in a science which is concerned with facts.

Why do I focus upon Kohler? In an important article, Henle (1978) describes Kohler's "courageous struggle against the Nazis to try to save the Psychological Institute of the University of Berlin." Her documentation of his struggle covers the period from 1933 to August 1935, when he finally resigned and left Germany. Kurt Lewin, the psychologist, a German Jew, had resigned and left for the United States. "Resigned" is actually a poor word since the Nazis came to power on January 30, 1933, and soon after this dismissed the Jewish professors from the university faculties. The great figures of science, including Albert Einstein, to the graduate students who were assistants—all of them were dismissed. The most astounding thing about the dismissals is that the colleagues of those dismissed did not protest. Their silence was deafening. During World War II, Kohler gave a lecture which Henle notes, and he stated: "Nothing astonished the Nazis so much as the cowardice of whole university faculties, which did not consist of Nazis. Naturally this corroborated the Nazis' contempt for the intellectual life."

Earlier, in April 1933, Kohler had written to Ralph Barton Perry, the American philosopher who was Edgar Pierce Professor of Philosophy at Harvard. Perry, an outstanding public service-oriented citizen, is often overlooked by behavioral scientists, but his books, especially *General Theory of Value* and *Realms of Value*, are seminal works and *General Theory of Value* is a standard treatise. Perry had studied under William James and wrote about James in an important book, *The Thought and Character of William James*. In his letter to Perry (as Henle reports), Kohler stated:

> . . . As to myself, my patriotism expects the Germans to behave better than any other people. This seems to me a sound form of patriotism. Unfortunately, it is very different from current nationalism which presupposes that the people are right and do right whatever they are and do. However, there will still be some fight during the next weeks. Don't judge the Germans before it is over.

But in late April 1933, Kohler realized that the fight had to begin and wrote the last anti-Nazi article that was to be published in a German newspaper while the Nazis were in power. Kohler expected that he would be arrested for this act and played chamber music the evening of the day the newspaper printed his article. But the Nazis did not arrest him.

By December 1933, the Nazis began to seriously interfere with Kohler's work, as they began to order inspections of his institute. Yet he stayed on and demanded autonomy. During this period (1933-1934) he traveled and lectured in Norway and Scotland and the United States, so he could have easily sought political exile. Instead, he sought retirement. He would not succumb to the directives of the Nazis. In 1935 he was told to sign an oath of loyalty to Hitler. Instead, he replied that he had retired and his retirement took precedence. He stated that he could only remain as director of the Psychological Institute of the University of Berlin if he was assured that he would not " . . . repeatedly be(ing) subjected to the kind of treatment that only a weakling with no sense of honor could tolerate." All of his efforts were devoted to saving the Psychological Institute, but by August 1935, he realized his efforts were futile and finally moved to the United States. Henle (1978, p. 944) notes in her report of Kohler's struggle: "Was that struggle in vain? I think not. For as we look back on it, it shows us once more what a human being can be."

When one views Kohler's struggle in light of his writings, one is struck by his emphasis on a system of values. Later, in the United States, Solomon Asch, also a Gestalt psychologist, stated that even in different cultures where there are differing perceptions of reality, people share the same problems of values and what is preferred behavior. He stated his ideas in 1952, after the barbarism of World War II (Asch, 1952), and placed a lot of credence in human reason. Behaviorists avoid the problem of values since all value is external. We "ought" to do things, say the behaviorists, because we have received social approval. B. F. Skinner avoids introspection and reflection. Mankind values survival and, therefore, that is the basic value as far as the behaviorist is concerned. The culture reinforces what is necessary for survival. This, of course, does not deal with freedom, dignity, compassion, self-sacrifice, and a host of other values which are important to reflective individuals.

If the study of various theorists and writers on obedience and compliance and our shared experiences of the last few years tell us anything, it is this: Obedience to authority and compliance at the expense of personal ethics is unique to no one age or nation. It is an issue every society must face. We in the United States, chastened by the disclosures of American conduct in Southeast Asia—the murder of civilians at My Lai, the secret bombing of hamlets; and the disclosure of widespread political sabotage and corruption—are finally learning this truth. Anyone concerned with personal ethics, social morality, and the very survival of mankind must examine these questions anew. Milgram (1974) concludes his study with greater insight, but also greater pessismism:

> And what have we seen? Not aggression, for there is no anger, vindictiveness, or hatred in those who shocked the victim. . . . Something far more dangerous is revealed: the capacity for man to abandon his humanity, indeed the inevitability that he does so, as he meshes his unique personality into a larger institutional structure. This is a fatal flaw nature has designed into us, and which in the long run gives our species only a modest chance of survival.

But Milgram did not carefully read the great figures of philosophy. Aristotle wrote in his *Treatise on Politics*

> In this particular, man differs from other animals, that he alone has a perception of good and evil, of just and unjust, and it is a participation of these common sentiments which forms a family and a city... for as by the completion of it man is the most excellent of all living beings, so without law and justice he would be the worst of all, for nothing is so difficult to subdue as injustice in arms: but these arms man is born with, namely, prudence and valor, which he may apply to the most opposite purposes, for he who abuses them will be the most wicked, the most cruel, the most lustful, and most gluttonous being imaginable.

Muller (1958, p. 8) noted that the ancient Greeks "developed a faith in mind as the distinctive essence of man; they enthroned the power of reason by which man might hope to dispel mystery and order his own life." And further, Muller notes that ancient man " . . . was always subject to the tyranny of supernatural powers that could be propitiated by priestly magic. Obedience to arbitrary authority was likewise the ruling principle in his social and political life. . . . The chief use of thought was not to analyze, inquire, or create but to conserve, to sanctify the status quo."

But in every time, there is an Aristotle or John Stuart Mill to help man free himself from tyranny. Hopefully, there will always be someone to help us use reason to move beyond the status quo:

> ... It is the peculiarity of man, in comparison with the rest of the animal world, that he alone possesses a perception of good and evil, of the just and the unjust, and of other similar qualities; and it is association in (a common perception of) these things which makes a family and a polis. . . . (1966, p. 378)   Aristotle
>
> ... Man, when perfected, is the best of animals; but if he be isolated from law and justice he is the worst of all. Injustice is all the graver when it is armed injustice; and man is furnished from birth with arms (such as for instance, language) which are intended to serve the purposes of moral prudence and virtue, but which may be used in preference for opposite ends. That is why, if he be without virtue, he is a most unholy and savage being, and worse than all others in the indulg-

ence of lust and gluttony. Justice (which is his salvation) belongs to the polis; for justice, which is the determination of what is just, is an ordering of the political association. (1966, p. 379)   Aristotle

Men, it has been well said, think in herds; it will be seen that they go mad in herds, while they only recover their senses slowly, and one by one. (Mackay, 1852)

Or perhaps Kurt Lewin (1948), the social psychologist, captured another way of confronting the problems of compliance when he wrote: "To believe in reason, is to believe in democracy, because it grants to the reasoning partners a status of equality.

REFERENCES

Allen, R.E. (ed.) *Greek Philosophy: Thales to Aristotle* New York: Free Press, 1966.
Am. Psych. Association *Code of ethics on experimental research*, Washington, D.C. APA, 1981.
Arendt, H. *Eichmann in Jerusalem: A report on the banality of evil.* New York: Viking Press, 1964.
Asch, S. E. *Social psychology.* Englewood Cliffs, N.J.: Prentice-Hall, 1952.
Berne, E. *Principles of group treatment.* New York: Oxford University Press, 1966.
Cooley, C. H. *Human nature and the social order (1922).* New York: Free Press, 1956.
Freud, S. *The Standard Edition of the Complete Psychological Works of Sigmund Freud.* (24 vol.). London: Hogarth Press and Institute of Psychoanalysis, 1953–1974.
Fromm, E. *Escape from freedom.* New York: Farrar and Rinehart, 1941.
Henle, M. One man against the Nazis—Wolfgang Kohler. *American Psychologist*, 1978, *33*: 939–944.
Jung, C. G. After the catastrophe. In *Collected Works of C. G. Jung* (Vol. 10) (2nd ed.). Princeton, N.J.: Princeton University Press, 1970, 194–217.
Epilogue to essays on contemporary events. In *Collected works of C. G. Jung* (Vol. 10) (2nd ed.). Princeton, N. J.: Princeton University Press, 1970, 227–243.

The fight with the shadow. In *Collected works of C. G. Jung* (Vol. 10) (2nd ed.). Princeton, N. J.: Princeton University Press, 1970, 218–226.

Wotan, In *Collected works of C. G. Jung* (Vol. 10) (2nd ed.). Princeton, N. J.: Princeton University Press, 1970, 179–193.

Kelman, H. C., & Lawrence, L. H. Assignment of responsibility in the case of Lt. Calley: Preliminary report on a national survey, *Journal of Social Issues*, 1972, *28*(1):177–212.

Kilham, W., & Mann, L. Levels of destructive obedience as a function of transmitter and executant roles in the Milgram obedience paradigm. *Journal of Personality and Social Psychology*, 1974, *29*:696–702.

Kohler, W. *The place of value in a world of facts*. New York: Liverwright, 1938.

Lewin, K. *Resolving social conflicts*. New York: Harper Bros., 1948.

Mackay, C. *Extraordinary popular delusions and the madness of crowds*. London: Richard Bentley, 1852(2nd edition)

Mantell, D. M. The potential for violence in Germany. *Journal of Social Issues*, 1971, *27*: 101–112.

McKeon, R. (Ed.) The Basic Works of Aristotle. New York: Random House, 1941.

Mead, G. H. *Mind, self and society*. Chicago: University of Chicago Press, 1934.

Milgram, S. *Obedience to authority*. New York: Harper and Row, 1974.

Mill, J. S. *On liberty (1859)*. Indianapolis, Ind.: Library of Liberal Arts, 1956.

Moreno, J. L. *Psychodrama*, New York: Beacon House, 1946.

Muller, H. *The loom of history*. New York: Harper and Bros., 1958.

New English Bible, Acts 2:44, New York: Oxford University Press, 1971.

Perry, R. B. General Theory of Value New York: Longmans Green & Co. 1926.

Perry, R. B. Realms of value. Cambridge, Mass.: Harvard University Press, 1954.

Rotenstreich, N. *Holocaust and rebirth*. Lecture delivered at Yad Vashem, Jerusalem, Israel 1974.

Shanab, M. E., & Yahya, K. A. Behavioral study of obedience in children. *Journal of Personality and Social Psychology*, 1977, *33*: 523–536.

Shelley, P. B. The Complete Poetical Works of Shelley. Boston: Houghton Miflin Company, Cambridge Edition.

Sheridan, C. L., & King, R. G. Obedience to authority with an authentic victim. *Proceedings of the American Psychological Association*, 1972, 7: 165–166.

Skinner, B. F. Science and Human Behavior. New York: Macmillan, 1953.

Strauss, A. (Ed.). *The social psychology of Geroge Herbert Mead.* Chicago: University of Chicago Press, Phoenix Books, 1956.

Szasz, T. *The myth of mental illness: Foundations of a theory of personal conduct.* New York: Harper and Bros., 1961.

Talmon, J. L. *Holocaust and rebirth: A Symposium.* The Riverside Press: Cambridge, 1813.

Webster's collegiate dictionary (5th ed.). Springfield, Mass.: G. & C. Merriam Co., 1945.

SUGGESTED READINGS

Heider, F. *The psychology of interpersonal relatons.* New York: Wiley, 1958.

Shaver, K. G. *An introduction to attribution processes.* Cambridge, Mass.: Winthrop, 1975.

Chapter 2

COMPLIANCE AND CONFORMITY IN AN AGE OF SINCERITY

Kurt W. Back

ETHICS, POLITICS AND THE PSYCHOLOGY OF COMPLIANCE

Compliance is an ethical as well as a psychological problem. When, if ever, is a person justified in acting in compliance with an order in opposition to his own beliefs? Is an immoral act justified if it is performed under duress? Is a system which exacts compliance ever justified? What is the price we pay for a system where enforcement of compliance is tabooed? Is it subtle or not so subtle pressure to a uniformity of beliefs? Values on questions such as these influence theories and research of scientists in any society, even if they try to be as objective as possible.

Values dealing with compliance arise at two levels—as compliance within the political system and within personal relations. A basic orientation in a society underlies the justification of compliance on both levels, but it is not completely deterministic. We can examine each level separately and note congruences and discrepancies.

The aim of this chapter is to assess the place of outward compliance as compared with internalized conformity in current society. To understand this we have to trace the shift from reliance on compliance toward conformity in modern times, its meaning, and cost. Before going into this analysis, let us consider two modern examples of dealing with compliance which show the range of opinions in recent times.

Two Studies

The first example is a classical experiment on opinion change by Kelman (1958). To simplify the experiment and to avoid pre- and posttesting, Kelman used an opinion to which he knew practically all of his subjects would be opposed. He used a black college in Maryland at the time when the Supreme Court's opinion in *Brown vs. the Board of Education* was expected. The opinion advocated in the change experiment was that, even if the Supreme Court decision was in favor of integration, there was still a role for purely black colleges and that a certain amount of segregation should be maintained—an opinion that few black college students at that time could be expected to have. The influence message was given to different groups of students in four different ways: One was a powerful source, a trustee who had given money to the school and could be expected to do so again, but who had stated that he would give money only to institutions where the students agreed with his opinions. The second was a black student leader whose opinions were backed by an opinion poll of black students. The third was a prestigious professor, an expert in race relations and known to be favorable to the aspirations of black students. The fourth, the control group, was the man on the street with a Southern accent who also expressed some racist opinions. The basic message, after the introduction of the speakers, was identical from all four sources. The subject groups were further subdivided for different posttests. One group was asked immediately after the message, and participants were also required to sign the questionnaires. The second group was given anonymous questionnaires immediately after the message, and the third group was given the same questions a few weeks later in a very different setting, where the questions were a part of a larger questionnaire and the questionnaire ostensibly had no connection with the original message. In general, the results were what could be expected. The control group showed hardly any changes in any condition; the group listening to the trustee showed the largest changes in the "signed" condition but no changes in the other two; the student leader was ahead of the professor in the situation where the questionnaire was identified with the message, but the professor caught up and even surpassed the student a little in the later administration. Kelman reasoned cogently that in the first situation the *mechanism of compliance* persisted as long as power could be exerted. The second he called the *mechanism of identification* with the attractive source of the message. It was effective as long as people remembered with whom they identified. The third mechanism, though not so powerful, was *internalization*. Whatever was retained was retained as part of the person.

This study presents a good definition of the three processes. But what interests us here is the fact that Kelman took the results of the compliance condition as obvious and not particularly interesting and spent much thought and later research in following up the distinction between identification and internalization. Looking at the functioning of political systems, one could easily take the opposite position. Society works because people comply to its rules and to its power relations, and we really do not know how far their actions would conform to their opinions if left completely alone. It might be just as important to understand the conditions of this compliance, how it affects individuals, and what the interpersonal dynamics of agreement between different aspects of a person's reactions and attitudes are. In this chapter I shall contrast compliance with conformity, which may include identification as well as internalization.

In contrast to Kelman's position is that of the Polish poet and social critic, Milosz (1951). Milosz describes the survival of the Polish people under German and Communist occupation. He makes the point that survival is practically dependent on the ability to separate one's actions towards a regime from one's feelings and attitudes about it. Furthermore, he gives case studies to show the experiences of individuals who were more or less successful in keeping up this separation. Milosz explains a principle which comes from the Eastern European experience and was introduced by the Turkish rulers, which they call *ketman*. Ketman is the principle propounded by some Islamic mystics who had been persecuted for their beliefs. They developed the rule that mystical knowledge is only for the enlightened person and should not be given to the multitude; therefore, the enlightened person should not share his ideas with the multitude, but only with other enlightened people—in effect, people with whom it is safe to talk. The principle of ketman, therefore, accepts compliance for compliance's sake and states that it is not only inconvenient, but wrong, to act according to one's deep-seated beliefs and to express those beliefs in ordinary life. Milosz then shows the importance of the principle of ketman in recent European history.

The contrast between these two points of view is fundamental. Both look at the same phenomena and agree on their import, but they judge them differently. One point of view says that compliance without conformity is not important. It expresses the position that it should not be a means of social control, but should be, at best, only a temporary expedient. It implies that there is something wrong with people whose actions do not correspond with their beliefs. The opposite point of view accepts compliance as a general technique in the social world. Its proponents accept the inner resistance as the only way to survive in the world as it is and to keep one's integrity and ideas alive under oppression. And finally, this attitude of preserving one's beliefs, unsupported by action, is considered clever and indeed superior. This second point of view may look opportunistic and even cynical. However, looking at the prevalence of appropriate situations, it has been the more widespread view than the view that one should be of one piece, attitude, and behavior. There is certainly some case to be made that the first point of view is an invention of, and has become important primarily in, modern western society.

Sincerity and Individualism

The decline of compliance, of enforced agreement with others, and the corresponding emphasis on conformity as the basis of the function of the polity, as well as of interpersonal relations, deserves further exposition. Before discussing the place of compliance in today's world, we shall trace some of the evidence of this change.

One aspect of this change is the development of new values, such as sincerity. Lionel Trilling (1971) has made a strong case for the invention of sincerity as a new value in modern Europe. Sincerity is the belief that people should act the way they feel without putting up a front. He posits, as one reason for this rare occurrence, the invention of a new value, that is, the rapid mobility of modern society which came with the expansion of the middle classes. In a society where it became difficult to establish another person's status by some outward sign, it became necessary to require that people should not only act in a certain way but that their actions should reflect both their social position and represent something of themselves. This new value also coincided with the new concept of the individual as unique and not simply a set of obligations to society. The later Middle Ages has shown in the selection of heroes, in fiction as well as fact, their new appeal. Previously, protagonists complied, either to social standards or to prophesied fate. Now they would exhibit their individual commitments, as Abelard and especially Héloïse. Even mythic heroes would be individuals, not simple representatives of fate and ritual. Campbell (1968), the prominent mythologist, has noted that Parsifal is the first hero who shows prophesies about fate to be untrue. Traditional wisdom said that one cannot reach the Grail a second time after losing it, and that nobody who looks for it can find it. But Parsifal succeeds in both. By becoming individuals, these heroes and heroines also accept responsibility for their actions. They do not comply to outside influences, but act independently or change throughout their entire lives. They act without a mask—sincerely. (Literally, *sincere* means *sine cera*, without wax, that is, without a mask.) A virtue contrasting with sincerity is heroism. Heroes make great effort in putting up a front, in acting through required rules, independent of their own emotions. We can trust that heroes do not always feel valiant, courageous, and courteous, but they are even more admired in medieval romances for acting that way. Nobody cares about their real feelings. Again, we find that at the beginning of the modern period, one of the greatest literary works is a satire on this heroic attitude, namely, *Don Quixote*. Sancho Panza represents the more honest, sincere point of view of acting according to his feelings, and he shows up the knightly imagination and posturing as quite insane. As Moreno (1969) points out, Don Quixote is undone by the modern technique of self-confrontation: by having a knight not fight him but show him a mirror by which he can accept his own nature and discard his mask. A figure similar to Sancho Panza, Shakespeare's Falstaff, is also shown quite sympathetically as an honest, self-indulgent coward. He is more sympathetic than he would have been drawn in an heroic time. We can certainly see him in a better light than Homer's Thersites, the pacifist soldier who dares to express the private's universal desire for going home.

THE RELIGION AND POLITICS OF SINCERITY

Changes in interpersonal relations find their parallels in the norms of the political system: in acceptance of freedom of religion; in guarantees of the freedoms of dissent and speech; and in general, in the limitations on the state to enforce compliance. With sincerity as a standard of conduct, people might appreciate a consistent dissident more than an outward conformer who harbors deviant thoughts. However, tolerance of outward dissent means a shift from compliance to conformity as the base of social control. Compliance is not necessarily a response to terrorism. It requires only an acceptance of the forms. Sincerity in individuals has been related closely to political ideas of tolerance and freedom. But conformity, if enforced, can and has led to the most violent of wars, of religious or ideological conflict. The modern period cannot be idealized as a period of continuous progress, but also includes the strongest repressions and cruelty. Both of these are only two sides of the development of the new idea that behavior should represent one's thoughts. We can trace this development in the field where it started first, namely in religion.

The power of the Roman Catholic Church was one of the main features of the Middle Ages. The Church controlled the whole life of the people, through its cannonical law and its rituals, enforcing them through clerical as well as secular authorities. However, looking at the situation closely, we can see that the influence was mainly an outward compliance. People had to acknowledge the truth of the teachings of the Church, participate in the ritual, and do nothing too different from the institutional conditions of the Church. However, there is even disagreement as to how far the conversion to Christianity had gone and how far there was still the survival of older beliefs. The recurring persecution of dissidents and the persecution of heretics and witches would point to a large dissident group. For instance, there is still disagreement as to how far witchcraft actually existed as an adherence to the nature cults or whether belief in witchcraft represented fear of the unknown and of strangers (Cohn, 1975; Murray, 1962). However, whatever the basis of the belief, the medieval church was willing to tolerate witchcraft and did not prosecute alleged witches. The real effort to eradicate belief in witches, to eradicate the beliefs as well as the cults themselves, happened later in the sixteenth and seventeenth centuries. This was possibly forced conversion caused by the population expansion and colonization of previously uncontrolled areas, or it may have been a reaction to insecurity, xenophobia, leading to enforced conformity. Whatever it was is not important for our purposes here. In any case, the previous accommodation was broken by the need of the dominant group to assure itself of more continuity than outward compliance would manifest.

Similar developments can be seen within the religious institutions themselves. The impressive rituals and buildings which characterized medieval Christianity's hold over the general population did not seem to be enough any more. Ignatius of Loyola (1618) codified a technique to assure individual control through small group technique, constant confessions, meditation, and discussions. The methods of Loyola's exercises look strangely similar to other group techniques for therapy or self-realization used today. Similar techniques of small group control were used by the Protestants, e.g., Calvinists, as were used by the Roman Catholic Church. The small Protestant denominations wanted pure beliefs and not simply outward conformity or outward compliance. An example is the emphasis of the Puritans on preaching, which is an attempt to convince by internalization, as opposed to the ritual of the established Anglican Church, which would induce compliance but leave reasoning untouched.

The religious struggles to enforce conformity and sincere belief led finally to mutual exhaustion. The different denominations and sects were finally forced to accept each other's existence in the name of tolerance. However, within each group, more than compliance was required. In each denomination, new movements appeared which tried to find new techniques to expand personal control of the adherents beyond the ritual control of the state-connected establishment. John Wesley's group dynamic, for instance, was codified later in Methodism, whose very name pays an ironic tribute to the importance of the method of influence over dogma and rituals (Watson, 1978).

The religious wars of the sixteenth and seventeenth centuries finally convinced the rulers that enforcing compliance to religious beliefs was not possible. This assumption led to the tolerance of the eighteenth century, the Age of Reason, which accepted religious tolerance and is the basis for today's concept of freedom of religion. At the same time that tolerance increased, however, we also find the strength of the new evangelical movement. Here, not only are the ritualists adhering to the religious beliefs, but a person's behavior within as well as outside the home, the sincerity of belief, and all aspects of morals and behavior were enforced.

Even in relations with non-European beliefs, the same change occurred. The eighteenth century adventurers were brash, aggressive, and not particularly convinced of the superiority of their own culture or their own ideas. They reinspected the existence of other cultures even though they might not have been willing to combine them with their own. The colonizers of the nineteenth century acted as transmitters of the culture of the beliefs of European civilization. The missionary followed the trader and the soldier in this new colonization. It was not enough to accept the symbols of the conquest, but an effort was made to penetrate the ideas and the ideals of the colonial power as well.

When later other values started to supersede the importance of religious missions, the same missionary spirit prevailed. The apostles of the Age of Reason were just as intolerant in their way as religious apostles had been. The blessings of European scientific education, for instance, were found superior and substituted for those who did not belong to European culture. Macaulay, who as a historian exalts the religious compromise in the eighteenth century, was instrumental in exporting the current dogmas of the English Age of Reason into Indian education and banishing the local Moslem and Hindu "superstitions." In this way, conformity to new European ideas was assured. It is ironic that the internalization of European ideas—nationalistic, liberal, or marxist—led to the movement which ended the Age of Colonialism (Clive, 1973).

In general, the decline of religious wars was followed by a rise in conflict on other principles, political ideology, nationality, or adherence to an economic system. Some cultural groups, such as language groups, which had lived together peacefully or at least in indifference to one another, became concerned over the exclusive use of language, control of education, and the rights of the minority language. In political determination, there was a shift from authoritarian government where a minority clings to power and the rest of the population is only required to acquiesce and comply, to totalitarianism, where the group in power imposes its beliefs on the total population, trying to control the most minute details of their lives.

The Language of Sincerity

We find the same process of tolerance and totalitarianism in the control of expression. Censorship of topics which could attack the secular or spiritual authorities was relaxed and freedom of speech became a natural right. However, in the name of equality censorship on minute matters of grammar and expression were introduced to avoid racism and sexism. Today, a writer can easily write "shit," but can get into trouble if he uses "man" or "he."

The control of expression shows the difference between compliance and conformity in the interpersonal field. Censorship, as we know it and usually understand it, refers to certain topics which cannot be expressed or can be expressed only in paraphrase. One cannot attack some of the tenets of the dominant religion; one cannot discuss the sex act or anything else connected with it; one cannot describe violence in too great detail. There is hardly any indication, however, of the manner in which topics which are allowed should be treated. Control on the forms of language, grammar, syntax, and diction, correspond to an attempt to impose conformity, controlling the categories of thought and the use of different categories. One does not have to accept the extreme of the Whorfian hypothesis—that language determines the categories of thought—to acknowledge that there is a systematic abolishing of some way of speaking or a systematic forcing to do so will have some effect on the thought of the population concerned. However, in his creation of "Newspeak" in *1984*, Orwell tried to show systematic impoverishment of a language. Orwell also makes a point of working through the language for social control, that conformity is only needed among the intellectuals, the experts in language, for it to influence the rest of the population. For the "proles," compliance is sufficient to ensure dictatorial control. In the same way, Roland Barthes (1976) shows in his book, *Sade/Fourier/Loyola*, that innovators who want a radical change of society or who want to create a special kind of society for themselves have to invent a new language or at least new categorizations of terms which will encompass the whole existence of life, not only as it is, but as it should be. Sade's society of cruelty, Fourier's exact terminology and control of the social units, and Loyola's exact descriptions of the ways of spiritual search and the exact description of heaven and hell, as known today mainly through Joyce's parody in *Portrait of the Artist as a Young Man*, create a new world, simply through the use of language. In the new world, what is important is not outward compliance, although compliance is important, but adherence of the whole person who cannot think in any other way anymore.

The Role of Rhetoric

A similar development occurred closer to the fields of our concerns, that is, in the analysis and teaching of influence. This can be called the transition from rhetoric to social psychology. Rhetoric was developed in the Greek city states with voters on public affairs and of the judges for personal fate and was an important part of life. The importance of immediate consent as contrasted with long-range convictions is clear. In the art of swaying an audience, techniques to marshall one's arguments and defend them became of utmost importance for one's position in society and even sometimes in one's life. But concentrating on the means of swaying one's audience, without regard for the subject matter, was also viewed as immoral, or we may say insincere. In fact, we can see in the conflict about rhetoric and influence between the Sophists and Socrates an early intimation of all the problems of compliance and conformity in modern psychology (Guthrie, 1971).

The moral claim of the rhetorician, of course, is that the form is just designed to bring out the true state of affairs, clearly and convincingly, thus enlightening the audience and producing what in modern parlance would be called internalization. However, in practical terms the aim is to ensure immediate success. For the two adversaries it is also clear that not both of them can be right, but both of them might be taught the same techniques to make their point. The celebrated conflict in *Plato's Dialogues,* such as *Gorgias,* turned on the question of whether or not techniques alone could be taught or whether they spring out naturally in the search for truth. A group of brilliant debaters and professional teachers of rhetoric appeared who called themselves "wise men" or Sophists. They claimed they had the wisdom to teach anybody how to prevail in debate or in court, and correspondingly, that there were no immutable truths to be discovered. Truth was a matter of consensus and attitudes and "man is the measure of all things." Their opponents contended the opposite point of view: that truth was immutable but not easy to discover; not techniques but only careful debate, indeed, would lead to the direction of the truth. This group called themselves more modestly "friends of wisdom" or philosophers (Phaidon). They are represented in opposition to the Sophists in Socrates or Plato. We know the views of philosophers partly because Plato's brilliant writing has prevailed and the Sophists have fallen into disrepute. However, although the Sophists lost, the practice of rhetoric prevailed and can be seen in later Roman rhetoricians. In fact, rhetoric was qualified and became the mainstay of the medieval curriculum; the trivium included three fields—rhetoric, logic, and grammar, that is, the field of communication. Only in modern times have some considered the fields belonging to the trivium as not important and use *trivial* as a belittling term (White, 1978).

Social control, whose goal is mainly compliance, has at its disposal a variety of mechanisms. One of them is pure force or the threat of force which can assure compliance to command. The ability to control behavior has a secondary advantage because continued compliance may even cause a change in requisite beliefs. The durable insistence on requisite performance becomes part of the compliant society and the decline of this society leads to preference for other means of social control. Rhetoric is milder in comparison: it is partly based on the ideal of rational discourse embellished with emotional overtones which is the essence of the program of complete internalization. However, in its form and in its insistence on form, rhetoric tries to influence people for immediate action—the principle of compliance for short-term change. Compliance societies can use this approach to ensure the benefits conformity brings with it.

Until very modern times, therefore, rhetoric has been a method parallel to violence in social control. Rhetoric has at least a semblance of going deeper than force in inducing behavior. It provides a chance to convince a person by rational or emotional argument, for the present occasion, but prepares the audience to be receptive later to the same opinion. Rhetoric is generally used to convince one's peer group to give a token of approval and in unusual cases to stimulate a crowd into specific action. It is the perfect complement for the authoritarian or feudal society that is based on compliance. It has been frequently pointed out by modern historians that traditional acquiescence of the feudal order was really a thin cover over widespread discontent of the populace and that recurring peasant revolts are evidence of this fact. It is also true that these revolts failed, partly by being violently suppressed, and partly by seduction of the leaders of the revolt through the superior rhetorical abilities of the courtiers. The latter is reflected in the recurrent stories of revolutionaries being betrayed by glib-talking aristocrats and, later, broken promises. Skill in rhetoric complemented the ruling circle's coersive power. Shakespeare, in his Roman plays, especially *Julius Caesar,* shows contemptuously the power of rhetoric in the hands of a skilled orator.

The intermediate position of rhetoric is seen by its fate in the early modern period. The conflicts of the reformation and the counter reformation were at least as intense concerning the manner of conducting a service as about questions of dogma. Conduct of the service, with its importance on the influence of the believer, is of a social psychological as well as religious interest. One of the points at issue, especially in England during the early seventeenth century, was the emphasis on preaching. The Church was mainly interested in a minimum of social cohesion. This could be best accomplished by the symbols of established ritual. The Puritans, on the other hand, believed in stronger influences on their members and built their services around a strong speaker whose sermon could rouse and change many members of the community. Rhetoric in the forms of the sermons of great preachers became important. The seventeenth and eighteenth centuries brought a late reblossoming of religious eloquence. What is striking, however, is the intensity of opposition of the proponents of what are essentially psychological techniques. The violent opposition of the Puritans against any ritual, which included the widespread destruction of ritualistic decoration and artwork in the churches, was followed by the repression in preaching and the strong control over the amount of sermons when the Church of England regained power.

During the period of revolution and reaction which started in the late eighteenth century, rhetoric shifted to the political arena. The great orators of France, England, and the United States filled the legislatures and popular meetings and achieved fame with their ability. Current complaints about the decline of the caliber of the speakers in our political debates are more than modern nostalgia for the giants of the good old days. It also reflects the audience reaction which would not honor somebody just for being a good speaker, without consideration of the content. Even when we imitate the oratorical contests of older times, such as in a debate for presidential candidates, we do not listen in appreciation of oratorical skill. We want to go beyond the skill, if any, and always apprehend the real person. This may be the reason that most of the arranged affairs based on the older model of appreciation—of compliant behavior and conviction through rhetoric—usually fall very flat. Belief in the virtue of sincerity now has precedence over pure appreciation of the oratorical science. One may even be suspicious of too polished a speaker who sounds like a commercial. Or, to speak in more modern communication terms, we have depreciated the value of the structure of the message.

Persuasion

With this background on the historical context and political significance of compliance we can now turn to current social psychological analysis of the influence process. Let us now recall Kelman's experiment. The striking aspect of the study was that all the messages were identical. The same message was used to assure superficial compliance as well as all the more intensive conformity. The only difference was the relation of the speaker to the audience. The difference in the results of the study correspond to these relationships and were independent of the speech itself. In this respect, the experiment is not unique in the social psychological studies on influence. On the contrary, the tradition of social psychological experiments is to pay little attention to the content of the message or the construction of the argument itself. Even in field studies of influence, such as the study of mass media, there is little attempt at relating effects to virtuosity in constructing a speech. The closest that scientists usually come to doing so is in some studies of content analysis where certain scenes or appeals are related to the effect on the audience. However, techniques are frequently identified in a pejorative sense. Only bad people would use tricks of this kind. The techniques are related to the structure of the speech in the same way an orator would teach or analyze the architecture of the whole speech. In this way, the decline of rhetoric looks like a quite serious social change that links to changes in social control and value of individual conduct.

The contrast between traditional work on verbal persuasion and modern social psychology is so strong that it is worthwhile to consider this change in greater detail. This new trend is not more than half a century old and has corresponded with the culmination of the recognition and insistence on conformity between attitudes and action. In the political arena, this development has led to two contrasting directions. One is increased tolerance and freedom, which has made it possible to express one's feelings and to act freely in accordance with one's beliefs: the other is totalitarianism, which tries to indoctrinate everybody in such a way that feelings correspond with beliefs. The attention given to sincerity leads either to the insistence that political authority allows expression of individuals or that compliance to political authority implies surrender of belief. A combination of these two has been called *totalitarian democracy* (Talmon, 1952). Here the state is seen as an expression of individual beliefs and is, therefore, entitled to require complete conformity from its loyal citizens. The rise of totalitarian democracy had led to the excesses of the nineteenth and twentieth centuries with which we are all too familiar. It has also led people outside these societies to wonder how these beliefs and actions were possible. The experience in totalitarian countries in the early twentieth century brought poignantly the question of compliance and conformity into focus. The direction of the study of influence and conformity was, therefore, colored by the problems of the time. The depth of convictions, really the importance of participation, the responsibility of people for incomprehensibly cruel acts, behavior under excessive stress, all these can be seen as questions of current social problems at different levels of outside influence or of a contrast between compliance and conformity.

Social Psychological Theories

Attitudes and Actions

In current social psychological classification this topic has been studied under the heading of the relation between attitude and action, with a number of central questions: Can attitudes determine action? Can a change in attitudes also lead to a change in action? Or, in the opposite direction, can one have a subject perform some action without changing the basic attitudes and orientations? The classic experiment which poses this question was done by LaPiere in 1934. LaPiere (1934) traveled with a young Chinese couple across the country, stopping with them in many hotels without incident. After this, he wrote to the places where he had stayed and asked them whether they were catering to Orientals. Most of the innkeepers said they would not. Many explanations of these findings suggest themselves, and in a recent review of the whole topic the author admitted that the reason for the particular outcome was still not understood (Schuman & Johnson, 1976).

In this case the behavior was more prosocial and unprejudiced and the corresponding attitude was disproved by the investigator. The social implications of the contrast between behavior and attitudes are frequently not so simple. Sometimes we want to believe that people are not really as bad as they act, but sometimes we might be satisfied to make people behave in a prosocial way, whatever they may think. Sometimes we may want to believe that people act sincerely and that we can trust them to act consistently. At times, even, we want to believe in sincere behavior for its own sake, as a supreme good. As human beings, as well as investigators, we differ in the value of purely compliant behavior and we have different investments in the question of whether it occurs or not. In addition, just as there are different theories about the social implications of consistent and inconsistent behavior, there are different psychological theories about this relationship. The assumed attitude-action link has its implications about theories of human nature, the independence of thought, and the unity of the organism. Theories in social psychology and research supporting them support almost any relationship between compliance and conformity and attitudes and actions. We shall give some representative examples to indicate the whole range.

Persuasion Theory

A common-sense approach would say that people normally will act according to their attitudes: this is the domain of persuasion theory (Crawford, 1974). It is the theory most congenial to a society believing in sincerity as a general standard. Basically, it means that a certain general disposition which we call *attitude* or *opinion* would result in acts which look consistent with them, unless there are definite reasons to oppose them. Attitudes predict behavior; this relationship can be used for practical purposes. Politicians could inquire into voting intentions or general political attitudes to predict votes or cooperation with a certain policy. Marketers could inquire into attitudes toward certain products or certain qualities of products to predict purchases. They could also try to change attitudes in order to induce changes in the corresponding behavior. Compliance here would be looked at as a mechanism which would interfere with the natural relationship. For instance, terrorism could change voting intentions or rationing could interfere with buying habits.

Persuasion theory looks especially reasonable, but research results are generally not as clear-cut as one might expect. In most research studies we find low to medium correlations between attitudes and behavior, typically around .30. One way of increasing this correlation has been to make the attitudes more and more specific, all directed toward the expected behavior. Thus, general approval of a candidate might give less correlation with a vote than approval of the specific candidate for this position, or a statement of immediate intention to vote, or even a statement on voting day of the intention to go out and vote for the candidate (Crespi, 1977). Similarly, general interest in restricting the size of one's family might have less to do with actual birth control use than intention to use a specific method or a woman's statement that she is going to take a birth control pill in the next 5 minutes. This improvement can be taken too far, as is clear from the examples. Attitudes are useful concepts if taken as tendencies, as predictors of a variety of behavior. If we go to very specific attitudes (as in the last term of each sequence), then we have only behavioral intentions, practically indirect measures of observable behavior. This leads us far from human behavior (Fishbein & Ajzen, 1975).

Some cognitive theorists have accepted the low relationship and become moderate in their claims. The fact is that attitudes and corresponding behavior are almost exclusively positively related and to a nonnegligible degree. If we have no further information, we can use attitudes, even the most general ones, as predictors. Changing attitudes may be the most feasible way of eliciting an increase in desirable behavior, given moral and legal limitations. This method is also congruent with the value of sincerity in the society. An initial disappointment at the low correlations in research and at failures of cognitive theory, we find resignation and acceptance of the limitations of this approach.

Balance Theory: Dissonance

If one is disappointed with cognitive theory, other possibilities are open. One is to take a neutral stance, to assume congruence between attitude and actions without presupposing a direction of influence. Collectively, these theories are called *balance theories*. Some of the most striking experimental work has been done under the guise of dissonance theory (Festinger, 1957). Dissonance theory assumes that people want to be consistent and have a consistent view of the world as well as of their own actions. If a person has two cognitions which seem to be inconsistent, dissonance will result, with a consequent effort to reduce it. The individual will try to bring the cognitions into consonance by finding a mechanism by which he can convince himself that the two cognitions are not really dissonant or by changing one of the two. If one of the two cognitions is about one's own beliefs and one is a recognition of one's own actions, one of them would have to change. Dissonance theory has recognized that the usual way is to make one's actions conform to one's own beliefs. In this, it predicts the same facts as persuasion theory, and experiments which prove this fact cannot be considered relevant to the proof of the theory. Dissonance experiments frequently try to change attitudes by changing behavior. This is done by making the subject act in opposition to his own attitudes and then showing that attitudes will change to conform to behavior. Examples are experiments where required behaviors are such acts as writing an essay opposed to one's beliefs, to convince someone else of a fact known to be untrue, or undergoing a disagreeable experience for the sake of insufficient rewards. These experiments then show that people will change their opinion and the direction of their beliefs in the direction of their influence attempts, or may assume that the reward was sufficient to undergo the deprivation, or that the deprivation was not so big. Thus, in these experiments, compliance will eventually lead to conformity by changing attitudes such that a person again becomes sincere. Experiments investigating the conditions under which compliance will not actuate a change in attitudes show that these are the conditions under which the person can convince himself that his behavior did not necessarily occur in violation of beliefs. Some conditions in this case are overwhelming force or overwhelming bribe. People in these cases could then say that they were coerced or bought off and that their actions did not necessarily violate their beliefs. Thus, the best way, according to this theory, to ensure conformity after compliance is to induce the behavior with the minimum possible force. On the other hand, if one wants to keep one's beliefs, the best way is to imagine oneself to be under strong duress.

Dissonance theory, as well as similar balance theories, assumes a strong value of consistency. The adherence to this value might differ between individuals and also between societies. Thus, Milosz's notion of ketman is very acceptable under habitual situations of oppression and even under less extreme conditions in societies with a strong hierarchical structure. It might be quite reasonable to act in certain ways to achieve a superior status whatever one's opinions are. In such a society the incongruity between actions and private opinions in terms of dissonance theory would be that the actions were induced by overwhelming force. If that is the usual behavior in the society, the theory would not be very effective there. In societies where sincerity has a high value, however, dissonant behavior becomes hypocritical, and would be condemned. We can see this value of sincerity from the vantage point of the nineteenth century writer Hawthorne, in symbolizing the Puritan society of 200 years before his time in *The Scarlet Letter*. He used a physical symbol of the scarlet letter which is an outward sign of acceptance of a deviate from the norm in society. On the other hand, the novel established the conditions under which compliance will lead to conformity, that is, the conditions under which minimum pressures are exerted. This prescription responds to the ideas of a democratic society which uses legislation to avoid force. Brehm and Cohen (1962), using the context of dissonance theory, predicted that legislatures which would integrate schools and facilities with minimum pressure toward integration would eventually change attitudes toward integration better than Reconstruction did where military force was used. The events bore out this prediction, at least partially.

Dissonance theory and other balance theories are mainly supplements to cognitive theories. They accept the close relationship between attitude and action and say that a change in attitude means a change in action and vice versa. They do see that the relation can go in either direction. Therefore, compliance is a mechanism of control and can be effective and lead eventually to a corresponding change in behavior and attitude.

Behavior Modification

Another tradition in today's psychology, however, proposes to dispense with attitudes and theory. This is the tradition of behavior modification (Wolpe & Lazarus, 1966). The model here does not assume anything about the interior mechanism of a person or attitudes which lead to permanent behavior. It represents the individual as a kind of black box where certain stimuli conditions are entered and certain behavior is expressed. By giving rewards such as tokens to preferred behavior, behavior can be changed and even fixated for a long period of time. Most of the work on behavioral theory had been done in a therapeutic way, with disturbed or retarded people; further, much of the work is based on animal experimentation. Here, a cognitive model based on normal humans would interfere. People who really tried to figure out the schedule might not react to it but try to manipulate the situation in a way superior to the experimenter. Thus, behavior shaping with normal subjects is done in a way that prevents the subject from attending too closely. Mannerisms of speech can be reinforced by nodding without the subject's being aware of the connection. It is possible that many therapeutic interviews are shaped in this way. The therapist, by reinforcing certain topics by almost imperceptible signs, or by following them up with questions, will shape the patient's utterances in the direction of his own theories. The patient will produce more and more material on this topic and also be convinced of the correctness of the therapist's theory and its applicability to his own problem (Frank, 1961). In this way, compliance would lead to conformity, although behavior therapists, who are not concerned with attitudes, would not put it that way.

Behavior theory has been founded and promoted by Skinner. He has been in the forefront of the discussion of its social implications. Predictably, he does not hold with the culture of sincerity. He looks at social systems mainly according to their outcome and elicits behavior which is socially valuable through the different control mechanisms. One of his books, *Beyond Freedom and Dignity* (1971), shows his negative view of the values which derive from appreciation of sincerity. One may say that Skinner represents a psychological theory which relates to a time when sincerity is not seen as being important. He is trying to show that a humane society may be possible, based completely on a compliance model. The relative strength of conformity and compliance is a question of social context and the norms of the society. The dilemma cannot be decided through a psychological theory.

Symbolic Interaction and Person Perception

More sociologically oriented theoreticians would also doubt whether there really is a justification for a concept to define something inside a person such as attitude. This position is represented by those theorists who call themselves *symbolic interactionists* and allied groups. Their interest is only in the interaction process and its regularities and their technique is mainly observation. They can easily dispense with any inference of what happens within a person: in fact, they would say that the whole idea of attitudes is only a methodological artifact of people who want to study attitudes. By administering questionnaires, the researcher creates certain consistencies. It is the questioner who creates attitudes, not the subject who would have them. In this extreme of nominalism, one does not worry about derived concepts of attitudes and convictions, and the question of sincerity is irrelevant (Blumer, 1969).

Theoretical analysis has carried pretty far from the common-sense point of view that people have beliefs and act accordingly, or if they do not, we would like to know why. This naive assessment has been tested in research on person perception. In experiments in judging people it has been shown that it does make a difference whether one assumes the person has acted in accordance with the social or physical demands of the situation or not. Concordance is assumed to be natural and does not lead to any inferences about any deep or lasting aspects of the personality. Actions which seem natural in the situation are attributed to the actor's personality (Jones, Kanouse, Kelley, Nisbett, Valins, & Weiner, 1972). It is relevant for theoretical reasons whether there is a concept called attitude which leads to consistency needs, and the belief in attitudes does make a difference to most people in their interactions with others.

COMPLIANCE IN THE LABORATORY

In the social psychology laboratory we study the role of conformity and compliance, and questions regarding this role are not only important for abstract scientific knowledge but for social and ethical understanding within the society. We have seen how the issue of attitudes and behavior was initiated in LaPiere's study—which was really a study of racial prejudice—and this experiment has shown itself to be impervious to current theoretical interpretations. A current impasse is illustrated by a more recent experiment which also speaks to current research use and social concerns. This is Milgram's study of obedience.

The setting of Milgram's study (1974) is a psychological laboratory where the subjects are told they are trainers for people in some behavior-shaping experiments. They are shaping and training people by administering shocks to them for wrong answers. If the trainees persist in the wrong answers, the shock becomes stronger and stronger. The so-called trainers then are told by the experimenter to set the scales to the higher and higher voltage. In the meantime, the ostensible trainees, who are of course confederates, show pain and anxiety and also physical damage including to the heart. In the whole series of experiments, Milgram could show that practically all the subjects would comply to the instructions and started torturing the supposed trainees. Again, we find a variety of possible explanations. One can say that the subjects did trust the real experimenter and the university auspices and believed that no damages could occur in a sanctioned study. If one wants to, one can also say that most people are sadistic and do conform to their basic nature. Thus, some explanations are in the direction of compliance that people do obey some commands, even against their stronger beliefs: others that they really conform to their basic nature.

This experiment, like many others, can be fitted into different schemes, which depend on social and ethical norms and deeply-held beliefs. Would we be happier if the study showed that there is no basic nature of people, that people react only to the situation in which they find themselves, or whether people act against their own beliefs under a slight stimulation such as embarrassment of refusal? Or would we want rather to believe those people were sincere and really felt that they should do what they were doing? Perhaps, in this case, the reaction to the research was more revealing than the research itself. It can lead us to a reassessment of the value of sincerity.

The delicate balance between conformity and compliance pervades a society. With the heightened value of sincerity, these conflicts are closer to the surface than they might be in other conditions. The principal way in which this conflict is exposed is by accepting freedom of expression and action by consensus, while insisting on complete, whole agreement with one's actions. Sometimes we all do things we would rather not do, but we would prefer that everybody else would act according to their beliefs. This enforcement of sincerity has guided analysis in the laboratory and theories of the social psychologist. It guides the treatment of the individual as well as the moral values and constitution of the society.

Psychotherapy

Classical psychotherapy is based on an image of internal dynamics which is partly repressed, and the therapist has to bring out its natural feature for the understanding and cure of the patient. This does not mean, however, that the therapist is simply freeing the unconscious dynamic from restrictions—in other words, from compliant behavior. In psychiatric terminology, the superego, although its cost can be repressive, cannot be eliminated completely. It has to be readjusted to function in a healthy manner. In defining this healthy manner, the therapist defines the balance between conformity and compliance for mental health. The same conflict which we have found in our society occurs between therapies and different schools of therapy. Psychotherapy has come to its real fruition together with the cult of sincerity, and both are open to the same strictures. Psychotherapy could be used to produce a completely conforming society by manipulating people to conform completely. It also can be abused by creating self-fulfillment to lead to a completely unrestrained society, a society with a complete lack of compliance. Thus, psychiatry can be attacked as leading to manipulation of man as being in the service of the power structure or leading to chaos in society through the cult of self-gratification.

Like social theorists, psychiatrists are willing to avoid either extreme and struggle with the actual limits of roles in self-expression. They have been aware of the tension at least since Freud called attention to the discontent of civilization. The need for limits for some areas of life where compliance is useful is clear and so is the repressive cost of expanding this area too far. The acceptance of rules is civilization: this is the cost of living in society. By giving up the societal rules, life in society does not become autonomous, but on the contrary, more rigid rules are imposed by the stronger. The subtle rigidity of those institutions of current society which stress freedom, self-fulfillment, and authenticity as slogans are a case in point.

Conclusion

This short excursion into psychologists' work with individuals has brought the social problems of conformity and compliance into even stronger relief. The totally unrestrained nonsocial individual is just as much a fiction as the abstract concept of society. Impulse, attitude, and opinion cannot be translated completely into action for either a functioning individual or a functioning society. Therapy can help those persons for whom the adjustment has been too painful or unworkable. For the rest of the population, we may expect variability which we can call character, personality, or personal morality.

Changes in society impinge on the individual from the opposite direction. Personal preferences for consistency may be violated by authoritarian demands for actions extremely different from one's belief or by totalitarian demands to adapt opinions to enforced actions. These demands come from different sources as we noted in the rise of sincerity. Yesterday's enforcer of compliance may look benign today, when yesterday's defenders of freedom from compliance demand complete sincerity in belief and action. The change may be so rapid that one is confused as to where the sources of the danger of conformity may be. Psychotherapists had to struggle against academic censorship shortly before they imposed their values on the therapeutic society. It is no accident that Trilling gave his lectures on sincerity when he was himself in conflict about defining the autonomy of the individual against the demands of the New Left. Having fought totalitarianism and authoritarianism for decades, he felt too fatigued to engage himself again, but felt the conflict sufficiently enough to be painfully aware of the recent virtue of sincerity (Podhoretz, 1979).

Developing a creative balance between conformity and compliance, or between attitudes and actions, or ego and superego, is the test of the maturing of the individual. It would be an optimistic conclusion if we could discern a similar trend. However, if there is such a trend, it is certainly masked by serious disturbances. One may find some evidence of increasing restraint in interpersonal relations—of compliance in a way which leads to individual freedom. The sociologist and the social philosopher, Norbert Elias, has drawn attention to this long-range improvement in civilized behavior in his book, *The Civilizing Function* (1978). Analyzing personal conduct, he finds by and large an increase in civilized behavior in this sense. He is vividly conscious of deflections and perversions of this trend—the book is dedicated to his parents who perished in Auschwitz. In spite of all, Elias sees a maturing, civilizing trend in society. We may take heart in the everyday struggle in the society.

REFERENCES

Barthes, R. *Sade/Fourier/Loyola*. New York: Farrar, Straus and Giroux, 1976.

Blumer, H. J. *Symbolic interactionism.* Englewood Cliffs, N.J.: Prentice-Hall, 1969.

Brehm, J. W., & Cohen, A. R. *Explorations in cognitive dissonance.* New York: Wiley, 1962.

Campbell, J. *The masks of god: Creative mythology.* New York: Viking Press, 1968.

Clive, J. *Thomas Babington Macaulay.* London: Secker and Warburg, 1973.

Cohn, N. *Europe's inner demons.* London: Sussex University Press, 1975.

Crawford, T. J. Theories of attitude change and the "beyond family planning" debate: The case for the persuasion approach in population policy. *Journal of Social Issues,* 1974, *30* (4): 211–233.

Crespi, I. Attitude measurement, theory and prediction. *Public Opinion Quarterly,* 1977, *41:* 285–294.

Elias, N. *The civilizing process.* New York: Urizen Press, 1978.

Festinger, L. *A theory of cognitive dissonance.* Evanston, Ill: Row, Peterson, 1957.

Fishbein, M., & Ajzen, I. *Belief, attitude, intention and behavior.* Reading, Mass: Addison-Wesley, 1975.

Frank, J. *Persuasion and healing.* Baltimore: Johns Hopkins, 1961.

Guthrie, W. K. *Sophists.* Cambridge: Cambridge University Press, 1971.

Hawthorne, N. *The Scarlet Letter.* Boston: Tickner Reed Co., 1852.

Jones, E. E., Kanouse, D. E., Kelley, H. H., Nisbett, R. E., Valins, S., & Weiner, B. *Attribution: Perceiving the causes of behavior.* Morristown, N. J.: General Learning, 1972.

Joyce, J. *Portrait of the artist as a young man.* London: The Egoist Press, 1916.

Kelman, H. Compliance, identification and internalization: Three processes of opinion change. *Journal of Conflict Resolution,* 1958, *2:* 51–60.

LaPiere, R. T. Attitudes vs. actions. *Social Forces,* 1934, *13:* 230–237.

Loyola, I. *A manual of devout meditation.* Ilkley, England: Scolar Press, 1976 (from 1618 original).

Milgram, S. *Obedience to authority.* New York: Harper and Row, 1974.

Milosz, C. *The captive mind.* New York: Vintage, 1951.

Moreno, J. The concept of here and now, hic et nunc: Small groups and their relations to action research. *Group Psychotherapy,* 1969, *22* (3–4): 139–141.

Murray, M. *The Witch-cult in Western Europe.* New York: Oxford University Press, 1962.
Orwell, G. *1984.* New York: Harcourt, Brace & Jovanovich, 1949.
Podhoretz, N. *Breaking ranks.* New York: Harper and Row, 1979.
Schuman, H., & Johnson, M. P. Attitude and behavior. *Annual Review of Sociology,* 1976, *3*: 161–207.
Skinner, B. F. *Beyond freedom and dignity.* New York: Knopf, 1971.
Talmon, J. L. *The origins of totalitarian democracy.* London: Secker and Warburg, 1952.
Trilling, L. *Sincerity and authenticity.* Cambridge, Mass: Harvard University Press, 1971.
Watson, D. L. *The origins and significance of the early Methodist class meetings.* Unpublished doctoral dissertation, Duke University, 1978.
White, L., Jr. Science and the sense of self: The medieval background of a modern confrontation. *Daedalus,* 1978, *107* (2) (Spring): 47–71.
Wolpe, J., & Lazarus, A. A. *Behavior therapy technique: A guide to the treatment of neuroses.* London: Pergamon Press, 1966.

Chapter 3

COMPLIANCE?

Between Freedom and Compulsion

Raymond Battegay

THE CONFLICT OF NORMS

Each group in our society has at present its own social norm. These norms may be very different. Children who grow up in the small family of today with its norm of nonparticipation with individuals of other families come to the kindergarten with a norm demanding them to participate in other children's pleasure and play. When they leave this milieu to go to school again, another norm has to be observed. It is no longer the norm that the children should feel well and comfortable, but now it begins to be directed towards performance. Children are no longer able to live out their own fantasies and drives, but they have to fulfill the aim-directed expectancies of teachers. This new norm is contrary to that of the kindergarten. Whereas this school norm demands performance at any price, the mass media demonstrate to the young people a norm of leisure. Already, that contrast makes it difficult for them to know to which norm they should comply.

But also other norms interfere with this norm of demands which is characteristic of the school system. If the young person has to visit a doctor, he or she hears that relaxation is the most important thing in the world. If a boy or a girl has to visit a religious center the churchman or other religious people tell him or her that nothing other than love counts in the human existence. When he or she asks, why, then, in the name of religion crusades or wars were fought, he or she receives no intelligible answer. This leads to a conflict of norms in young people of which others, especially educators, seem to know very little.

Thus, children and adolescents have to grow up with many different norms which continuously demand a new compliance, without adults caring much about the tensions linked with this demand of a changing adaption to divergent norms.

Until World War II Western countries predominantly observed one main norm, oriented toward the Ten Commandments, which had become part of the Jewish-Christian religion. After World War II, mankind appeared to lose faith in religion and the effectiveness of the church weakened. Religion and the Christian-Jewish norm no longer governed Western civilization. We have to admit also that today a general norm covers all other norms of diverse small groups, but this norm seems to be only a superficial one, which includes only a certain behavior, mainly a result of the influences of the mass media. But in-depth, the conflict of norms in a small group is experienced consciously or unconsciously by our youth. Each child or young person must therefore feel the responsibility to follow this or that norm. It is no longer self-evident to which norm the youngsters should belong; they always have to decide afresh to which norm they are prepared to comply.

THE NECESSITY FOR A CONTINUOUSLY RENEWED DECISION

Many of those who have to grow up in our society and undergo socialization suffer in a world which is, as Riesman (1950) says, an other-directed one. They have a difficult time finding their own way. In each group, young people are expected to adapt themselves to the demands of the collective. They are never allowed to live in a manner which comes from within themselves. In Europe, in 1968, the student revolt against the universities was a dramatic signal that at least academic youth no longer accepted or complied with the authoritarian structures of the universities. The effect of this revolution did not last long. A restoration of old power structures ensued and only a few meaningless rights remained for the students; for example, the right to discuss the problems of universities with professors, whereas in reality students are rarely allowed to vote along with the authorities responsible for the universities. The revolution against the outer-directed world, against compliance, was not a lasting success. Again, young people had to adapt themselves to the written or unwritten directives and laws of the authorities. It *seems* that those who grow up can decide in a free way for this or for that norm. In fact, they expect that they should comply—wherever they are—to a unitary behavior norm which is regarded at the moment as modern.

A New Kind of Superego

In encounters with students as well as patients, we observe that very often they no longer have a superego in which authority figures of the past are introjected. Their anxieties prove that their superegos are much more formed by the anonymous norms which characterize our modern society.

The fact that most examinations are no longer executed verbally by a teacher or a professor alone with a student but are very often done by means of a multiple-choice procedure is typical for this anonymous collective authority represented in the superego of our time. Nowadays, we often observe in students, not fears concerning the authoritarian personality of a professor, but anxieties concerned with the anonymous system of examination in which no personal authority assumes responsibility. Therefore, it is not possible for students to enter into a dialogue either with their superego or with a responsible authority.

One of our patients, a man aged 29, was 2 years younger than his sister and 5 years older than his brother. He was overprotected by his mother and felt he was always tormented by his peer groups. This feeling was so pervasive that he remained an outsider in spite of his desire to have contact with comrades. Even in his short-lasting matrimonial life of 4 years, he experienced the nearness of a person as too demanding. When he came to our outpatient clinic, he was brought after 10 individual psychotherapy sessions, with his consent, to a seminar which approximately 20 physicians and psychologists attended. He seemed to suffer from anxiety, trembled, and said that in this situation as in earlier similar situations he felt that he should satisfy the whole anonymous group, which he experienced as demanding his adaptation.

This narcissistically disturbed man who was overprotected in his childhood felt this impersonal collective norm in a really dominating way. Less pronounced, all members of our modern society feel this impersonal superego. In a very imposing way, society is increasingly becoming more superficial. Transcendental belief is lacking.

Narcissistically disturbed people expect, on the one hand, a great deal from society, but on the other hand are disappointed in those whom they encounter. This derives partly from the fact that they feel in principle an obligation to adapt themselves to generally accepted norms of behavior without any foundation. Rules are only oriented toward behavior and not toward a content which could fulfill and guide them. This collective superego does not give them a direction in their lives. It is felt only as a categorical imperative (Kant, 1781), which does not consider them as human beings with their own needs, but only as members of a collective who should not demand too much attention from the others.

Bettelheim (1973), describing collective education in the kibbutzim, shows that the children and juveniles who grow up in these settlements do not show a superego in which the parental figures are introjected, but much more a type of superego in which the peer group gives the basis for its structure. In the kibbutzim, the group of children and juveniles of the same age plays a much more important role than the parents, since the children live most of their time in the children's house and not together with mother and father. Their compliance to the peer group goes so far that they relinquish their individual desires, if they notice that the peer group does not tolerate them. This adaptation to the group has its good side, since it helps to minimize disturbances, but it has also a doubtful aspect, since the members cannot develop a strong individuality even if they have a constitutionally determined strong ego structure. The compliance to the group superego means also that the members very often renounce individual intellectual development which can cause tension within themselves and between them and the ideology of the kibbutz.

COMPLIANCE TO A GROUP

From what has been said about the collective settlements, we have already implied what may be going on when an individual enters a group. The group with its own norms of behavior demands a certain compliance from each individual. If the group is considered to be more important than the participating individuals, there is the danger that they have to submit themselves to a collective norm which would thus turn into an ideology no longer open for constructive criticism. Therefore, the members become obliged to follow the demands of those who purport to be the representatives of this collective norm. In other words, the ideology dominates the participating members as is the case in a dictatorial system. Even if this general norm should sound very humane and should strive to create greater equality between human beings, such a unitarian ideology is dangerous for the individuals who submit themselves to it since it is easily possible that all other opinions are regarded as obsolete. In such a group each member who has an individual attitude towards the group will be regarded as in a position of "anomia" (Durkheim, 1893; Merton, 1957), and everybody in an outsider position risks being regarded as disturbing, or to be put in jail, or in (misused) psychiatric institutions as an "enemy of the people," as the Norwegian dramatist Henrik Ibsen (1956/1968) says. Any small or large group submitted totally to an ideologic norm exposes itself to the danger of developing an inhuman system. Such a group, obeying a totalitarian norm, runs great risk of petrifying. None of the members dares to propose changes. This means that such a group system is very rigid and, seen in the long term, must risk collapsing if new values and norms, which are not yet fulfilled in this group, show on the one hand their effectiveness and on the other the possibilities of a free human life. It is this petrification which Andrei Amalrik (1977) referred to when he described the Soviet system and asked whether it could survive 1984. Only by arms, a strong army, and a secret police, with all the modern means of manipulation at their disposal, can such a petrified ideologic system continue—one which has not renewed its theory born in the nineteenth century on economics and politics and has maintained its power since 1917. Therefore, we can say that the more a system adheres to an immobile norm, the more it is in jeopardy of being destroyed by its immobilism. Not even the best army of the world is able to conserve such an ideologically oriented system in the long term. Only a small or large group that is open to reforms of its norms is able to survive at length.

The Longer Arm of a Lever

Since the group is always an interactional system, the individual member also has the longer arm of a lever to reach the fulfillment of his desires. He can "use" parts of or the whole system and has then the result of the energies of the subgroup or of all members at his disposal. Therefore, with the interactional network of a group, the individual has an instrument at his disposal for eventually exerting more power toward a leader, but also eventually, with the leader together, toward people outside the group. This means that a small group has the possibility of imposing on the surrounding world which does not share its norm, i.e., or forcing the majority to comply with the minority.

Before the Nazis became powerful in Germany, they, as a political group, tried to get power and abused their own group structure and their aggressive ideology in a malfunctioning democratic system with the aim of submitting the whole nation to their domination. With the interactional system of their party and with the help of many others who were friendly with them and in principle were attached to this political group, the Nazis had a long arm of a lever to act in the sense of destruction of a badly organized state which was not prepared to combat such a well-organized fighting and terrorizing group.

In each group the participating individuals extend their narcissism more or less to the others and, on this basis, they undergo a process of identification which represents an active ego performance. The narcissistic fusion tendencies in the members of a group particularly can lead to a more or less compact collective which may be strong enough to impose their opinion on the others. We have observed this in our times, e.g., a movement of religious groups in Iran where the members have undergone fusion to such a degree with a leader and the other members that many of the surrounding society have aligned themselves totally. The leader succeeded, together with his group of followers from outside the country, in changing the state and expelling the Shah. The emotions of the group led to an induction of emotions in the people in such a way that what reminded them of the old political system was flooded over.

Milgram's experiments (1966, 1974) at Yale University have shown how far obedience can go when individuals are submitted to the pressure of a leader. Sixty-five percent of the subjects of an examined sample of an average population were ready to punish individuals, who made programmed faults, in a standardized experiment with electric shocks up to 450 volts, when they were told to do so by the leader. Apparently, they did not dare to resist him when he was near them. It could be proved with experiments that people were more easily ready to resist the leader when he only gave the order by phone from another room or when the individual to whom they should apply the electric shock was visible or touchable. The experiment, which seems not quite morally defensible, shows, however, that individuals who are submitted to a potent leader and are not able to resist are in danger of fulfilling orders, even when they know or feel that they are doing something inhuman. After the experiences in totalitarian states, however, it must be urged that each person with normal intelligence should be aware of this danger if they are integrated in a group and submitted to a leader, even if they might be fascinated emotionally by the leader and his ideology.

But also in a well-functioning society, it is possible for the group to extend pressure, for example, on the parliament and on the whole state. The system of the group gives the participants, and especially the leading members of the group, the opportunity to use the group as a means of pressure which may impose the opinion of the minority on the others. However, as long as a well-established democratic supervision by the parliament and the population functions, there is no real danger linked with it, since in this case the large group is able to buffer the pressure of the small group. We know how difficult it may be to resist in our Western countries, but it is even more so in countries where children are drilled to obedience to the appeal of a potent leader. We have to rethink our whole educational system and give our children and juveniles the opportunity from kindergarten on to recognize the dangers and advantages, not only of when the interactional system of a group is misused by a leader, but also the possibilities which the group system offers to help to solve problems.

The Educational System

If we stress the necessity of offering children self-experience in groups, we think that we can train them to find better means for solving their problems in social reality. For this purpose, skilled teachers who know the dynamics of groups from their own training in self-experience should be at the disposal of each class. Such self-experience sessions, e.g., lasting 2 hrs a week, should be introduced in each school timetable, so that the children may learn, in addition to mathematics, languages, and so forth, for their development and formation (in addition to the information they receive), what a social reality represents and what help they can expect from a group. We do not want to say that children should learn to adapt themselves to a group with such a group experience. We do, however, think that schoolgirls and boys in this way would gain an opportunity to develop insight into their own unconscious tendencies and the possibility of preserving and cultivating their individuality in and through the experience of the group. S. R. Slavson (1950) wrote that modern democracy is not the triumph of the free individual, but of the free group. Therefore, we can say that the group in modern society represents, with its manifold demands toward the individual and with its multiple norms, a frame of similar thinking and feeling of people, who help participating individuals by division of work and emotions to survive and to defend themselves against the necessity to comply to society at any price.

THE PROTECTING GROUP

From our experiences with group psychotherapy we know that the group is experienced as protective, after an initial phase of exploration in which anxieties come up. Demands on the individual do not cause much harm because they can be discussed with the other members. With the aid of the others, the participants succeed in maintaining their position without being forced to comply to outside pressure. Since smaller groups in general have a better cohesion than larger groups, the smaller ones usually are better able to maintain their own atmosphere and norm than the larger ones. From history and our own time, we know that small nations with a well-organized group structure often resist outside pressure better than others. The group cohesion gives a feeling of protection and security to the members. In huge countries a feeling of power may rise in the citizens, but perhaps in the smaller ones, in which their composition by small groups is still visible, cohesion in general is of a higher degree and people may feel more secure. Thus, we can say that the well-structured group protects against being compelled to comply to outside groups. However, as was already mentioned, a certain compliance is also necessary in a small group, even of seven to nine members, as in group psychotherapy. If there is no common denominator, no common norm exists—and no group and no group psychotherapy is possible. Individuals who are totally negative toward any kind of compliance are not suitable for a group and cannot be integrated into a psychotherapeutic group. Without the ability to comply, an individual is asocial and from the psychiatric point of view neurotically disturbed in his communication. Especially individuals who do not have enough self-confidence, who have no consistent self (Kohut, 1971) as a central representation, are frequently not able to comply, or they wish to undergo a fusion with people close to them. They do not find the desirable middle between resistance and compliance, between distance and closeness.

Compulsion and Freedom

In everyday life we always live as if no outer or inner necessities but only free decisions would drive us to our actions. Already what we have said about people who do not have a consistent self and do not have a healthy narcissism shows that at least our inner conditions may force us to a certain compliance with regard to our possibilities. We cannot achieve more than our forces permit us. Many people think that they are hungrier than they are actually able to eat, and as many individuals have aims which are far too high for them. In the course of time they have to comply to their limitations—to make peace with them—or they will be continuously disappointed because they cannot accept the gap between their desires and their real possibilities in the social reality. But also, the facts of the outside world, the rhythms of the seasons, of day and night, the influences of the political and socioeconomical conditions, the structure and the pattern of communications of the family in which the individual grows up, all these have a decisive influence on our existence.

Our capacity to verbalize, the kind of verbalization, our affectivity, our conceptualization of the world, and our behavior are to a large extent the product of compliance to the norms of the surrounding groups during socialization. We have therefore to ask ourselves, what in our existence is the result of our free will.

If we question ourselves on the matter of compulsion and freedom in human existence, we turn up deeper and deeper problems. We can put the question to the investigator of behavior Eibl-Eibesfeldt (1973)—whether or not the human being is not totally "preprogrammed," determined by the genetic code, which attributes to the desoxyribonucleic acids of our chromosomes this power, that the human being in former times attributed to an extraterrestrial creator. From our human experience, we can say that these preprogrammed processes are not alone decisive. They can apparently be comprehended by experience, learning, and conception of life to those functional entities which represent the specificity of each individual. By this statement, we mean that our human life is not only the result of a compliance to preexisting conditions, but also to a certain extent, the result of the free possibilities of each individual. This freedom, however, goes only as far as the conditions which each individual brings with him permit.

THE POINT OF VIEW OF PSYCHOANALYSIS

Sigmund Freud (1916–1917, 1923) considered the ego as the integrating instance in our psyche which should coordinate the different parts of our psychic life and of our different life realizations. It is this ego which Freud differentiated from the id with its drives and from the superego which contains the social norms as "introjects" in our fantasies. Freud knew that this scheme of psychic instances is only a model for thinking. He knew that what he designated as ego corresponds only to the human desire to overcome our ignorance concerning the integrative functions in the experience and in the life of the human being. The ego means that the individual has an instance which helps him to live his life in a more or less individual manner and to control to a certain degree the drives and the influences from the superego, on the one hand, and of the actual surrounding world on the other. The ego has the central function for the individual to assimilate intrapsychic and outside material, and at the same time to resist inner and outer stimuli against any compliance by establishing a filter, regardless of where it would be demanded. Heinz Kohut (1971, 1977) has drawn our attention to the fact that with the instances of ego, id, and superego we cannot yet understand the functioning of the human psyche. He speaks of the central representation, the self, with its narcissistic libido, if we want, from the warming energy which gives a self-value, a self-esteem to our whole life. It is this self which enables the human being to feel good in his body and to recognize his behavior and his actions emotionally as belonging to himself. If it is intact, this self gives him the power not to become dependent on other objects, not to make a total fusion with others, which would be necessary if a narcissistic lack would have to be fulfilled. Therefore, we can say that only an individual with a consistent self is capable of choosing in a free way, whether he wants to live integrated into a group, or into society, or even whether he wants to adapt himself totally to it, or whether he desires to follow a more or less independent way.

Dependence on Neurophysiological Conditions

Until now, neurophysiology and psychology have not delivered findings which would prove the ego, the id, and the superego or the self as representation of the physiological self-esteem. In a neurophysiological sense we have to suppose that the ego-functions and the self-functions are the result of the individual energies and effects of the 14 to 15 billion ganglia which compose our brain. If we say that the ego and the self are the subjective—integrative and self-fulfilling functions having their basis in the complex physiology of our central nervous system, we have not yet said much. Concerning the realm and the limits of the human liberty to decide from this aspect, we can only speculate and nobody can tell us whether our life means a total compliance to determined factors or whether it goes on in a free and undetermined way. Are we simply manipulated objects of the genetic code and the nervous system, determined by it, or are we free individuals who are able to activate the functional pathways of our brain by means of free choice? From our life experience we may suppose that we can only choose between some possibilities inherent in ourselves. However, we are never sure what this choosing instance is and whether our apparently free choice is really independent or whether it is not forced at least more or less to comply to the functional state of our body.

The Influence of the Past

Psychoanalysis has opened our eyes to the fact that the human being is highly dependent on the problems of his childhood which are emotionally not yet solved. What he believes to be the product of his free decision is often only the result of a compliance. With Watzlawick, Beavin, and Jackson (1967) we can say that human communications are only too often going on after analogous, in their essence always repeating, patterns and not in digital modalities, which would correspond to the new conditions. In other words, there is a human tendency to comply to patterns of behavior of the past more than to the actual conditions. But usually we live as if we could choose one of our possibilities in a free way, as if we were not determined by our early experiences and conditions of life, and as if we were not submitted to conditions from the inside or the outside. Apparently, we need this illusion of a totally free decision, otherwise we would be much less motivated for our activities. We would not take the many risks we do if we did not misunderstand the real realm of our freedom in an illusionary way. This illusion of freedom and this neglect of our necessity to comply to inner or outer conditions, at least in a certain way, seem to have an activating function towards productivity as well as towards imprudent, thoughtless, and premature actions.

Freedom by Reason and Consciousness

If we have spoken about an illusion of freedom, we must exemplify this statement again. The human being is characterized—in comparison to the animal—preponderantly by the fact that he is conscious of his life. Immanuel Kant (1781) has said that the human being by means of his reason is able to come out of the guardianship of nature into a state of freedom. His words, written in the eighteenth century, cannot by subscribed to today without critical remarks. On the one hand, the human being has made more progress than could be imagined in the past, but on the other hand, he proves to be extremely dependent on his unresolved aggressions and other drives in our time. He complied to these forces, especially when he was misled by political leaders. But still today, we may say that the human being, if he is trained and motivated, is able to be a critical and conscious observer of himself. He is not forced to identify himself with all his drive tendencies or with his acts, not even with his integrative ego. Even men and women who are not accustomed to thinking can become conscious of the limits of their freedom, if their behavior patterns clash with those of others, and ask themselves whether their action was right or not. They live more or less consciously in the direction of a central motive which they have, often unknown to themselves, taken over from the norms of their early family. This introjection of the surrounding norms leads to the superego, as Freud (1916–1917, 1923) stressed. On the one hand, this instance of conscience gives the human being a certain freedom from his drives. He is, therefore, not absolutely forced to comply with them. On the other hand, the submission to the superego also means a compliance, because it contains, as was already said, the norms of behavior and value of childhood. The human being feels forced to swing between the drives and impulses which act in him as biological energies and the expectations of society. In this field of forces he lives once more free and once more forced to comply.

However, if we consider the human being as dependent on his drives, we cannot necessarily say that he is unfree. Perhaps such an individual feels especially free—free from the judgments and prejudices of the society. In the same way, we may consider a man as free or unfree if he complies more or less totally to his surroundings. He then shall be free of his drives, but unfree, if we think of the fact that the fulfillment of the drives belongs to the human life and the unfulfillment of them lets him lose possibilities of a free development of his personality.

Chance or Necessity

Our entire lives are going on in this antinomy of freedom and compulsion. Freedom must not only mean free choice of possibilities, it comes also from the chance of probability. The French philosopher Jacques Monod (1970) entitled his book on this subject *Chance and Necessity* (*Le hasard et la nécessité*) and put the words of a Greek philosopher at the beginning: "All that exists in the world, is the fruit of necessity." What seems to be the result of freedom could also be a choice following the rules of probability. Monod, however, goes on in a very convincing way and says that the man who once was entirely dependent on the traditions of his tribe and on his group knows by now what power he possesses. As Monod says, scientific knowledge has given man possibilities—to take his destiny in his own hands but also to destroy the world.

Whatever the political system may have been, the human being has never recognized the fact that he alone is responsible for himself. As always man would tend to follow mystic fantasies because he could not bear his sole responsibility in the universe;

therefore, he would develop ideologies as defense mechanisms against his anxieties, as has been the case since archaic times. Therefore, the human being should become aware of the fact that he has the power not to comply to the natural forces and that, at least to a certain degree, he is able to overcome his own nature and the forces of the surrounding world. Even gravitation does not any longer mean that man is forced to comply to it. Monod characterizes religion also as a defense mechanism. His approach seems to me to be an all too simplistic point of view, since we have to consider that the world is experienced not only in a rational way, but also by means of the emotions and drives through the medium of the unconscious. Even natural sciences do not deliver an indivisible truth. We have to consider it a fact that we shall never find the absolute truth, but always only partial truths coming out of different aspects, even when they seem to contradict themselves. It is natural that we agree with Monod when he shows the necessity for the human being to recognize his responsibility. This means that man today cannot say that he is forced to comply to internal or external powers and, therefore, he has to recognize the weight of his decisions.

THE HUMAN RESPONSIBILITY TOWARDS THE LAW

The question of freedom and compulsion—from determinism and indeterminism of life—is especially seen in connection with the penal law. If the judges condemn a man who offends the law, they admit by that at least a relative freedom of decision. But as Dukor (1960) states so rightly, this question of determinism or indeterminism must be regarded today as too simple a way of consideration. It is not easy to judge when and where in the human life determinism—and with that compliance preponderantly to the genetic code but also to social conditions—predominates and where the human freedom of decision begins.

As soon as the child becomes conscious of himself, and thus with his ego, not entirely dependent on the drives of his id and his superego, which demand blind obedience to drives or to authority, i.e., as soon as it is possible for him to be his own observer, beginning from his tenth to eleventh year, it will be possible for him, in the normal case, to decide for this or that possibility in or outside of himself.

As psychiatrists, we would not have to examine the responsibility of a man before the law if he was regarded as entirely determined. If we assume an individual to be responsible for a certain action, we assume that he would be free to make up his mind for this or that possibility, even if a certain disturbance of the personality would be present. That will not mean that a man will be recommended to the courts for a heavy punishment—"Responsibility before the law" only means that a criminal act is not due to psychosis, a very severe neurosis, or an outstanding abnormal character, which would be preponderantly determined. We say with the statement that a man who has to be judged is responsible before this law, whether he would have had the chance to decide in a more or less free way for another option than the criminal one. The judge, however, can take into consideration mitigating circumstances which may have influenced such a man in a negative way.

In our human society we cannot but recognize a normal man within his responsibility, and by this, within his free possibilities of decision, even if it should be a fiction, i.e., even if, from an absolute point of view, human beings would be entirely determined. The admittance of a total determination would endanger our human society and our survival. Indeed, it is our experience of everyday life that with our constitutions we can develop possibilities to a social or to an antisocial aim. If we admitted a total determination of man, nothing would fascinate us in our existence—only the feeling of at least a certain possibility of free decision motivates us to act, to create. In education we therefore shall have to make sure early on that those who grow up in our society are able to recognize, on the one hand, the boundaries of their freedom of decision, and on the other hand, the realm in which they can fulfill themselves in a free and responsible way by means of work.

Freedom and Compulsion in Education

If we ask ourselves how to educate our children, it appears that we give them our beliefs and doctrines on the one hand, without being sufficiently aware of what they can do with them in an always changing world. On the other hand, we cannot disregard our own values in the education of our children. Later on, they should be better able to withdraw from us and to develop strong egos. This is after we have given them clear coordinates within which they can grow up in security and from which they can break away and develop in an independent way without fear that they will destroy their parents in the process.

Modern psychology urges that adolescents receive that unconditional understanding which should give them the chance to develop most of the possibilities existing in their personality in an utterly free atmosphere. Old authoritarian relationships in the family are disappearing. The traditional order system in the schools which was based on compliance and discipline is questioned. But nowadays, the adolescents complain that nobody dares to face them and that nobody wants to take any responsibility for them. Thus, on the one hand, the youth have obtained a freedom that could not have been imagined in earlier times, but on the other hand, the juveniles can no longer measure their attitudes in the exchange of opinions with authorities.

Compulsion and School Systems

If we want to train the children who are growing up to be responsible citizens, it is not possible to drill them to absolute obedience in schools. Schoolchildren should be much more encouraged than is the case today to participate actively in their classes. Teachers should be eager to take responsibility for pupils and to give them alternately the chance to study a certain realm of knowledge and to teach it to the classmates. Furthermore, schoolchildren should be motivated more than they are today for group work and, thus, for coping with others in a responsible way. Children and juveniles would learn much more willingly if they could cooperate actively than if they had to comply with teachers. Compulsion and compliance do not lead to free citizens. Only the free decision to work in a responsible way gives to our youth the possibility of acquiring knowledge and social experience as well. If we constantly stress that our youth should grow up in a free way, we shall have to take care to enable them to train themselves for free decisions and to bear their freedom in a world which is always more directed by norms.

The pure conveyance of facts in schools is therefore not thought suitable since the half-life period of knowledge is much shorter than it was 10, 50, or 100 years ago. In former times what was learned in school could be maintained almost throughout the whole life, but what is taught today is only valid for a few years. The teaching systems should have the aim to teach children and juveniles how to acquire different branches of knowledge with free effort in the later years of life. The school should, therefore, not be centered on the learning content as much as it is today, but much more on the methods with which students later on will be able to learn on their own in a responsible way. This is how they could prepare themselves early on to pursue their personal and professional lives with a feeling of freedom without having to fear being forced to comply to outside demands and normative rules.

From Outside-Motility to Inner Motion

In his now classical studies on babies, René Spitz (1965) has shown that a mask designed with eyes, a nose, and a mouth makes a three-month-old baby laugh, but only on condition that the mask is moved. The child remains motionless without this movement. This smile of the three-month-old child already shows the prime importance of the motility in our life in order to be "moved" inwardly.

The Harlows (1967) have raised a group of monkeys with an iron-wire mother surrogate which was equipped with milk bottles and a control group with an artificial fur mother surrogate. The small monkeys reared by the fur mother grew up normally and sought her protection in dangerous situations, even when the two investigators covered the fur mother with a nylon cloth. Apparently, the eyesight contact with the "warm" fur was sufficient after they had gotten in touch with the fur beforehand. The little monkeys, however, who were with their iron-wire mother neither took refuge with her nor did they breed later on. I am indebted to Prof. G. Benedetti (1967) for the reports on experiments, apparently of the Harlows', in which the iron-wire mother was not fixed at a particular place anymore, but moved, and the small monkeys developed almost as normally as those who grew up with a fur mother surrogate. These experiments and the observations of Spitz prove the importance of the outer movement—and of outer stimulation—on inner psychic activity and the development of the human being and the animal.

Taking these experiments into account, we have to consider whether we have lost something decisive for our own inner motion and thereupon for our feeling of freedom due to the widespread lack of movement in the present time. Our experience in psychiatry shows that the human being feels much freer if he takes regular exercise. This knowledge is not new. As is known, a basic principle of education in antiquity was: *Mens sana in corpore sano* ("Healthy mental activity in a healthy body"). Therefore, we have to assume that compliance to the many sitting jobs of today and the lack of movement linked with it not only stimulate the rise of circulatory diseases but also take us to the point where we are not free enough to be active in our fantasies. If we speak about inner freedom, we always have to think about the fact that a life which goes on more or less without muscular action may also lead to an inner compliance tendency or to an increase in inner tension and aggressivity. Not merely because of pollution but also for reasons of mental health, it is important not to be always passively transported by motorcars. A population is only able to feel inwardly free if it has the opportunity to move and if it is not tied unconditionally to a vehicle.

RESTRICTION OF FREEDOM AND AGGRESSION

It has been shown that persons who transform little of their inner energy into movement are exposed to the danger of not being able to control their own aggressions any longer. However, we do not agree with Erich Fromm (1973) who makes a distinction between a benign and a malignant aggression as if they were of a totally different genesis. Fromm believes that only the benign aggression has an anatomic substratum in the brain but not the malignant, destructive one. He says that this malignant aggression is a passion based on the structure of the character of the concerned person. We must point out in reply to Fromm that there is only *one* neurophysiological substratum in the brain for the benign as well as for the malignant aggression, as W. R. Hess' (1954) investigations about the fury of the cats have shown. If the human being is inclined to destructive aggression, more than any other living creature, we must assume that the aggression, originally serving him to defend himself and to develop a gripping interest, is pent up and undergoes a change in quality if it cannot be realized. Moreover, we have to suppose that this density of living together, to which modern man is forced, comes to the point where he does not anymore have the freedom to put his aggressions into action or use them in a socially constructive way in free nature. He has to restrain himself constantly and to comply to the many others surrounding him. He is always reminded of the many social norms so that the aggression is bottled up to the point where it bursts forth in a destructive way.

As observations of group behavior of wild rats have shown (Barnett, 1969), the reciprocal aggressions increased the denser the interactions of the rats became. Reciprocal intolerance was observed which drove these wild-living rats to expulsion of others, particularly of their offspring. It became apparent in a mice experiment that the smaller the cage was, or the more the mice were forced to interact because of lack of room, the more the aggressions of each animal increased (Charpentier, 1969).

Christian (1963) has observed that in a cage with an increasing population of mice, a progressive increase of hypophyseal-adrenocortical reactions and a decrease of the reproductional functions occur in both male and female animals. The growth of the mice is increasingly hindered by growing density of the population. Furthermore, it could be shown that the mortality rate grows with growing density of the population, i.e., sudden deaths occur. Presumably there is a connection between the sudden deaths of these mice and the exhaustion through permanent mobilization of glucose as a result of continuously repeated stimulation of the adrenal medulla, so that the animals die of a lack of sugar (hypoglycemia). With a growing density of living together and increasing interactions, there will not only be a growing aggressivity but also an intensified tension in the sense of stress of the endocrine-hormonal system, i.e., of an alarm syndrome which leads also to an impairment of the functions of procreation. These observations in the animal experiment prove, on the one hand, the psychophysical unity and, on the other hand, that, as shown in the animal experiments, there is a limit to the number of interactions above which they can no longer comply to the situation, but get aggressive against others in their area.

Modern man is far too unaware of the effects of this restriction of space, the accumulation of human beings in blocks of flats which are built so closely to each other and which leave them no chance of moving around freely. No doubt this limitation of freedom of space contains the risk of accumulated aggression which can go so far as to the evolution of destructive behavior. Not only is it that the big cities offer refuge to frustrated and intolerant people, but also the high density of living together in narrow space may have contributed to the fact that there are almost no boundaries for aggression as the growing criminality rates in the metropolitan milieu shows. The limitation of freedom in space can lead to an accumulation of aggression and then to a loss of control towards aggression. Therefore, we have to intensify the prophylactic steps in childhood and youth. If we neglect this duty, mankind is threatened and may perish by his own aggression.

Freedom in Games

If mankind continues to exploit the earth and leave less and less free space in the urban areas, responsible people—and who would not want to be one of them—know that it is not only a matter of leaving enough oxygen and procuring men the necessary energy. What they need principally is an area where they can move around freely and where they can free themselves from the necessity to adapt constantly to modern civilization. Such a free area, which must be retained in cities and areas around them, should not only offer the possibility for walking or for sport, but also offer the opportunity for people to find each other for games.

The Swiss psychologist, Piaget (1935), found out that the game is not simply the result of a free development of the naive, childlike fantasy. The game also has the function of practicing anticipation of the accomplishments of reality. While playing, the child is preparing himself to take over his duties in life. If adults play games, it will free them from the serious-mindedness of everyday worries. They also learn how to get along with other people. The cultivation of communication is often not sufficient in professional life and, thus, while playing games people have the possibility to integrate themselves into a group or to play with a partner without offending him. In the game, children as well as adults learn, on the one hand, to get to know the possibilities of their development, and on the other hand, to perceive those limits where fantasy finds its real boundaries in its realization.

Psychotropic Drugs: A Help?

It is not surprising that modern man so often needs so many psychotropic drugs if his living space gets smaller and smaller and the contradictory norms get more and more oppressive. We do not want to fight against the use of psychotropic drugs, since we have to take into consideration that many people would not be able to bear the dense and hectic life in the modern world if they could not get some distance from it or calm down, order their thoughts, or elevate their mood, with the help of tranquilizers, neuroleptics, or antidepressants. It has to be assumed that the number of psychosomatic diseases would also increase if it were not possible for the jeopardized people to obtain some liberation by complying to these drugs. One often speaks of a chemical straitjacket which results from these psychotropic agents. No doubt, there can also be a misuse of such active agents. Nevertheless, we have to say that the psychotropic drugs, conscientiously prescribed and applied, might give back the inner peace, the feeling of freedom, and in fact the freedom from inner constraint to emotionally tense neurotics, depressed people, and schizophrenics. Nowadays, if such people must enter a hospital for treatment at all, they can return to society quickly, while in earlier times they often suffered for years and years and/or remained in the hospital for a long time. The psychotropic drugs, applied parallel to psychotherapy, allow disturbed people at least a certain freedom, since otherwise their disease would prevail, i.e., the compliance to these agents on the one hand, gives them at least a certain freedom on the other hand. Even if interhuman surroundings were positively minded, somehow they would be submitted to an inner constraint. It is easier for people who are treated with these drugs to see their way through the social norms and regulations. Thus, they will neither attract attention by disorderliness nor by anomia (Durkheim, 1893; Merton, 1957). Like that, they do not risk being expelled from interhuman relationships. Modern psychiatry with the introduction of modern psychotropic drugs in 1952 (Delay and Deniker, 1952; Hamon, 1952) has contributed to a new feeling of freedom to man when he is stricken with an illness, which quite often has not only its roots in childhood experience and in social conditions, but also has genetic and biochemical roots.

The Freedom of the Mentally Ill Patient

Antipsychiatrists like Basaglia (1968/1971) and others demand the abolition of psychiatry and the delegation of the responsibility for the mentally sick persons directly to the people. Indeed, the treatment of the psychically ill people, as well as of the physically ill patients, should take place as long as possible within society more than is practiced nowadays in many places. Nevertheless, it will be necessary to maintain possibilities of hospitalization and outpatient treatment facilities where the patient can find an appropriate professional and humanly adequate treatment. If the mentally sick patients are "treated" only in and by the surrounding environment, there would be the danger that the persons treated would have to comply to the surrounding social groups, on the one hand, and on the other hand, would not be able to behave themselves according to the norms.

Thomas Szasz (1961) speaks of the psychiatrist as a "social manipulator" of human beings, influencing persons through punishment, constraint, or any other influence, to play a certain game or to interrupt it. In this connection we have to point out in reply to Szasz that since Sigmund Freud psychiatry has achieved fundamental knowledge for the liberation of mankind from this former bondage towards his own desires of instinctivity. Further, Heinz Kohut's (1971–1977) investigations about the self and the self-identity of the human being have contributed to the fact that narcissism is not despised anymore. It has been realized that the way to the others is only through self-realization. Psychoanalysis and with that psychiatry have come back to the knowledge which is already found in the third book of Moses, 19:18: "Thou shalt love thy neighbor as thyself." Today, we know that incorrect behavior of compliance and feelings of insufficiency cultivated by the society only lead to resentment and aggression. On the contrary, the care for a self-realization contributes to the fact that human beings find their way and from there are able to help the people in their neighborhood to take their self-realization in their own hands.

Obedience

As I have stressed, human freedom is limited by the compulsion which forces men to comply to visible or invisible social rules. If the human being would be absolutely free to decide to go whichever way he would like, as Jean Paul Sartre designates it in his drama *The Flies* for Orestes, then he would again feel perpetually compelled to decide and to act. He would suffer from anxiety since he would have to make new decisions all the time and to comply to this necessity. If, however, in a group or a political system everything is decided in an authoritarian way by a leader, man again experiences anxiety because he fears rightly, that the has no choice and looses "his way." If man feels weak, he would often like to be led. He thinks he saves himself the anxiety in this way, but often realizes too late that with this attitude he gives up his freedom and his own platform. Blind obedience means that the human being cannot follow his own inclinations. The Milgram (1966, 1974) experiments have proved how dangerous such unconditional obedience may be when they showed that 65 percent of an average population remain obedient, even when they are ordered to apply an electric shock of 450 volts in response to a mistake made by a subject in training. That the shock was not given by those who ran the experiment does not change the fact that so many people taking part in the experiment were really prepared to give such a big electric shock. Absolute obedience, as we have seen in the Manson "family" or in the Temple sect of Rev. Jones in Guyana—due to a total narcissistic fusion of the participants with the leader and of the leader with the members—leads to the danger that the life of others, or of the members, or both are threatened. In their dependence and obedience to the leader, they experience him as omnipotent and omniscient, attribute to him and in this way to themselves more right than to other men, and easily fall into criminality. Therefore, the beginning of such movements must be hindered, since afterwards it may be too late to free the members who have already undergone a total compliance towards the leader and the whole collectivity. We can in this respect no longer call such a collective a group, since a group would be linked with differentiated roles; but rather, a crowd in a more or less small or large frame, the members having lost individuality and having totally complied to the leader and the totality.

Unlimited freedom causes man anxiety as well as dependence and compulsion. Perhaps mankind always had the tendency to comply to a god or several gods, because man does not want to be forced to live in this total freedom, which would force him to make new decisions throughout his life. As much as the human being may long for a total freedom, he knows, at least unconsciously, that as Bally (1945) formulates it, he can only feel free if he experiences a certain order which gives his life a certain system with boundaries for himself, the others, and the leader.

SECURITY AND FREE CREATIVITY

The integration into a system with its structures, the furtherance of a common aim on one hand, and the protection of the human freedom of decision on the other hand will give to man a secure feeling in life, as well as the freedom which permits him to find his own way of living.

Often human beings tend toward too much security. More and more in their anxiety they try to ensure and to reassure themselves. They are often afraid of every risk. But again, a danger can result from such an attitude: it is that of monotony, which may itself lead to the feeling of being unfulfilled and to breakthrough of uncontroled drives. Only if man is able to maintain his creativity will he experience his existence as a human one, and he then will be able to ally himself with others to accomplish great achievements. Every individual is given the task of recognizing the realm of freedom of decision open to him and the responsibilities linked with it. Only in this way, via his individuation, which was so well described by C. G. Jung (1967), will his unique individuality be guaranteed and also the cognitive process which shows him the limits of human freedom within the social network.

Perhaps we are not sufficiently aware of the fact that only by training and growing experience we can recognize where our realm of free decision is and where the limiting structures in the social system are. Until the beginning of the twentieth century children and young people had the opportunity for manifold interactions within their large families, and in this way they were able to become aware of the possibilities of experiencing freedom or limits within a social system. In the small families of today, it is less possible to undergo such a social learning process. We, therefore, should have to provide opportunities for young people in our schools and in all other institutions and systems where adults come together in large numbers for furthering communications. We do not think that contents of solutions should be offered in such hours, but rather a training in methods for furthering communications. By such measures many neurotic developments could be prohibited and, therefore, a primary prevention could be accomplished, at least to a certain extent.

With the same aim in mind, men should be trained not to withdraw from their neighbors. Only in a communicative frame will it be possible, especially for those who are growing up, to feel on the one hand free and on the other hand to integrate themselves into the social system. Therefore, we may ask what man would be without realization of his free fantasy. But what would he be, if he would only live for his freedom? Within his boundaries he will have to learn to recognize his free space, in which he can realize his creativity, in which again and again he has to dip into and to produce his works (Balint, 1968). In this way it will be possible for men to accept social norms without feeling forced to comply totally to surrounding patterns of behavior and/or ideologies.

Conclusion

Men, and especially those who are in the process of growing up in our society with its many and manifold ideologies, live in a conflict of norms. In every group they feel that they are expected to comply to the demands of the collective. But who is at the top of the communities? Certainly, even in democracies, not always those who represent the best, the majority, and the rights of the minorities. Often those to whom the structures of power appeal the most, climb to the highest positions in the state and not those who are the advocates of humanity. Considering this fact, it is necessary that our children and juveniles should be trained early, also in the kindergartens and schools, to recognize and to utilize the possibilities open to them and be ready not always to follow old ways but to decide newly in each situation about their next steps. Even the superego has changed its content in the last few years. It has changed more and more from a personal one to a representation of anonymous and collective demands. Total compliance to it would lead to an abolishment of all free possibilities of development. People often fear that they will get into a position of anomia, in a group or in society, in which they would be experienced as violators of the social rules. It may be important for them to think over their position if this individual way does not lead more to their personal development and their individual contribution to society than a way in which they would have to comply totally to the expectations of the others. But it could also be the case that they should stick to their opinion and thus remain strongholds of freedom.

In a group with its system of interactions there are, however, also possibilities of cooperation which provide an individual with possibilities of influence and freedom. The group represents a securing, protecting milieu. But the human beings should also recognize the dangers linked with it. If the members totally extend their narcissism onto the leader and the group, they may become dependent on him and on the others and no longer be ready to take the individual responsibility for themselves. Especially individuals who have no consistent self often tend to undergo a fusion with a strong leader. They will have to learn to accept their own anxieties and to try to learn to live on their own. Our genetic code represents to a certain degree a compulsion. But within this genetic determination there is space for individual decision, since human beings have always at least to decide which of the many inherited possibilities they would like to choose. Psychoanalysis has always stressed this possibility of man to change his way of life even though its founder discovered that we are also determined to a more or less high degree by the experiences of early childhood. Reason and consciousness can lead to a certain control of the tendency of man to always repeat in an analogous way the behavior patterns of the past. Total compliance to genetic or early life conditions would lead to a dangerous abolishment of human freedom. We are not only a product of conditioning, we can not say that we are only a—human—animal. Man has learned during his history to overcome to a certain degree his genetic code (Portmann, 1970), and the way he is determined by tradition and culture and to achieve the possibility of free creativity, of exercising new ways in his games. The modern man sometimes wants to escape this freedom by drugs or by submission to political systems in which compulsion frees from the necessity of decisions. But he will always recognize, perhaps though too late, that only when he is ready to bear the risk of freedom recognizing a certain order and the right of all men to have a life in peace with controlled aggression, will he not be forced to undergo a total compliance to inner or outside conditions and be ready for a permanent and creative renewal of his personality.

REFERENCES

Amalrik, A. *L'Union Soviétique survivra-t-elle 1984 (The Soviet Union will she survive 1984)*. Librairie generale Française, Paris. 1977.

Balint, M., Bally, G. *The basic fault: Therapeutic aspects of regression*. London: Tavistock, 1968.

Barnett, S. A., Basaglia, E. Grouping and dispersive behavior among wild rats. In S. Garattini, & E. B. Siff (Eds.), *Aggressive behavior*. Amsterdam: Excerpta Medica Foundation, 1969, 86.

Benedetti, G. Personal communication, 1967.

Bettelheim, B. *The children of the dream*. London: Macmillian, 1969.

Charpentier, J. Analysis and measurement of aggressive behavior in mice. In S. Garattini, & E. B. Sigg (Eds.), *Aggressive behavior*, Amsterdam: Excerpta Medica Foundation, 1969, 86.

Christian, J. J., Delay, J., Deniker, P. Endocrine adaptive mechanisms and the physiologic regulation of population growth. In W. V. Mayer, and R. G. van Gedler (Eds.), *Physiological. Mammalogy*. New York, London: Academic Press, 1963, 189.

Dukor, B. *Freiheit, Zurechnungsfähigkeit, Strafe (Freedom, responsibility before the law, punishment)* (Polis Vol. 7) Zurich: EVZ, 1960, 1.

Durkheim, E. *Les régles de la méthode sociologique (The Rules of the Sociological Method.)*. Paris: Felix Alcan, 1893 (9. Aufl. 1938).

Eibl-Eibesfeldt, I. *Der programmierte Mensch. (The preprogrammed human being)* (3. Aufl.). Molden: Wien, München, Zürich, 1973.

Freud, S. *The ego and the id*. (standard ed.) (Vol. 18). 1923, 23.

———. *Introductory lectures on psychoanalysis*. (standard ed.) (Vols. 15 and 16). 1916–1917.

Fromm, E. *The anatomy of human destructiveness*. New York, Chicago, San Francisco: Holt, Rinehart and Winston, 1973.

Hamon, J., Paraire, J. Harlow, H. S., and Harlow, M. K. Reifungsfaktoren im sozialen Verhalten (Factors of maturation in social behavior). *Psyche., 21:* 193, 1967.

Hess, W. R. *Das Zwischenhirn (The interbrain)*. Basel: Schwabe, 1954.

Ibsen, H. *Ein Volksfeind (An enemy of the people)*, translated from the Norwegian. Stuttgart: Reclam Jun, 1956, 1968.

Jung, C. G. Theoretische Ueberlegungen zum Wesen des Psychischen (Theoretical consideration about the essence of the psychic life). *Gesammelte Werke, 8,* Zurich: Rascher, 1967, 185.

Kant, I. *Kritik der reinen Vernunft (Criticism of the pure reason)*. Riga: Johann Friedrich Hartknoch, 1781.

———. Mutmasslicher Anfang der Menschengeschichte (Probably beginning of the history of mankind). In *Immanuel Kants populäre schriften*. Deutsche Bibliothek: Berlin, 1914.

Kohut, H. *The analysis of the self*. New York: International University Press, 1971.

———. *The restoration of the self.* New York: International Universities Press, 1977.

Merton, R. K. *Social theory and social structure.* Glencoe, Ill.: Free Press, 1957.

Milgram, S. *Obedience to authority.* New York: Harper & Row, 1974.

———. Personality characteristics associated with obedience towards authoritative command. *Journal of Experimental Research in Personality,* 1965, *1*: 282.

Monod, J. *Le hasard et la nécessité, essai sur la philosophie naturelle de la biologie moderne (The chance and the necessity, essay on the natural philosophy of modern biology).* Paris: Editions du Seuil, 1970.

Moses, Third book of Moses, 19:18.

Piaget, J. Les théories de l'imitation (The theories of imitation) *Cahiers de pédegogie experimentale et de Psychologie de l'enfant,* 1935, *6*: 13.

Portmann, A. The taste of a basic anthropology. In *Main currents in modern thoughts, 27* (1): 3, 1970.

Riesman, D. *The lonely crowd.* New Haven, Conn.: Yale University Press, 1950.

Sartre, J. P., Slavson, S. R. *Analytic group psychotherapy.* New York: Columbia University Press, 1950.

Spitz, R. A. *The first year of life.* New York: Universities Press, 1965.

Szasz, T. *The myth of mental illness.* New York: Harper & Row, 1961.

Watzlawick, P., Beavin, J. H., Jackson, D. D. *Pragmatics of human communications.* New York: W. W. Norton, 1967.

Chapter 4

RELIGION AND COMPLIANCE

E. Mansell Pattison

This chapter focuses on the function of religion in human behavior. The thesis I wish to pursue is that compliance with religion beliefs, attitudes, and practices can be a tremendous force for *either* good or evil in human affairs. This is so clearly illustrated in events of a few years ago, during which we saw the destructive influence of religious compliance in the mass suicide of the Jonestown community in Guyana, while almost concurrently the Nobel Peace Prize was awarded to Sister Teresa for her lifelong compliance with Christian teachings in service to the miserably poor, outcasts, and untouchables in the slums of Calcutta. I shall illustrate my thesis at several levels of human operations: the cultural level; the intermediary social network of social relations; the family level; and in the individual.

HISTORICAL PERSPECTIVES

Religion has always loomed large in human affairs and continues to be even in our contemporary secularized society. A full century after the conventional scientific and philosophic wisdom of the day had declared the idea of God a "costly and unnecessary hypothesis," conventional religious movements are alive and well in contemporary America (Zaretsky & Leone, 1974). Even more striking is the tremendous upsurge of new religions whose devotees vehemently reject traditional and conventional religious beliefs and practices (Needleman, 1970; Needleman & Baker, 1978). To a significant extent this renewed religious concern is neither a surfacing of continued conventional religion nor a revival of traditional religion, but a "new religious consciousness" in the culture (Glock & Bellah, 1976; Wuthnow, 1976).

To understand this current religious consciousness we must hark back to the prevailing consciousness of mid-nineteenth century Western thought. The notion of *cultural evolutionism* was the reigning Zeitgeist: whether we turn to biological, philosophical, or social thought, all was of the same fabric. Recent historical analysis reveals that Freud's attitudes toward religion and culture were largely influenced and determined by this Zeitgeist (Wallace, 1980). In essence, human culture was viewed as a process of cultural evolution. Culture was ever developing toward new and higher forms of social organization. Older social beliefs, forms, and practices were giving way to a new social order based upon rational scientific data. Western civilization was the apogee of such evolution, leading toward the utopia of a rational scientific society.

Among the intellectual cognoscenti of that time, conventional wisdom held that religion had been a necessary and useful force for social cohesion in primitive societies. But now progressive evolution of the social order rendered religion obsolescent. Religious faith and belief were perceived as atavistic, anachronistic, magical, and naive. Religious structuring of behavior was viewed as coercive, constrictive, and obstructive of the continued development of a society based on rationalism and scientism. In sum, religion was viewed with perhaps benign tolerance, beyond the merit of skepticism, and above all an epiphenomenon scientifically demonstrated to be irrelevant to a mature human society.

As historian John Dillenberger (1960) has clearly described, there was a 500-year debate in critical Western thought over the constitution of an overarching *weltanschauung* or world view. The issues were more profound than a simple battle of science versus religion, extending into the definition of reality, meaning, matter, and substance, the essence of society, and the nature of man. And above all, it was a debate over where the locus of grounding for human behavior was to be found. As Dillenberger points out, the religious assumptive weltanschauung gradually gave way, and by the last decades of the nineteenth century the scientific weltanschauung held intellectual sway. This is not to say that popular and conventional religion did not remain, particularly in America, but rather that a superficial patina of "civil religion" (Bellah, 1975) remained. This patina of religiosity, however, did not command the commitment of life and action, serving more to obscure to the common mind the radical degree to which a scientific consciousness now informed our behavior.

Not all of the intellectual world took these changes in Western consciousness with sanguine and enthusiastic acceptance. With remarkable and foretelling prescience Jean-Paul Sartre (1947) explicated the problems for the new human society:

> The existentialist is strongly opposed to a certain kind of secular ethics which would like to abolish God with the least possible expense. . . . The existentialist, on the contrary, thinks it very distressing that God does not exist, because all possibility of finding values in a heaven of ideas disappears along with Him: there can no longer be an *a priori* Good, since there is no infinite and perfect consciousness to think it. . . . Indeed, everything is permissible if God does not exist, and as a result man is forlorn, because neither within him nor without does he find anything to cling to. . . . I find myself suddenly alone without help, engaged in a world for which I bear the whole responsibility. (pp. 21 ff.)

Sartre saw the fabric of society rent apart by the loss of religion, and not stitched together again by the seamstresses of science. The themes of existential angst, the philosophy of the absurd, the sociology of the lonely crowd, the ennui of the workless weekends, all manifest the central notion of the existential man of freedom. Man is totally free of coercion and compliance. The consequence is social isolation, aloneness, the loss of meaningful social bonds.

This leads us to a central tension: existence in relationship involves commitment, compliance to the demands and expectations of others, the willingness to submit to personal and social coercion. The excesses of social coercion and compliance are set in bas relief by the excesses of lack of social coercion and compliance. The sociologist Philip Rieff (1966) describes the ebb and flow between social commitment which becomes constrictive and social commitment which is nourishing. He describes negative communities that require no commitment and offer no symbolic integrative values in contrast to positive communities which demand commitment and offer symbolic integration. He concludes:

> To speak of a moral culture would be redundant. Every culture has two main functions: (1) to organize the moral demands that make men intelligible and trustworthy to each other, thus rendering the world intelligible and trustworthy; (2) to organize the expressive remissions by which men release themselves in some degree from the strain of conforming to the controlling symbolic, internalized variant readings of culture that constitute invidual character. The process by which a culture changes at its profoundest level may be traced in the shifting balance of controls and releases which constitute a system of moral demands. (p. 28)

Note that Rieff does not subscribe to a progressive evolution that will cut the Gordian knot of tension between controls and releases. Rather, human society reflects a fluctuation between the need to provide more control, coercion, and compliance, and the need to alleviate such.

These basic cultural processes are at the center of religion. Indeed, anthropologists have seen religion as a central organizing process of culture. The late Harvard anthropologist, Clyde Kluckhohn (1966) comments:

> There is a need for a moral order. Human life is necessarily a moral life precisely because it is a social life, and in the case of

the human animal the minimum requirements for predictability of social behavior that will insure some stability and continuity are not taken care of automatically by biologically inherited instincts, as is the case with the bees and the ants. Hence there must be generally accepted standards of conduct, and these values are more compelling if they are invested with divine authority and continually symbolized in rites that appeal to the senses. (p. iv)

Sartre challenged the scientific consciousness on philosophical grounds, but he also wrote after two world wars and genocide. Can the scientific weltanschauung hold a society together? Is such a grounding of being sufficient, not just on logical grounds, but in terms of human experience and action? Or is it possible that both tough-minded logical empiricism and obdurate philosophical existentialism are manners of rationalization, while in everyday life the very exponents of nonreligious groundings exemplify in their lives the rootings in the dirt for nourishing substance?

I suggest that the current new religious consciousness is just such a manifestation—a growing sense of the need for groundings which are experienced in meaningful commitments and symbolized in shared religious manifestations. This interpretation is supported by the observations of religious historian Martin Marty (1977):

> The age-old dogfight between science and religion is entering a strange new phase—strangest of all, in place of the ancient set piece between belief and unbelief, we are now seeing internecine warfare between old school religionists and a newer breed of theologians cautiously open to scientific advances, and between hard core, slide rule scientists and their colleagues who are open to the new findings about mind and consciousness. Both the theologians and the scientists are warring among themselves.... Scientists and theologians of conviction, whether they be conservative or liberal, positivist or not, now do link in subterranean ways, or they meet in alliances across party lines in what once was no-man's-land. (p. 25)

The struggle over the "consciousness of our world" is spreading out to the man in the street. We have witnessed the immense popularity in the past two decades of movies, plays, and books about magic, mysticism, and supernaturalism. The man in the street no longer has a consciousness committed to the infallibility of science. Even if that man on the street is not religious today in the conventional sense, surely many consider the mystical, the transcendental, the cosmic, the supernatural, and even the religious as not incidental to their lives.

A number of social scientists have interpreted this return to a supernaturalistic cosmology in a secular culture much along the lines already described. S. K. Pande (1968), a non-Western psychiatrist, noted that the scientific Western cosmology created "deficits in the Western way of life . . . negative psychological implications . . . , and Western psychotherapy, especially the psychoanalytic model, as a symbolic and substantive undertaking to correct them" (p. 432). This theme is underscored by Henri Ellenberger (1970) in his history of Western psychotherapy, where he notes that psychotherapy was a response to cosmological problems of the educated elite: "By the end of the nineteenth century the upper classes could no longer be content with the existing method of hypnotic and suggestive therapy and demanded a new, nonauthoritarian psychotherapy that would explain to the patient what was going on in his own mind" (p. 887).

The problem, of course, is that we now live in a postmodern age in which people no longer find the cosmology of the Western scientific ethos satisfactory. The current rise of supernaturalism in our culture—belief in demonology, possession, exorcism, and the gamut of supernaturalistic cosmologies now popular—is not unpredictable. Social conditions were ripe in the Western world for the reemergence of supernaturalism. These conditions include a society perceived as oppressive; trust in social institutions has disintegrated; social protest has been realistically dangerous; and a mood of hopeless impotence has emerged. Such social conditions certainly typified the late 1960's when the wild hope of social activism faded and people withdrew into personal privatism and supernaturalism.

The Spanish anthropologist Baroja (1964) notes that the breakdown of Western rationalism has brought us full circle back to medieval supernaturalism, because: "Ours is no period of calm, with an optimistic view of public morality and religious philosophy and beliefs. It is an age of existentialism and an existential way of life, which leads man to break down the barriers and conventions and face up to his own angst" (p. 257). The existential consciousness of our day is the stark sense of alienated and singular responsibility for everything. Historian Judith Neaman (1975) finds it not surprising that psychiatry is becoming more biological just at the time when our society is becoming more metaphysical. She recalls that, in every culture, a period of hyperrationalism is followed by a renewal of supernaturalism. For with the rationalism and ultimately the existentialism comes too much responsibility—too much to bear. Psychiatry brought man from outer reality into himself and only himself, and left man there. Neaman concludes:

> The legacy of the Middle Ages was the increasing interiorization of the self and a concomitant increase in responsibility for human action. These ideas were consummated in the twentieth century beliefs that we are responsible not only for our own actions but also for our own guilts, fears, and obsessions. The fantasy of the 1970's has been a wish to return to an age of exorcism. (p. 190)

Similarly, in her study of new religious movements, anthropologist Erika Bourguignon (1973) finds: "There is a wish to find alternative ways of living, and thus not only modify society, but modify the self" (p. 352).

In summary, we are the inheritors of an intellectual legacy of the idea of cultural evolution. That legacy interpreted religion primarily in terms of an oppressive, constrictive, and unduly coercive social force that exacted destructive compliance in the behavior of adherents. From that perspective it might seem puzzling that both intellectuals and the common man might deliberately resurrect the supernatural. However, we have also seen that the intellectual legacy was naive. The question before us is not whether religion imposes compliance, but rather what compliance does religion command to either good or evil ends?

The Definition of Religion

To discuss the functions of religion, we must clarify what we mean by religion. In my review of psychiatry and religion (Pattison, 1978), I reported an analysis of the literature in which I found a substantial conceptual and empirical differentiation in the forms and functions of religion.

Religion is a complex phenomenon. It is multivariate in form and function. Consequently, to pose the question of the effect or influence of religion on this or that human behavior is not very productive. Rather, we must define specific religious factors that may influence human behavior. More often, no one religious factor operates in isolation but in permutations or combinations of multiple religious factors. It is rather like asking how parents influence children. Obviously they do, but through multiple and interactive variables.

The most well-known set of religious variables was constructed by Glock and Stark (1965). They proposed five major dimensions of religion:

1. Ideological: Refers to commitment to a group or movement as a social process
2. Intellectual: Refers to specific sets of beliefs, explanations, or cognitive structuring of meaning and value
3. Experiential: Refers to the feelings one experiences, which may be entirely personal, or structured group activities which produce specific experiences
4. Sacramental: Refers to participation in symbolic rituals
5. Consequential: Refers to religiously defined standards of conduct

Upon examination, it is obvious that each religious dimension has a different import for human conduct. In contemporary America we can find both conventional religious denominations and new religious sects, cults, and groups which primarily emphasize one of the five dimensions to the relative exclusion of all others. Thus when we say a person is religious or ask of the influence of religion, we must qualify our inquiry to a specific dimension.

More current qualitative research underway is aimed to clarify operational means of measurement of these multidimensions of religious commitment (Roof, 1979). Without such specificity, our inquiry into the functions of religion remain rather imprecise generalizations, with many exceptions easily noted. Consequently, our subsequent discussion is more general than desirable, and can only intimate directions of more precise research.

RELIGION AND CULTURAL COMPLIANCE

The potency of religion in the influence of human behavior is related to the level of cultural organization and complexity. On the one extreme, we have the small face-to-face village which is the existent society and the culture, even if there be similar villages nearby. Here, there is a low differentiation of social roles and a relatively homogeneous social existence. In such a society, religion is the culture and culture is the religion. Religion is infused into every aspect of daily life and provides an overarching structure for existence. Here, "religion-culture" defines meaning and action to everything. All of life is ipso facto religious. In such "small societies" there is relative uniformity and conformity. There is early and rigorous socialization into the religious beliefs and practices, for they are the warp and woof of existence. One could scarcely function without being religious. Although deviant behavior can and does occur, the limits of deviancy are severely constrained by the survival needs of the society. In turn, substantial deviancy from the religious-cultural norms is high risk for survival. Where else can one go and survive?

Somewhere intermediate is the small-town phenomenon as part of a large and differentiated culture. The small town retains the essential social homogeneity of the village. Religion and culture are one, despite the superficial variations between local denominations. The social history of small towns in America (Lingeman, 1980) reflects the paramount importance of immediate personal interaction and insulation from the pluralistic values and life styles of urban industrialized society. Lingeman (1980) notes that the insular small-town society first came under attack at the turn of the twentieth century when economic subsistence and viability in these small societies were compromised by larger socioeconomic developments on a national scale. Seeking survival in the urban society, the expatriates might feel displaced and long to return to the security and safety of the structured religious culture of the small town. Others, like Sinclair Lewis in *Main Street* and Edgar Lee Masters in *Spoon River Anthology* satirized the coercive social structure of small-town religious culture. The perceived oppression of small-town mores, however, is from the perspective of the cosmopolitan and pluralistic culture of urban society.

In this case, deviancy from the small-town cultural construction of reality becomes possible and feasible for two reasons. First, there is an available alternative reality of urban society against which to measure the small-town reality. Second, there is an alternative culture to which the small-town deviant can flee—and even be nondeviant in the alternative society.

The same process has obtained in urban areas in both Europe and America, in which small-town religious culture has been re-created in *urban villages,* more often termed shtetls, barrios, ghettos, or the _____ *ethnic community.* Urban villagers function with the same tensions of cultural collision as their country village cousins. Some members find comfort, solidity, support, and meaning in the urban village, while others find it stifling and coercive.

The point is obvious here that the village structure is maintained, whether in country or city, by a uniform religious culture which maintains a viable structure of meaning and demands relatively homogeneous behavior of community members. High compliance is required to maintain village viability in the face of the larger impinging cosmopolitan culture. Personal value is lodged in shared beliefs and values, shared styles of behavior, and shared ideology. Your social role is determined before your birth and remains with you throughout life. Who you are in the established continuity of social order is more important than what you do. Therefore, the social task is to learn your ascribed role and live in it. Such is the nature of compliance to a predestined social role.

In contrast, the urban cosmopolitan culture is not based on continuity or on similarity. This is a highly differentiated society of multiple tasks and roles. Social role is achieved and lost with equal rapidity. Beliefs, values, and ideologies take a distant second place to the immediate utilitarian performance of tasks which anonymously link with the tasks of others. As a result, the structure and function of the utilitarian culture is not threatened by divergent and pluralistic beliefs, values, and ideologies. Even deviant behavior does not threaten the culture or the individual—"just so long as you get your job done." Thus, a religious culture is not necessary for the production of goods and instrumental services. Religious compliance is intrinsically less relevant to the instrumental achievement tasks. Religion and culture can be separated. And for this reason, religion is indeed increasingly irrelevant to urban man, and religion is less potent. On the other hand, the very anonymity of the impersonal urban society role performance makes religion all the more relevant to personal meaning and personal social relations. This process leads to highly "personalized religion"—typical American concepts of personal relations between man and God. Yet this option, too, fails to address the need for "social religion" which links fellow man to fellow man. Again, this is reflected in the characteristic nature of religious resurgence which stresses religion community. In this latter case, we arrive at religious compliance with norms of personal conduct, but not religious norms which define the totality of all events and behavior.

The functions of religious compliance in directing behavior and modifying deviance can be seen as a system of human guidance. The linking of religious systems to psychological function in each of the previously mentioned levels of cultural organization is described in detail in *Religious Systems and Psychotherapy* (Cox, 1973). In summary, religious compliance is both strong and central to the agrarian peasant culture. Religious compliance is attenuated in the urban or country small-town society. While religious compliance is impotent and irrelevant to urban utilitarian achievement culture, the relevance of religious compliance to personal meaning and interpersonal relations becomes paramount.

To the extent that a religious organization addresses the multiple spheres of life activity, the greater such a religious structure will impact on the lives of people. The one extreme case would be the religious commune which withdraws from the urban society and establishes a separate religious culture. Here, there is the demand for total religious compliance in a total religious community. At the other extreme is the case of civil religion, which addresses no specific aspect of actual life behavior. Here, there are no norms to comply with or any social religious structure which can exact social compliance.

RELIGION AND SOCIAL NETWORK COMPLIANCE

The next level of social organization is what is now termed the *social network* (Pattison, 1977; Pattison, Llamas, & Hurd, 1979). People are not linked amorphously to culture at large. Rather, each person is embedded in a finite number of social relations of about 1,500 to 2,000 persons. I shall briefly describe the nature of social network structure, and then proceed to illustrate some issues of religious compliance at this level, particularly in religious cults.

People are linked to each other in a variety of patterns, termed *networks*. Depending upon the specific social action, we can trace these networks throughout this finite number of people. Thus, there are rumor networks, political networks, informational networks, work networks, friendships networks, and so forth. Not all people are involved in all the networks, and many people in a network, which is an invisible social construct after all, do not know one another, nor are they aware that they belong to the same social network. Yet their social actions influence one another, and through appropriate social action the invisible social links can be made visible to all—as, for example, a community response to a disaster or a political action campaign.

I shall discuss only personal networks here. That is, the networks of social relations identified with one person who is consciously related to a finite number of persons. Even though all these persons do not know one another, they are all socially related to the identified subject. This is called an *egocentric* network. And, even more limited, I shall discuss only the persons deemed most *important* to the individuals who comprise the *intimate psychosocial network* of the individual. This limited group of people, about 25 persons in normal networks, we find to be a basic social unit of function.

In order to study the personal psychosocial network, we have devised the Pattison Psychosocial Inventory. This consists of three major elements. First, we ask subjects to simply list all the people who are important to them, regardless of whether they like the persons or not, arranged in four subgroups of family, relatives, friends-neighbors, and social-work associates. Second, the subject specifies which people have ongoing relationships between them, apart from their relation to the subject—these are the links or *connections* in the network. Third, the subject rates the nature and quality of interaction between the subject and each person on five variables that have been shown to be critical elements of significant interpersonal relationships. The first variable is contact; there is a high degree of *interaction*, whether face to face, by telephone, or by letter. In other words, the normal person invests in those with whom he has frequent contact. Second, the relationship has a strong *emotional intensity*. The degree of valued investment is reflected in the intensity of feeling toward the other. Third, the emotion is *positive*. Negative important relationships are maintained only in the face of constraint, e.g., a boss or spouse. Fourth, the relationship has an *instrumental base*, i.e., the other person is not only positively valued but can be counted on to provide concrete assistance. Fifth, the relationship is *symmetrically reciprocal*. The other person returns a strong positive emotional feeling and may count on you to, in turn, provide instrumental assistance. So there is an affective and instrumental quid pro quo and mutual exchange of both positive feelings and instrumental assistance between the subject and the others in his personal network.

With this method we have studied a national sample of normal populations and a wide variety of persons with different types of psychopathology. We have discovered three main types of personal social networks. First is a highly replicable social network for normal persons. Second is a "neurotic-type" network common to persons with neurotic disorders, alcoholics, and suicide attempters. Third is a "psychotic-type" network common to acute and chronic schizophrenics and manic-depressives, sociopaths, and heroin addicts.

The normal network has about 25 persons. There are five or six persons in each subgroup of family, relatives, friend-neighbors, social-work associates. In a normal network, each person relates to about six other persons apart from the subject. The relationships are rated highly on each of the five variables of interaction. That is, the relationships have frequent contact, positive and intense emotional investment, provide instrumental assistance, and are symmetrically reciprocal.

What does this normal social network provide the subject? First, it provides a relatively consistent set of norms and social expectations for the management of intercurrent stress. Second, individuals and groups can be readily mobilized in the network to respond to the subject when under stress. Third, there is a rather continuous flow of positive emotional support to the subject. Fourth, the network provides ready and available instrumental assistance to the subject. Fifth, the network is relatively conflict-free and tends to be stress-reducing, rather than stress-inducing or stress-maintaining. Sixth, the network is semipermeable across multiple areas of life interaction, so that the subject is consistently reinforced in function throughout his lifespace, yet not subject to a single group of people who might impose a closed "group tyranny." Seventh, the network consists of selected persons drawn from a larger pool of other relatives, friends-neighbors, social-work associates, so that the loss or addition of important persons in the network can be readily accommodated. In sum, the normal social network is a flexible and responsive social resource in which the person is embedded.

Our data reveal that effective personal function is intimately linked to one's intimate psychosocial network. It is noteworthy that *healthy networks have a moderate degree of compliance* built into their structure. Neurotic networks are characterized by low compliance and psychotic networks by excessive and coercive compliance. The significance of these variations in compliance is highlighted in the following excerpts from my study of relgous youth cults (Pattison, 1980).

Religious youth cults offer a religious healing system in opposition to standard mental health norms and methods. These religious youth cults proclaim a superior route to insight, understanding, satisfying relationships with others, and peace with self and the world. They do not offer psychotherapy but growth and learning. They do not offer mental health but health of the whole person. They do not intend to help one cope with reality but, rather, offer a new sense of reality. They are alternative healing systems that share many of the *goals* of the mental health system, but differ radically in method, content, and context. Many young people deliberately turn *away* from traditional psychotherapies and look *toward* a religious cult as the answer for what we might consider mental health problems of anxiety, depression, apathy, disinterest, meaninglessness, isolation, and confusion.

Religious cults are not new phenomena. There is a circular pattern in which religious protest movements arise out of social alienation as socially isolated cults, move into partial social accommodation as sects, achieve social respectability as denominations, and lose social relevance as homogenized civil religion. This, in turn, creates an existential vacuum within which the new cultic movements are spawned. What may seem an exotic cult may be a religious movement in one of several stages of social accommodation. Similarly, there is a spectrum of religious youth movements in the United States today. Our concern here is with one end of the spectrum that I shall define as *cult,* as follows: they are primarily composed of young adults, with an explicit religious orientation, offering a radical world view in distinction from the common culture, with explicit sanctions in regard to one's behavior, with a strong emphasis on separatism from the world at large that is reflected in some degree of small group communality—ranging from total community living to frequent communal gatherings.

Although strikingly different in theological content, they demonstrate similar sociological characteristics. There are cults derived from eastern mysticism, such as the Hare Krishna, the Divine Light Mission, the lovers of Meher Baba; syncretistic derivations from mainline Protestantism such as the Moonies; and extentions of fundamentalism as in the Jesus People. All are derivative forms of major cultural religions but without participation in the larger culture, for the devotees live in a "separate reality."

Although our data is sparse, the scattered studies reveal that those attracted to religious youth cults are not the ethnic poor from our urban ghettos or rural backwaters. Rather, these are middle-class, affluent, educated, and sophisticated youth. Indeed, part of the popular uproar about such religious youth cults comes from bewildered parents, educators, and mental health professionals, who cannot comprehend why these youth who have been socialized into the mainstream of society with many seeming advantages should turn their backs on their cultural heritage to enter such a separate reality.

Studies of youth cult members reveal relatively similar psychological patterns. Devotees show increased anxiety, decreased personal integration, and increased impulse expression. However, after conversion and participation in the life style of the cult, these youth demonstrate a reduction in anxiety and depression, increased personal integration, and improved behavioral patterns of life. One could interpret such data to indicate that the participants are "neurotic," and that these cults provide "psychotherapy." An equally tenable interpretation is that these young people exhibit emotional responses to the "existential dyslocation" in life which is ameliorated through an "existential resolution" provided by the religious cult.

The youth who turn from psychotherapy toward religious cults are the harbingers of the shift in Western cosmologies now under way. These youth no longer "buy into" the Western scientific rationalism of their parents. They face an existential angst which the Western modes of psychotherapy do not address. It is not surprising to see new supernaturalistic social organizations form which address the existential situation of these youth. These youth cults arise out of conventional cultural religions but depart from the cosmological moorings of the conventional religions, whether Eastern or Western.

The sociological distinction of these youth cults, then, is the separate reality of a new cosmology, where the devotees come from the bourgeoisie. In contrast, the poor and ethnic minorities form religious cults which protest the conventional cosmology of the culture, while the socially marginal and inept join cults which are merely offbeat transformations of popular culture such as Scientology, Theosophy, astrology, or the Church of Satan.

A seond major theme is the radical change in family structure. The religious youth cults are an alternative family structure for youth who find themselves lacking a viable family structure. As the religious framework of family structure lost much of its strength due to secularization, family, filial, and parental ties were considerably weakened. At the same time, the extended family kinship system was being eroded by industrialization and urbanization. As a result, there was increasing nuclearization of family structure, such that, in the middle class, the nuclear family became the conventional model of family life. There was great concern that the isolated nuclear family would not long exist without the instrumental and affective supports of the extended kinship system.

It is not that the youth lost their nuclear families. In fact, many of the youthful devotees proclaim that they love and respect their parents—but that is not enough for them. The problem lies in the fact that the nuclear family alone is separated from the ongoing processes of society. The nuclear family may provide affective ties, but it appears irrelevant to the instrumental nature of modern bureaucratic society. As Kenneth Keniston (1960) has stated: "... there is a loss of a sense of historical relatedness, the loss of traditional community, and the intact task, and perhaps most important, the loss of a compelling positive vision of the individual and collective future" (p. 475).

It is noteworthy that the religious youth cults have not recruited membership from the working classes and ethnic classes where the extended family kinship system, often with strong religious ideologies, still remains a modal family structure. The extended family kinship system is a social institution which integrates the young into the culture. The extended family kinship system provided continuity of values, continuity of capital and property, continuity of technical skills, and continuity of life styles across generations. But, though the extended family system provided for integration in the culture, it was a system that was essentially conservative in nature and changed only slowly over time. Not only did the extended family system disintegrate with the rapid expansion of technology and social movement, but its inflexibility made it nonadaptive to periods of rapid social change. It is striking that so many young people look with nostalgia back toward the old extended family kinship system and attempt to re-create that family structure in communes. However, the communes as reconstituted extended kinship structures do not survive for long because, like the extended kinship system, they represent an anachronistic social structure that is not malleable and adaptive to rapid shifts in social roles, skills, economics, and so forth.

Among the religious youth cults, those which are most communal in structure (such as the Moonies) tend to hold their devotees for relatively short periods of time, from a few months to a few years. However, those youth cults which are more culturally integrative (like Meher Baba and the Jesus People) are likely to develop longer-term participants who also live and work in the dominant culture. Those religious youth cults which replicate the extended kinship system are less viable institutions, whereas the cults which approximate the normal social network systems I described are likely to attain longer-term viability.

Relatively recent studies of the new wave of consciousness among the youth who are joining religious cults reveals both a set of deprivations which these youth experience and a search for new social structures which will promote integration into the culture. Sociologist Charles Glock (1964) defines four major deprivations of these youth: social, organismic, ethical and psychic. It is striking that the traditional extended family kinship system provided for social, organismic, ethical, and psychic well-being, whereas many of the middle-class youth of today have experienced loss of the social supports of the kinship system, organismic loss, often associated with drug use, ethic losses due to secularization, and, finally, many psychic symptoms as noted earlier. We have seen that the normal social network provides social support, promotes organismic health, probably will generate ethical norms, and provides for psychic well-being.

Let us focus our analysis now on the youth cults. Here, we find a social system that begins to look curiously much like our normal social network systems. Many of the youth cults are organized into small, functional units of around 30 people. They emphasize both affective and instrumental ties between the members. There is strong social support with opportunities for frequent interaction. There are usually strong interdictions against drug use and the active promotion of healthful life styles. They generate strong ethic norms, built on explicit religious ideologies.

And, as we have seen before, there are indications of salutary psychic improvement in the psychological adaptation of the devotees. It is no wonder that the names used by these youth cults indicate the nature of their social structure: the Family of God, the Children of God, the Holy Family, and so on.

There has been a loss of symbols in Western psychotherapy. The mystery, awe, and sense of transcendence in the process of healing have been demystified as psychotherapy is promoted as a science. In contrast, we see a rich symbolization of healing in the altered states of consciousness and rites of mysticism and meditation so central to the religious youth cults. Such experiences may not be pathological regressive states but rather transformational symbolic experiences of the new cosmology of the youth, which may be ego-integrative.

Finally, how do we interpret psychic symptoms? Where the social network is not adequate, a person is likely to experience inability to cope with life stress, hence generating symptoms of psychic distress and behavioral dysfunction. The problem is not just personal neurosis, but rather an ineffective social network for adaptation. The data on devotees of religious cults reveal psychic distress among these youth. This is not surprising where the social network of an extended family system has proven inadequate. However, when they affiliate with an adequate social network—a religious youth cult—we observe a decrease in psychic symptoms and improvement in life adaptation.

These interpretations are supported by a recent comprehensive study of religious sects and cults sponsored by the Province of Ontario (Hill, 1980). That report finds that there are indeed casualties, particularly among the highly coercive total community groups. But importantly, such casualties were already emotionally high-risk subjects. Further, recruitment into such groups is not just through bald coercion, but a series of differential decision points to deepen one's affiliation.

In sum, we may suggest that a moderate degree of participant compliance is characteristic of the healthy and normal social network. Obviously, some people seek even stronger social affiliation where the compliance is more total. To many observers, such willingness to submit to rigid norms of total compliance seem onerous at best, and frightening to some. Yet the Hill report found the casualty reports highly exaggerated. Even more striking was the finding that excommune members, dropouts, and the disenchanted were *not* universally negative in their judgments of sect participation. Rather, they reported personal benefits and substantial elements of satisfaction, even though they did not choose to remain within the religious culture.

Religious Compliance and the Family

Religious beliefs, values, attitudes, and practices are an integral part of family life in some manner for most American families. In fact, social scientists assert an interdependent link between family and religion. For example, family sociologist C.C. Zimmerman (1974) says:

> Religion is a collective and not an individual fact. Thus the family is only partly subservient to individual wishes. It is also a religious and legal-political institution. When a couple join in matrimony the biological mating has religious and political significance. The moral and political rights, obligations and duties of the couple and their children are also altered. Family, society, and civilization intertwine through religious beliefs. This system of interrelationships explains why times such as the present see a concurrent weakening of faiths, family relations, and public order. (p. 2)

Although there is an apparent diminution in the strength and vitality of family and religion in our culture, this may be more apparent that real. From an historical perspective, Zimmerman observes that during periods of rapid social change both families and religion tend to decline in strength and together reemerge with social reconsolidation. He predicted the emerging vitality of both family and religion which we now see.

I shall focus on some of the major psychodynamic patterns involving religion in the family. I shall describe four major psychosocial aspects of religion, with clinical examples for each.

Sacralization

This refers to the patterning of family structure and function provided by a religious framework. The religious structure defines beliefs, attitudes, values, and interactions of family life. This may include the choice of a marital mate from a specific religious background; patterns of courtship; the nature of marital vows and marital expectations; the expected roles of mother, father, children, and kin; patterns of childrearing; patterns of worship, recreation, and education; methods of resolving conflict and defining desirable mode of interpersonal interaction. In other words, there is a "sacred order" which provides not only overarching beliefs and values, but also defines the social patterning of the family down to very specific details of behavior. Thus, religion is not merely an epiphenomenon of family belief, but is an intrinsic part of the structure, order, and dynamic of family life and function.

The advantage of sacralization is that it provides a high degree of consensual agreement among family members about roles, behaviors, and goals. Thus, we may expect high degrees of social cohesion and the capacity to mobilize the family unit to cope with stress and crisis in an effective manner.

Example: A young family was confronted with a major crisis when one of their children suffered severe brain damage in a car accident. Both parents and children immediately responded to this family trauma in terms of their religious belief that the event was within the province of God's will for their family. Each family member supported the other in emotional ways and immediately reassigned family tasks so that the injured child could be cared for. In addition, other kin and friends who shared the same religious perspective reinforced the emotional coping style of the family and quickly provided concrete assistance in everyday family tasks.

In this case there was no great emotional decompensation on the part of any family member, nor the family as a unit. Crisis intervention from mental health agencies was not needed, because adequate coping capacity was present within the family and their extended kin and friend support systems in the church.

The disadvantage of sacralization is that the specific sacred order in the family may not be adaptive to the needs of the family or to the changing sociocultural milieu of the family. Thus, when change in family function is required, it may be seen as a threat to the established social order. Thus, the family capacity to adapt and respond may be restricted or compromised.

Example: A middle-aged family with five children had centered their life in a small urban Mennonite church. Both parents were professionals who still maintained a strong allegiance to a rural conservative Mennonite life style. As a result, the young children were sent to urban schools dressed in rural Mennonite clothes, and required to act in accord with rural Mennonite social traditions. Although the parents were able to tolerate the social conflict of living in two different cultural worlds, the children could not. Soon the children began to exhibit school phobias, nightmares, and manifest neurotic symptoms. In this case, individual psychotherapy with the children had been of little avail. Only when the family was able to address the implicit sacralization of family function was change effected in the family life style with resolution of the children's symptoms.

Family Coalitions with the Supernatural

In this situation religious figures, such as God, Christ, a saint, the Virgin Mary, angels, or devils, may be invoked as personal beings who are drawn into the personal interactions between family members. Parents may comfort children by telling them that angels will watch over their bed at night, or threaten children by the punishment of the devil. Coalition with a supernatural figure may be made by a family member to gain additional strength in family arguments, to gain extra power, control, authority, or sanction.

The advantage to such a coalition, when developed at a somewhat abstract and general level, is that is provides a common source of overarching values that may command family member commitment beyond the immediate narcissistic positions of each family member. Thus, parents are to be obeyed, children treated with respect, and marital partner treated justly, not just on the basis of personal power, personal proclivity, or personal need, but because of Godly sanctions. An eloquent statement of this view is provided by Regina W. Wieman (1941) in her book *The Family Lives Its Religion*, where she says: "The family that lives for the sake of great things itself becomes great. . . . Complete commitment to the Creativity of God is the great source of security, of freedom, of richness, and of meaning for the family."

Example: A middle-aged family was faced with a request to provide emergency shelter for two orphaned children. Each family member was faced with different personal problems in this situation. In a family conference, after consideration of the individual personal conflicts, the family sought a resolution on the basis of their shared religious commitments, rather than on personal need and conflict. The disadvantages of coalitions lie in the opportunity for avoidance of personal responsibility and the projection of power and authority to an invisible family member with whom there cannot be joint family interaction. Instances of family myth and family mystification lead to implicit "curses" on family members due to such coalitions with the supernatural.

Example: A little girl came home from Sunday school and immediately began to brush her teeth. When her parents told her it was not necessary to brush her teeth, she vigorously opposed them, saying that she had learned in Sunday school that Jesus would cry if she did not brush her teeth. And since she did not want Jesus to cry she was going to brush her teeth regardless of what her parents said.

Example: A seven-year old boy was consistently annoying his parents, teachers, and family friends. Whenever he was reproached, he would reply that he was an evil person inhabited by a devil who made him do all these annoying things. So he could not change.

Example: A young couple came for marital counseling. The wife stated that her first love was Jesus Christ, who was telling her how to treat her husband. Therefore, she had no need to pay any attention to her husband's opinions.

In these examples it is evident one cannot dismiss such coalitions out of hand as mere superstitions, but must appreciate the dynamic function of such coalitions.

Religious Conflict as a Projection of Family Conflict

It is not unusual to find religious issues used as a "stalking horse" to present and represent an underlying family conflict. As Draper, Meyer, Parzen, and Samuelson (1965) have shown, religious ideas, values, and concepts can be a rich and accurate reflection of psychodynamics. Especially in deeply devout or strongly religious families, religious metaphor may be a dominant mode of family communication. On the other hand, I have seen many ostensibly nonreligious families who have employed religious metaphor and symbol as a convenient arena for projection of family conflict.

Example: A young Jewish family with no ostensible religious commitments suddenly began to bring violent religious disagreements to family therapy sessions. On the surface the issue was whether to provide a Bar Mitzvah for the children. Soon the family was engaged in an intense and rather bitter exploration of what religion meant to each family member. In this process, a latent strong difference in religious orientation between two families of origin was uncovered, which in turn was embodied in a basic conflict between mother and father over patterns and responsibilities of childrearing. And this in turn emanated from basic conflicts around marital trust, sharing, and reciprocity. Although this family subsequently developed a rather strong religious commitment, conflict over their religious commitment subsided when the underlying family conflict was uncovered.

This example is instructive, in that there was genuine religious movement occurring in this family, which was being distorted by the spurious projection of family conflict into their religious exploration.

Family Conflict as a Projection of Religious Conflict

Not all religious conflict is a projection of other family conflict, however. For just the reverse can occur, in which religious conflict in its own right can produce disruption of effective family function. Perhaps the most striking example is the fact that marriages of mixed religious background have much higher probabilities for marital conflict, dissatisfaction, and divorce. Differing degrees of religious commitment and religious practice may serve as the nidus for conflict. For example, a husband may become jealous of a wife who spends time in religious work to the seeming neglect of her husband. Or, there may be fundamental differences in religious frame of reference where husband and wife really have divergent views of life.

Example: A young couple sought marital counseling because of mutual dissatisfaction with the marriage. Both had experienced a religious conversion as Jesus People, and both were engaged in similar religious vocations. Yet in the 6 years of marriage the wife had developed a profound religious commitment, whereas the husband maintained only a superficial allegiance to the allegedly shared religious viewpoint. Although they had shared a similar life style at the onset of marriage, it was clear that they had grown quite apart in religious life style. The marital conflict arose directly out of now fundamentally different religious commitments.

Example: A middle-aged couple had reared four children in a devout, pietistic conservative Bretheren Church. As each child grew up through adolescence, they gave up any religious belief and refused any participation with the parents in the religious activities that had been the center of family life. Although the parents respected the autonomy of the children, strained and distant relationships resulted from the loss of shared religious commitments, for the parents maintained their intense religious life which was now discontinuous with their children.

In sum, religious compliance may play a major role in the structure and function of family life. As we have seen, such compliance can promote healthy and moral family function, or such compliance can be destructive.

Religious Compliance and the Individual

The effects of religion in relation to personality development, psychodynamics, and behavior have been extensively studied (Pattison, 1969; Pruyser, 1968; Strommen, 1971). Although there is a wealth of empirical and clinical data, one can draw no simple conclusions. The patterns of "being religious," as noted earlier, are critical to our interpretation. An important example of this problem is found in the research on the relationship between religion and prejudice. On the one hand was the pious assertion that devoutly religious persons should or would love everyone in the world, without prejudice. On the other hand, there was substantial data on the positive correlation between religiousity and prejudice. This paradox was considerably resolved by the work of Allport and Ross (1967) who found that some very religious people were much less prejudiced than agnostics, atheists, and irreligious, while other very religious people were much more prejudiced. The least prejudiced religious held to what Allport termed "intrinsic religion"—a commitment to universal norms and values of high moral intention. While the most prejudiced religious held to "extrinsic religions"—a commitment to a particularistic and ideological group membership norm. These two styles of being religious can be related to the norming and valuing processes of psychodynamics. I have termed the broader ego dynamics of this process "ego morality" (Pattison, 1968), to contrast with the superego morality functions which are more primitive and narrow.

Most clinicians are well acquainted with the development of the superego, which is the internalized injunctions of parental figures. The internalized superego norms are subsequently experienced as guilt feelings. This is often assumed to be the essence of conscience or moral norms. Indeed, religious norms may be internalized as unconscious contents of the superego. As a result, we can observe religiously determined compliant behavior, which is unconsciously determined coercion of the person. This represents a major source of extrinsic religious compliance. However, it can hardly be called morality, except in the most primitive sense. Such moral coercion is not necessarily moral in consequence. In fact, this type of religious psychodynamic often results in immoral behavior pursued in the name of religious morality, as in the religious zealot or the moral masochist. What we in fact have is not morality, but a private moral code of the unconscious, which is at best quasimorality or moralism.

In contrast, intrinsic religious morality is related to ego development and mature ego function. Edith Jacobson (1964) has described these functions thus:

The mature self-critical ego, though participating in this moral evaluation, also judges our ego functions and our practical relations to reality... evaluates behavior not only in terms of correct or incorrect, true or false, appropriate or inappropriate, reasonable or unreasonable... and ego goals.

The achievement of mature moral ego functions is shown by Kohlberg (1964) to be related to the following moral capacities of ego development:

1. The ability to withstand temptation and to behave honestly.
2. To act in conformance with social norms that require impulse control.
3. Capacity to defer immediate gratification in favor of more distant rewards.
4. Maintain focused attention on one task.
5. Ability to control unsocialized fantasies.

But formal moral capacity and actual moral behavior are not necessarily congruent. Moral performance is learned through the observation of older children and adults, leading to role imitation, role practice, and role learning. And most importantly, moral behavior is strongly determined by the social and situational context of significant others (Aronfreed, 1968).

Moral or prosocial behavior is based upon social learning and social reinforcement that catalyzes the translation of principle into action. Moral character is both an attribute of the person and a situational social response. Prosocial behavior results from affective and cognitive developmental integration of the self, along with socially learned and reinforced role behaviors.

In terms of religious compliance, we can see that where a religious system is primarily assimilated into a primitive superego structure we will find strong unconscious religious compliance, which may not necessarily be related to higher moral values or moral behavior. Whereas, a religious system that is assimilated into mature development of discriminative ego functions and provides social contexts supportive of actualization of high moral commitment may produce behavior in compliance with high ethical principles.

CONCLUSION

The thesis presented in this chapter is that compliance to norms of social organization and ethical precepts is central to the viability of society. Religion is perhaps the strongest force in human history around which norms of social organization are crystallized, for the definition of ethical precepts, and for enforcement of compliance to such norms and values. However, our analysis of religion reveals that religious compliance can be a force for human good or inhuman destruction. We are left with the age-old problem of man's inhumanity to man. Whence comes social evil into the world, and how might we promote social good? In their analysis of the roots of evil, Sanford and Comstock (1971) find the social tree of evil rooted in personal maldevelopment, in family dysfunction, in community dysfunction, and in the social sanction of dehumanization. At each of these levels, this chapter presents an analysis of both the beneficient and destructive aspects of religion.

I conclude that the simplistic proposal to either increase religious compliance or to eliminate religious compliance is an inadequate response. Rather, we must pursue the path of understanding how religious compliance can be best constructed for human good.

REFERENCES

Allport, G. W., & Ross, J. M. Personal religious orientation and prejudice. *Journal of Personality and Social Psychology*, 1967, 5:432–433.
Aronfreed, J. *Conduct and conscience: The socialization of internalized control over behavior.* New York: Academic Press, 1968.
Baroja, J. C. *The world of witches.* Chicago: University of Chicago Press, 1964.
Bellah, R. N. *The broken covenant: American civil religion in time of trial.* New York: Seabury Press, 1975.
Bourguignon, E. *Religion, altered states of consciousness, and social change.* Columbus: Ohio State University Press, 1973.
Cox, R. H. (Ed.) *Religious Systems and Psychotherapy.* Springfield, Ill: C. C. Thomas, 1973.

Dillenberger, J. *Protestant thought and natural science.* Garden City, N.Y.: Doubleday, 1960.

Draper, E., Meyer, G. G., Parzen, Z., & Samuelson, G. On the diagnostic value of religious ideation. *Archives of General Psychiatry,* 1965, *13*:202–207.

Ellenberger, H. F. *The discovery of the unconscious. The history and evolution of dynamic psychiatry.* New York: Basic Books, 1970.

Glock, C. Y. The role of deprivation in the origin and evolution of religious groups. In Lee, R., & M. Marty, (Eds.), *Religion and social conflict.* New York: Oxford University Press, 1964.

Glock, C. Y., & Bellah, R. N. (Eds.). *The new religious consciousness.* Berkeley: University of California Press, 1976.

Glock, C. Y., & Stark, R. *Religion and society in tension.* Chicago: Rand McNally, 1965.

Hill. D. G. *Study of mind development groups, sects and cults in Ontario.* Toronto: Report to the Ontario Government, 1980.

Jacobson, E. *The self and the object world.* New York: International Universities Press, 1964.

Keniston, K. *The uncommitted: Alienated youth in American society.* New York: Harcourt, Brace, and World, 1960.

Kluckhohn, C. Introduction. In W. A. Less, & E. Z. Vogt, (Eds.), *Reader in comparative religion: An anthropological approach.* New York: Harper & Row, 1966.

Kohlberg, L. Development of moral character and moral ideology. In M. L. Hoffman, & L. W. Hoffman, Eds.), *Review of child development research.* (Vol. 1) New York: Russell Sage Foundation, 1964.

Lingeman, R. *Small town America.* New York: G. P. Putnam's Sons, 1980.

Marty, M. E. Science versus religion: An old squabble simmers down. *Saturday Review of Literature,* 1977 Dec. 10:29–35.

Neaman, J. S. *Suggestion of the devil: The origins of madness.* New York: Anchor Books, 1975.

Needleman, J. *The new religions.* Garden City, N.Y.: Doubleday, 1970.

Needleman, J., & Baker, G. (Eds.). *Understanding the new religions.* New York: Seabury Press, 1978.

Pande, S. K. The mystique of western psychotherapy: An eastern interpretation. *Journal of Nervous and Mental Disease,* 1968, *146*:425–432.

Pattison, E. M. (Ed.). *Clinical psychiatry and religion.* Boston: Little, Brown, 1969.

———Ego morality: An emerging psychotherapeutic concept. *Psychoanalytic Review*, 1968, *55*:187–222.

———Psychiatry and religion circa 1978: Analysis of a decade. *Pastoral Psychology*, *27*:8–25; 119–141, 1978.

———Religious youth cults: Alternative healing social networks. *Journal of Religion and Health*, *19*:275–286, 1980.

———A theoretical-empirical base for social systems therapy. In E. Foulkes, Wintrub, R. W., Westmeyer, J., Favassa, A. R., (Eds.), *Current perspectives in cultural psychiatry*. New York: Spectrum, 1977.

Pattison, E. M., Llamas, R., & Hurd, G. Social network mediation of anxiety. *Psychiatry Annals*, 1979, *9*:56–67.

Pruyser, P. *A dynamic psychology of religion*. New York: Harper & Row, 1968.

Rieff, P. *The triumph of the therapeutic: Uses of faith after freud*. New York: Harper & Row, 1966.

Roof, W. C. Concepts and indicators of religious commitment: a critical review. In R. Wuthnow (Ed.), *The religious dimension: New directions in quantitative research*. New York: Academic Press, 1979.

Sanford, N., & Comstock, C. *Sanctions for evil*. San Francisco: Jossey-Bass, 1971.

Sartre, J. -P. *Existentialism and human emotions*. New York: Philosophical Library, 1947.

Strommen, M. P. *Research on religious development: A comprehensive handbook*. New York: Hawthorn Books, 1971.

Wallace, E. R., IV. Freud and cultural evolutionism. In E. R. Wallace IV, & Pressley, L. C. (Eds.), *Essays in the history of psychiatry*. Columbia, S.C.: W. S. Hall Psychiatric Institute, 1980.

Wieman, R. W. *The family lives its religion*. New York: Harper, 1941.

Wuthnow, R. *The consciousness reformation*. Berkeley: University of California Press, 1976.

Zaretsky, I. I., & Leone, M. P. (Eds.). *Religious movements in contemporary america*. Princeton: Princeton University Press, 1974.

Zimmerman, C. C. Family influence upon religion. *Journal of Comparative Family Studies*, 1974, *5*:1–16.

Chapter 5

THE HEALTHY SIDE OF COMPLIANCE

Joseph A. Braun

The meaning of the word *compliance* is tinged with contrasting affective colorations even within the confines of its dictionary definitions (*The Oxford English Dictionary*, 1961; *Webster's Third New International Dictionary*, 1976). Compliance in its most general sense is seen as an autoplastic yielding to external demands, regulations, and pressures. Compliance connotes a citizen's deference, conformity, allegiance, or cooperation with respect to the social order; on an interpersonal level, this facet of compliance is equated with courtesy, politeness, and a befitting civility.

The affective ambivalence associated with compliance grows from any perspective on the human condition that acknowledges that in any social order and system of regulations there are relative degrees of health and sickness, love and hate, good and evil. Under the shadow of the dark sides of these polarities, compliance takes on the meaning of a character weakness synonymous with obsequiousness, spinelessness, unworthy subservience, and deliberate confederation. Compliance of this latter magnitude is linked with the moral and criminal charges of conspiracy and reprehensible collusion.

Particularly with the perspicuity provided by philosophy, history, or geographical distance, noncompliance is often understandably seen as the only moral, existential response appropriate for a human being, even if such a stance would require heroic courage. Gruesome images of the Guyana mass killings and the Holocaust are stark reminders of mankind's puzzling compliance with surrounding forces of destruction.

If one pauses for reflection, though, one wonders whether this human quality of compliance has been excessively maligned by the pathology-bent eyes of the behavioral scientist. In the physical sciences compliance is "the reciprocal of stiffness" (Thewlis, 1973, p. 66); it is the quality of yielding to bending under stress without breaking and without being permanently deformed; the ability of an object to recover its normal shape when deforming forces are removed (Considine, 1976). In engineering and physics, then, compliance is recognized as a necessary quality of strength; even in 1793 a certain bridge's safety was attributed to its quality of compliancy (*The Oxford English Dictionary*, 1961).

The physicalistic usage of compliance can be metaphorized to human character study, granting emphasis to compliance as an adaptive strength, a highly favorable quality, the facility to bend with outside pressure, and to compromise with external reality but without breaking personal codes or beliefs. Qualities such as tolerance, perspective, flexibility, eclecticism, adaptability, openness, even quiet wisdom and transcendence, all come to mind as elaborations of this facet of compliance.

EXTERNAL AND INTERNAL COMPLIANCE

When speaking of the compliance of the human person as a possible adaptive strength, it would seem that an important distinction must be drawn between *external* compliance and *internal* compliance. External compliance can be understood as visible compliance, that which makes the authorities or even one's peers content, happy, or, more likely, simply inactive and unnoticing. External compliance involves the documentable conformance to all figurative speed limits, stop signs, and required or expected rituals. Internal compliance, on the other hand, rests on a person's inner allegiance to these demands, principles, and regulations. External compliance is not always based on an accompanying inner compliance, a point important to remember. For better or for worse, from integrity or from its absence, visible behavior can exist on a different track from loyalties, convictions, and ideals.

By way of illustrating the difference between external and internal compliance, I have often fantasized when reading of the Holocaust how and where, should history ever repeat itself, I would hide and nourish my Jewish friends in order to save them and to send them to freedom. At the same time I can picture myself at a parade, as expected, giving external compliance. Would I perhaps even keep a swastika-lined bumper sticker on my car to keep the local police looking the other way? Only a childhood sense of omnipotence could lead me to believe that external noncompliance or a combative vocalization of my inner noncompliance could buttress the political thrust of a totalitarian regime and at the same time preserve intact both my family and my humble mission of love for dear friends. To paraphrase the psychoanalyst, Wilhelm Stekel, living humbly for a cause seems generally to be more fruitful then dying nobly for one.

The Extrinsic and Intrinsic Institution

There is a second important distinction that must be made in this discussion of compliance. There is often, although not necessarily, a vast difference between the intrinsic essence of an institution towards which compliance is given and the extrinsic facets of the same institution. There are extrinsic and intrinsic aspects to the object of compliance, then, paralleling the subject's ability to give either external or internal compliance or both. Just as an individual's external and internal compliance may be in harmony, the extrinsic and intrinsic aspects of the institution may coincide. The two are often radically different, however, with the intrinsic essence most discernible only from within and often imperceptible from without.

When Rabbi Heschel (1965) wrote that the beginning of

religious living comes from the question of what to do with the feeling of awe and wonder for being alive, he expressed an intrinsic essence devoid of extrinsic regulations, robes, and rituals. Buber's (1958) I-thou theology and philosophy touches one with the simplicity of its essence of a religious and interpersonal ideal.

Both Heschel and Buber give internal compliance to what they experienced as the intrinsic aspects of their religion. Heschel also lived with external compliance to the extrinsic aspects of Judaism, to the law and the formal observances. By contrast, Buber refused to comply with Jewish religious law and to attend services; in his conviction that formal religion could so readily mask the true essence of belief, he could give neither internal nor external compliance to the extrinsic aspects of Judaism.

Clearly, then, internal compliance to the intrinsic institution may or may not be accompanied by external compliance to the extrinsic aspects. External compliance, when evidenced, need not be interpreted automatically as a thoughtless submissiveness; external compliance may be a natural outgrowth of an authentic and active inner compliance. Failure to consider these inner and outer aspects of both the compliant subject and the object of compliance can lead to oversimplification and erroneous judgment regarding compliance.

A Roman Catholic Christianity, for instance, only viewed extrinsically in terms of external compliance with canon law, papal statements, and scholasticism is bound to convey negative impressions of automatons hopelessly and joylessly struggling to integrate and comply with papal pronouncements against contraception and hearty marital sexuality. Such a view, however, fails to account for internal compliance with an intrinsic essence. Apparently naive talk about marriage by a celibate pope from an Eastern European culture will have as much effect on an inner-directed, American Catholic as one psychoanalyst's suicide will have on another practicing analyst. Regrets, compassion, as well as in-house jokes, will appear, but there will have been no shaking of the foundation; the essence as perceived and experienced by the insider has not at all been touched.

It will be illuminating to remain with a brief exploration of Catholicism, a stereotypical authoritarian structure. The inner theology of Catholicism speaks differently from its external appearances and readily acknowledges the dichotomy between the extrinsic and intrinsic institution. The noted moral theologian, Bernard Häring (1966) warns:

> We shall never arrive at a truly animated knowledge of the law, if the effort concerning moral knowledge is concentrated on the law or on human dictates and commands and nothing more. Superiors, including Church superiors, must do their best so that the subject is not left hanging to the letter of the law which is something external, but that he come to an inner vision of the good, both that demanded by the law and that which lies outside the law. (p.70)

Speaking specifically of the compliance required of a person in a formal religious vocation, Rahner (1966b) wrote in a similar spirit that even such vowed obedience should be viewed "not primarily as obedience to individual commands, nor is it even the abstract notion of a general readiness to fulfill such commands. Primarily, it is the permanent binding of oneself to a definite mode of life" (p. 216).

Religious obedience is thus not to be equated with the unidirectional obedience that children owe their parents. Rahner emphasizes the dialogical aspect of obedience, calling for the subject's own initiative and decisiveness and acknowledging the role of spontaneous and autonomous moral judgment by the subject, especially in the face of a command that may be wrong and destructive. Although persons must obey their own consciences, the external law is nevertheless seen as essential for the provision of some foundation of illumination, guidance, and objective truth, so that individual conscience does not degenerate into a private solipsistic voice (Häring, 1966; Rahner, 1966a). The dialogical tension between the external and the internal has been elucidated by Curran (1977), another prominent moral theologian:

> The fundamental law for the Christian and for the Church is the law of the Spirit, which is primarily an internal law. There is a need for external law in the Church, but this

external law must be in conformity with the demands of the internal law. . The external law might not always correspond to the demands of the Spirit here and now. (p. 89)

When a casual social acquaintance deepens into friendship, the external trappings fade in significance as the inner person becomes known and experienced. There is often surprise that others, appraising the friend only from the outside, arrive at very different impressions from the ones based on intimacy. Behind a public facade, even one of cold authority, may be a vibrant pulse that can be missed by the superficial judge.

A Basis for Unhealthy Compliance

Amid these considerations of the extrinsic and intrinsic aspects of institutions and of the person's own phenomenology of inner autonomy, the compliance of moral turpitude, unhealth, and destruction seems strangely out of place. The reason for this lack of fit is that in unhealthy compliance there really seems to be no internal compliance to any intrinsic essence or ideal and no external compliance to an institution with a heritage, lineage, and identity. Destructive and unhealthy compliance, at least in its most perverse forms, seems linked not with intrinsic institutions but with one person, a charismatic, often megalomanic and psychopathic leader, who *personally* becomes the compliant follower's object of allegiance. The leader *is* the institution, as it were, or else supplants an institution and its healthy heritage, a phenomenon so observable in religious and nonreligious cults and in cultish subgroups of larger institutions that are not in themselves cultish.

The unhealthy complier seems to relinquish the rights to inner noncompliance and to the freedom to perform even the subtlest act of external noncompliance. The leader in turn seems to value and to need this self-abnegating compliance. The extensive literature based on clinical work with so-called borderline conditions enlightens the understanding of unhealthy compliance. Failure in crucial early separation-individuation phases

(Masterson, 1976), with a pervasive lack of personal identity and a sense of self (Grinker & Werble, 1977) and a persistence of primitive object relations (Kernberg, 1975), are interrelated dimensions that are helpful in explaining both the drive toward a compliant stance and the need satisfaction and homeostasis granted when emptiness as a person is filled with a shared identity. This observation, however, is not meant to encourage the practice of perjuriously labeling and categorizing persons and behavior with the diagnostic category "borderline" (Appelbaum, 1979; Glazer, 1979).

Compliance in these unhealthy situations no longer can be understood primarily in idealogical, philosophical, or rational terms. The internal assent, the inner evaluative and belief process, seems not a major factor. Rather, cultural and psychological developmental deficits and forces in the compliant subjects constitute the primary framework to use in dealing conceptually with destructive compliance.

COMPLIANCE IN SERVICE OF FIDELITY AND LOVE

Internal compliance, as well as an autonomous external compliance, may be a natural, healthy expression and perpetuation of an integrated self. Compliance may be an act of fidelity and loyalty to an essence of oneself and of an external object or group that one has arrived at and touched in the process of healthy growth and individuation. Healthy compliance may be an act of commitment to, and continuity with, one's roots and personal history—a perpetuation of all that is meant by an individual's identity. Compliance may represent wholesome allegiance to, and stability of, personal relationships. In short, compliance may be one aspect of mature love.

The existential evolution behind a compliant stance must not be overlooked. A mental health practitioner, for example, may engage in a personal psychotherapeutic journey and have unveiled the forces of personal history unconsciously working in the present day. The same person, struggling with patients over protracted periods of time, becomes sensitized to the historical framework and unconscious material behind the patients' problematic behavior, cognition, affect, and character traits. Formal training in psychoanalysis is commenced and duly finished. Charlatanic narcissists with but one-tenth the requisite training and character integrity may represent themselves to the public and to their professional peers as "psychoanalysts," causing that well-trained, well-credentialed analyst to cringe. Political disputes, extremist stances, psychopathy, and megalomania may contaminate the psychoanalytic image even within official circles. The legitimately certified psychoanalyst nonetheless does not shed his or her identity, but internally complies willingly and fruitfully with the essential aspects of technique and theory and complies externally with organizational requirements and policies. As he or she becomes further involved in the training of psychoanalysts, friendships develop with teaching colleagues and with students, whose struggles and progress one shares. General compliance to the professional framework—not to be understood as an avoidance of some specific disagreements—is fueled now not just by one's professional identity but by a mature and responsible caring for many individuals in the personal network within the profession.

When such a personal commitment and affiliation is based on a genuine personal journey, compliance within the framework of that commitment may be an act of fidelity and caring. "There is a point," wrote Hammarskjöld (1964), "at which everything becomes simple and there is no longer any question of choice, because all you have staked will be lost if you look back. Life's point of no return" (p. 66).

By way of contrast, it seems that persons who are characterologically noncompliant in the conventional world, making much into an arena of protest and dissent although with a rationale, often are without love. The noncompliers often lack courtesy, politeness, kindness, and civility toward the individuals in their path. It seems more like the noncompliant person experiences others as inner objects to assist in some debacle. Noncompliance of this kind appears to be an act of narcissism. Healthy compliance by contrast may readily be experienced as a quiet respect and caring.

Even within the confines of a totalitarian regime, external compliance may be a requisite for the expression of love. The delicate balance becomes one of annihilative compliance with a danger of the loss of the human spirit and an equally annihilative noncompliance with its danger of the loss of life and of further restrictions on individual freedom.

COMPLIANCE IN SERVICE OF PRIORITIES AND CREATIVITY

Whether compliance is shaded positively or negatively is an issue of relativity and individual situations. For any person there will always be areas of compliance and noncompliance, just as there are life areas where activity dominates and those where passive acceptance is the prime way of adjusting. The problem, one of priorities and balances, is like the dilemma in the Alcoholics Anonymous prayer that begs for the wisdom to know the difference between what should be serenely accepted as unchangeable and what can and should be courageously changed. Even those persons noted for their noncompliance must have areas of compliance either in small matters of day-to-day survival or in issues of importance to other like-minded noncompliers.

The more intelligent and perceptive the individual, the more that person can see life's faults and failings. The more motivated and creative a person, the more perceptible is the mediocrity that permeates job performance and the general approach to living. Fighting small-minded little people and their petty concerns, however, and battling to reform all that is reformable can be sapping of personal energies.

Compliance with what is existent, customary, expected, needed, or required is often the substratum for an efficient use of time and for the constructive channeling of creative resources. Compliance in this context can be seen as an outgrowth of a healthy, mature ego. Conversely, noncompliance, especially external noncompliance, may be a defense against the creative use of time and energy.

If people want to ship their creative or necessary productions by railroad to every part of the country but refuse to comply with the standard guage of the track, they must first expend a staggering amount of money and time to rebuild millions of railroad cars and thousands of miles of track. Clearly, the consideration of priorities is an essential component of any compliance versus noncompliance dilemma and of any judgment concerning the health or pathology of compliant behavior. Compliance with the requisite format for a journal helps assure the publication of what is hopefully valuable material to be shared with and utilized by colleagues or the public. Compliance with a building inspector's request simply means that the new office, gallery, or study will be opened and utilizable on schedule.

Compliance with graduate school degree and dissertation reguirements assures one of the right of passage to entry-level positions in a career line and to further recognition and creative opportunities. How many haughty refusals to comply with dissertation requirements were not at all really adult stances against unreason but were rather refusals to face the adult responsible reality that the terminal degree would bring? From a psychodynamic stance, such noncompliance is often based on childlike omnipotence, self-destruction, or on a perpetuation of Oedipal and other family dynamics and identifications that would rather perpetuate fighting than quiet, independent functioning. Even in the presence of unreasonable demands or departmental politics, a mature ego free of destructive inner dynamics might easily look ahead to an autonomous selection and shaping of values, behavior, and creative output after the degree requirements had been fulfilled. Destructive compliance might be seen as existing only if, later in one's career, one identified with the aggressor, so to speak, and treated others the way one had hated to be treated.

Paradoxically, then, external compliance may be a necessary substructure for genuine creativity, attention to priorities, and inner autonomy. Similarly, true internal freedom is often being exercised under the cloak of compliance and submissiveness. It is possible for people to be totally externally compliant with external authority and yet, by the simple quality of their life existence, be totally and powerfully noncompliant with the essence of that same authority.

The American hostages in Iran are a monument to this paradox. So are missionaries who have gone to difficult lands not to overthrow a regime, change a culture, or radicalize the populus but to simply *be* and by that being make a powerful statement.

To balance the picture, however, it must be emphasized that

external and internal noncompliance may at other times be a loving, creative act of the highest order. It is often a responsible, sensitive, generative soul whose voice of external and internal noncompliance becomes either the first to raise the consciousness of the many or else becomes the formal articulator of the unspoken sentiments of all whose position does not grant the right to be heard as a profound and pertinent authority.

Conclusion

Compliance is a word with many applications and varied emotional colorations. Compliance does not possess the unipolar affective valence carried by words like murder, rape, torture, war, or terrorism. Subjective and existential, then, are the individual formulas that determine when compliance, external or internal, is necessary, contructive, desirable, or tolerable, and when it is destructive, intolerable, or even morally wrong.

References

Appelbaum, S. A. To define and decipher the borderline syndrome. *Psychotherapy: Theory, research, and practice,* 1979, *16*(4): 364–370.
Buber, M. *I and thou.* New York: Scribner's, 1958.
Considine, D. M. *Van Nostrand's scientific encyclopedia.* New York: Van Nostrand Reinhold, 1976.
Curran, C. E. *Themes in fundamental moral theology.* Notre Dame, Ind.: University of Notre Dame Press, 1977.
Glazer, M. W. The borderline personality diagnosis: some negative implications. *Psychotherapy: Theory, research and practice,* 1979, *16*(4): 376–380.
Grinker, R. R. and Werble, B. *The borderline patient.* New York: Jason Aronson, 1977.
Hammarskjöld, D. *Markings.* New York: Knopf, 1964.
Häring, B. An inner vision of the good. In *Obedience, the greatest freedom.* Boston: Daughters of St. Paul, 1966.
Heschel, A. J. *Who is man?* Stanford: Stanford University Press, 1965.

Kernberg, O. *Borderline conditions and pathological narcissism.* New York: Jason Aronson, 1975.

Masterson, J. F. *Psychotherapy of the borderline adult.* New York: Brunner/Mazel, 1976.

The Oxford English dictionary. Oxford: Clarendon Press, 1961.

Rahner, K. The appeal to conscience. In *Obedience, the greatest freedom.* Boston: Daughters of St. Paul, 1966. (a)

——Reflections on obedience. In *Obedience, the greatest freedom.* Boston: Daughters of St. Paul, 1966. (b)

Thewlis, J. *Concise dictionary of physics.* New York: Pergamon, 1973.

Webster's third new international dictionary. New York: G. & C. Merriam, 1976.

Chapter 6

DEMONIC POSSESSION

A Social Psychological Analysis

Nicholas P. Spanos

This chapter deals with Western European and colonial American manifestations of demonic possession that occurred during the Late Medieval-Early Modern Period. I shall begin by describing behaviors commonly associated with the possession notion during this period and shall then present two modern interpretations of these phenomena. The first interpretation holds that the possessed were suffering from various mental illnesses. The second suggests, instead, that possession cannot be understood adequately unless it is viewed in terms of its sociohistorical context. Such an analysis is consonant with modern social-learning and social-role formulations of behavior, but is much less compatible with traditional psychiatric interpretations.

CHARACTERISTICS OF THE DEMONICALLY POSSESSED

For the most part, the phenomenon of demonic possession emerged in Western Europe as an accompaniment to the spread of Christianity.[1] In the New Testament the notion that demons can enter the human body and take over its functioning is made explicit, possession is differentiated from physical illness, behavioral symptoms of this condition are specified, and numerous examples of possession and exorcism are recorded (Catherinet, 1972; McCasland, 1951). Among the most prominent symptoms displayed by the New Testament demoniacs, i.e., possessed persons, were convulsions, heightened intelligence with indications of clairvoyance, increased strength, sensory and motor deficits, and changes in personality (Catherinet, 1972; Lea, 1957). In the New Testament descriptions, individual demoniacs usually displayed only one, or occasionally a few, of these symptoms. By the Medieval and Late Medieval Periods, however, individual demoniacs usually displayed all or most of these behaviors (Boguet, 1603/1929; Kramer & Sprenger, 1489/1971).

The characteristics officially attributed to demons by the Medieval Church were, in large part, based on the New Testament descriptions of demoniacs. Thus, demons were incorporal; they could enter the body (but not the soul) of an individual and take over its functioning. They could travel quickly from place to place gaining knowledge of distant places, people, and foreign languages. They were more intelligent than humans. They could not foretell the future, for that was a prerogative held only by God. Nevertheless, because of their greater intelligence, coupled with the knowledge gained from distant travel, they were able to make shrewd and often accurate predictions of future events (Nauman, 1974; Robbins, 1959; Summers, 1956).

Although there were important local variations, the pattern of behaviors enacted by demoniacs had, by the sixteenth century, become fairly stereotyped. Among the most consistently occurring behaviors were convulsions, increased intelligence accompanied by clairvoyance and spontaneous amnesia, transcendent "feats," and the experience of the demonic behavior as occurring involuntarily.

Convulsions

The occurrence of convulsions, particularly during exorcisms soon before expulsion of the demon, was an almost invariable accompaniment of possession (McCasland, 1951; Oesterreich, 1966). The *Compendium Maleficarum*, the most authoritative witch hunting manual of the seventeenth century, put the matter as follows: "A man may very surely be known for a demoniac if he is disturbed [i.e., convulsed] when the exorcisms are read" (Guazzo, 1608/1970, p. 168). The following description of a seventeenth century nun possessed by the demon Asmodius provides an example of demonically induced convulsions:

> ... Asmodius was not long in manifesting his supeme rage shaking the girl backwards and forwards a number of times and making her strike like a hammer with such great rapidity that her teeth rattled and sound was forced out of her throat. That between these movements her face became completely unrecognizable, her glance furious, her tongue prodigiously large, long, and hanging down out of her mouth.... (Aubin, 1716, p. 226)

It is important to note that the onset and termination of convulsions were frequently a function of social cues. For instance, during the Salem witch trials of 1692, demoniacs convulsed whenever an accused witch looked in their direction and were relieved of their convulsions whenever they were touched by the accused (Brattle, 1692/1914; Lawson, 1693/1914). The same phenomenon occurred in Continental Europe and in England. For example, the young daughters of Robert Throckmorton claimed that old Mother Samuel had bewitched them. Although they often behaved normally:

> ... no sooner had Mother Samuel entered the hall but at one moment the said three children fell down upon the ground strangely tormented ... their bellies heaving up, their heads and heels still touching the ground as though they had been tumblers. *(The Most Strange and Admirable Discovery of the Three Witches of Warboys,* 1593/1972, p. 246)

Increased Intelligence, Clairvoyance, and Amnesia

The importance of heightened intellectual ability and clairvoyance in recognizing possession was continually stressed by both witch hunting and exorcism manuals (e.g., Guazzo, 1608/

1970; *A Manual of Exorcism,* 1720/1975). For instance, the *Compendium Maleficarum* held that:

> An even more certain sign is when a sick man speaks in foreign tongues unknown to him, or understands in those tongues; or when, being but ignorant, the patients argue about high and difficult questions; or when they discover hidden and long-forgotton matters, or future events, or the secrets of the inner conscience, such as the sins and imaginings of the bystanders. . . . It is a manifest sign when an ignorant man speaks literary and grammatical latin, or if without knowledge of the art he sings musically or says something of which he could never have had any knowledge. (Guazzo, 1608/1970, p. 168)

The type of evidence used to support claims of clairvoyance or other preternatural knowledge in demoniacs is illustrated by the following seventeenth century account reported in Glanvill's *Saducismus Triumphatus* (1689). It must be kept in mind that demoniacs were often thought to convulse when in proximity to a witch, even when they had no knowledge of the witch's presence.[2]

> ... but when the witch was brought in again, ... although she [the demoniac] could not possibly see her, she would be immediately senseless and like to be strangled, and so would continue till the witch were taken out, and then ... she would come again to her senses. That afterwards Mr. *Greatrix,* Mr. *Blackwell,* and some others, who would needs satisfy themselves in the influence of the witch's presence, tried it and found it several times. Although he did it with all possible privacy, and so as none could think it possible that the maid to know either of the witches coming in or going out. (Glanvill, 1689, p. 382)

Another common, although not invariable, manifestation of possession was spontaneous amnesia for events occuring during the demon's occupation of the body (Catherinet, 1972; Oesterreich, 1966). For instance, the following possessed girl experienced long "Ludicrous intervals" in which she appeared to be more intelligent than usual but later manifested amnesia for the events occurring during these intervals:

> Her Apprehension, Understanding, and Memory, was riper than ever in her life; any yet, when she was herself, she Could Remember the other Accidents of her Afflictions but forgot almost everything that passed in these Ludicrous Intervals. (Mather, 1693/1914, p. 272).

Other Transcendent Phenomena

The demonically possessed displayed not only intellectual enhancements and amnesia but also behaviors that were thought to transcend normal capacities (More, 1600). Examples of some of the more important of these follow:

> 1. *Insensitivity to pain:* "The insensibilityes of her bodie, during her extasies and furies tried by the prickings of long pinnes (sic), without any shew, that ever she made of feeling the same, either in the putting in of them, or in the taking out of them." (Hartwell, 1599, pp. 15–16)
> 2. *Predicting the future occurrence of their own "demonic attacks":* If they asked their possessing demon how many fits they should have the next day following, and the third day, or any day that week . . . and what manner of fits they should be, whether more grievous or less, how long every fit should continue . . . it [their demon] hath told them and not failed in one point." *(The Most Strange and Admirable Discovery of the Three Witches of Warboys,* 1593/1972, p. 261)
> 3. *Unusual strength:* " . . . she was again with violence and extremity seized by her fits in such a way that six persons could hardly hold her." (Willard, 1683/1974).
> 4. *Temporary and selective sensory-motor deficits:* Sometimes being taken in her fit she is but deaf only. . . . Sometimes also she can hear only, and not everybody, but someone whom she liketh and chooseth out from the rest; sometimes she seeth only, and as plainly as any other, but neither heareth nor speaketh anything, her teeth being set in her head; sometimes both hearing and seeing very well, and yet not

able to speak. *(The Most Strange and Admirable Discovery of the Three Witches of Warboys,* 1593/1972, p. 249)

Experienced Involuntariness

Some episodes of possession did not involve amnesia. From these it is clear that the demoniacs defined their possession as an event over which they could exercise no volitional control. They described their convulsions, contortions, blaspheming, and other behaviors as being carried out in spite rather than because of their wishes. For instance, Heinrick Kramer and James Sprenger, the fifteenth century authors of the infamous *Malleus Maleficarum* (1489), asked a demoniac why he did not restrain himself. The demoniac replied.

> I cannot help myself at all, for he the demon uses my limbs and organs, my neck, my tongue, and my lungs, whenever he pleases, causing me to speak or to cry out; and I hear the words as if they were spoken by myself, but I am altogether unable to restrain them; and when I try to engage in prayer he attacks me more violently, thrusting out my tongue. (pp. 131–132)

Possession was not only experienced as involuntary by the demoniac, it was defined as an involuntary occurrence by the society at large. Medieval cannon law classified possession as a species of demonically induced insanity. The possessed, like other insane, were not considered responsible for their actions (Neaman, 1975; Richter, 1959). Thus, the possessed saw themselves and were viewed by others as automatons controlled by a foreign agency that had temporarily set the normal personality in abeyance.

Psychiatric Interpretations

Most modern psychiatric historians argue that individuals labeled as demonically possessed were suffering from one or another type of mental illness (Cartwright & Biddiss, 1972;

Krohn, 1978; Roback, 1962; Veith, 1965, 1977; Zilboorg & Henry, 1941). This view may be summarized as follows: Demonic possession was a notion used by superstitious people of more credulous eras to explain behavioral dysfunctions that we now know were "really" hysteria (Hansen, 1969; Krohn, 1978; Veith, 1965), schizophrenia (Zilboorg & Henry, 1941), or the like. During and after the seventeenth century, demonic superstitions were gradually discarded, and mental illness came to be correctly diagnosed (Zilboorg & Henry, 1941).

Hysteria and Possession

By far the most common diagnostic label applied to historical cases of demonic possession is hysteria. The idea that manifestations of possession resulted from hysteria had been proposed by the early seventeenth century (Jorden, 1603), and it gained general credence in the medical community by the end of the nineteenth century (Cesbron, 1909; Charcot, 1889; Janet, 1925: Richet, 1887). According to Charcot, for example, demonically possessed, seventeenth century French nuns suffered from hysteria. He and his colleagues supported their contentions by pointing to the behavioral similarities between their own nineteenth century hysterical patients and the earlier French demoniacs (Charcot, 1889; Charcot & Marie, 1892; Charcot & Richer, 1887/1972).

Along similar lines, a number of nineteenth and twentieth century American historians and psychiatrists have interpreted New England possession cases in terms of hysteria. For instance, the reports of temporary blindness, choking sensations, and specters (visual images of ghosts, witches, etc.) given by colonial demoniacs have been interpreted as classic indicators of the "disease" hysteria (Caulfield, 1943; Demos, 1970; Hansen, 1969; Thompson, 1972). This view is clearly expressed by Hansen in the following passage:

> These symptoms are readily recognizable. The most cursory examination of the classic studies of hysteria—Charcot or Janet, or Breuer and Freud—will demonstrate that the afflicted girls of Salem were hysterical in the scientific sense of that term. . . . (1969, p. 22)

Unfortunately, for historians of psychiatry there is no single, unambiguous "scientific sense" in which the term hysteria is used. If the diagnostic labels of modern psychiatry were to be ranked for clarity, precision, and reliability, hysteria would surely be close to the bottom of the list (Chodoff & Lyons, 1958; Slater, 1965). Historically, this term has been associated with a vast hodgepoge of unusual and dramatic behaviors, including spontaneous amnesia, and fugue states, convulsions, sensory and motor deficits occurring in the absence of demonstrable organic pathology, heightened suggestibility, hallucinations, anorexia, a host of sexual disturbances, various language disfunctions, and a personality configuration variously described as vain, coquettish, frigid, and so on (Chodoff & Lyons, 1958; Chodoff, 1974; Janet, 1925). There is certainly no evidence to support the notion that the array of behaviors subsumed under this term reflect a unitary disease process (Mersky & Buhrich, 1975; Slater, 1965). In fact, Slater has gone so far as to argue that:

> No evidence has yet been offered that the patients diagnosed as suffering from "hysteria" are in medically significant terms anything more than a random selection.... The only thing "hysterical" patients can be shown to have in common is that they are all patients.... The diagnosis of "hysteria" is a disguise for ignorance and a fertile source of clinical error. (p. 1399)

Numerous hypotheses have been formulated concerning the etiology of hysteria. Given the range of behaviors subsumed under this term, it is not surprising that many of these hypotheses are inconsistent with one another (Abse, 1959; Guze, 1967; Krohn, 1978. Despite their differences, however, most of these hypotheses share a tendency to locate the primary causes of hysterical behavior in unconscious conflicts that were repressed during early childhood. Ongoing interpersonal factors that might play an important role in the production and maintenance of such behaviors are deemphasized. At best, situational variables are seen as triggering or reinforcing the repressed conflicts that are the "real" causes of hysterical symptoms (e.g., Fenichel, 1945; Krohn, 1978). This lack of serious concern for situational influences on behavior has sometimes led psychiatric writers to adopt and perpetuate serious historical inaccuracies. One such inaccuracy involves the confusion of demonic possession and witchcraft found in many standard psychiatric histories.

Witchcraft and Demonic Possession

Although the notion that people can be possessed by demons stretches back into antiquity, it did not become associated with witchcraft in Western European thought until the fifteenth century (Brown, 1970; Oesterreich, 1966). From the fifteenth through the seventeenth centuries, the ideas of the demoniac and the witch were kept distinct and served different social functions. The demoniac was frequently (but by no means always) construed as an individual smitten by witchcraft and was encouraged to accuse the witch who had caused her to become possessed (Oesterreich, 1966; Spanos, 1978). The person or persons accused by the demoniac were frequently defined as witches on the basis of such accusations and often subjected to legal torture and execution (Mandrou, 1968; Rosen, 1969). The demoniac was not accused of being a witch and, although sometimes treated harshly, was not subjected to systematic legal torture and was not executed. Because demonic possession was defined by canon law as a species of insanity and therefore as involuntary, it was usually treated by means of exorcism and/or prayer and fasting rather than by legal punishment (Boguet, 1603/1929; Kelly, 1974; Pickett, 1959). The witch, on the other hand, was construed as a sane individual who had voluntarily renounced God, made a pact with the Devil, and thereby deserved both torture and execution (Bodin, 1593; Kramer & Sprenger, 1486/1971; Roberts, 1616/1971).

Despite such important differences, witches and demoniacs have been confused by psychiatric writers since the early nineteenth century (e.g., Charcot, 1889; Esquirol, 1838/1965; Jacoby, 1912; Janet, 1924; Shryock, 1944; Veith, 1965). For instance, Roback (1962) stated incorrectly that: "during the sixteenth and seventeenth centuries, hundreds of thousands of the 'possessed' were burned.... Hysterics, largely women, would . . .

act as if they were really possessed. The only cure was burning, generally preceded by torture." (pp. 216–217).

The reason behind this confusion is not difficult to discern. Both witches and demoniacs were described as showing some similar symptoms. For instance, both were purportedly analgesic and sometimes reported bizarre sexual fantasies. From a psychiatric perspective, behaviors of this type are often taken to be symptoms of hysteria or some other mental disorder, and their primary causes are thereby relegated to the realm of unconscious motivation. For this reason, the very different social contexts in which these behaviors were displayed by witches and demoniacs, and the very different consequences that ensued when a demoniac as opposed to a witch enacted such behaviors, have simply remained unexamined.

The consequences of deemphasizing situational factors in accounts of demonic possession are often more subtle than major historical inaccuracies. More typically, such deemphasis simply leads to theoretical accounts that are unnecessarily complex and often incapable of being substantiated or disconfirmed. Such an account of New England possession cases has been presented by Demos (1970).

Demonic possession and oral fixation. Demos (1970) contended that the demoniacs of colonial New England were suffering from hysteria, and he attempted to account for their behavior by speculating about the "oral phase" of their development.

> It seems plausible, however, that many New England children were faced with some unspecified but extremely difficult psychic task in the first year or so of life. The outcome was that their aggressive drives were tied especially closely to the oral mode and driven underground. Years later, in accordance with changes in normal adolescence, instinctual energies of all types were greatly augmented; and this tended, as it so often does, to reactivate the earliest conflicts—the process that Freud vividly described as the "the return of the repressed." But these conflicts were no easier to deal with in adolescence than they had been earlier; hence the need for the twin defenses of projection and displacement. (Demos, 1970, p. 1325)

Demos (1970) does not tell us why it is plausible to assume that New England children (as opposed to any other) were faced with an "extremely difficult psychic task" early in life, and he provides no evidence concerning the nature of this unspecified task. He does, however, provide a content analysis of the recorded verbalizations of New England demoniacs. These verbal reports contained "oral themes," e.g., reports of being "bitten, pinched and pricked," and of seeing familiars, i.e., demons in the shape of small animals that did a witch's bidding, sucking witches teats. Demos (1970) also contended that many of the demoniacs underwent long fasts before and after their fits. For him, all of this constitutes convincing evidence of orally fixated individuals.

There is no question that New England demoniacs frequently reported being bitten and seeing familiars. However, an interpretation, much more parsimonious than "oral fixation," can account for these reports. Namely, these reports reflected the folklore of seventeenth century Puritan communities. Puritan demoniacs reported being bitten and seeing familiars, because these were the characteristics they had learned were applicable to those who had been bewitched.

The fact that Demos found very similar reports for the 50-year period from the initial Puritan settlements in New England to the time of the Salem Village witch panic, lends more credence to such a social-learning hypothesis than to one framed in terms of repressed conflicts. Furthermore, the "symptoms" catalogued by Demos (1970) were not specific to New England Puritan demoniacs. They occurred frequently in English cases of demonic possession and many occurred in continental cases as well. (Oesterreich, 1966; Robbins, 1959; Thomas, 1971).

With respect to the fasting that allegedly occurred among New England demoniacs, Demos is simply incorrect. There is evidence that fasting occurred in the cases of two Boston demoniacs, but it was never reported as occurring among the Salem demoniacs who made up the largest share of New England possession cases.

Demos' argument is based on the implicit assumption that certain adult behaviors, e.g., reports of oral activity can be used to accurately infer the nature of conflicts that purportedly occurred and were repressed at specific points during early development. There is, in fact, no convincing empirical evidence to support this assumption (O'Connor & Franks, 1960). Moreover, this assumption is, itself, based on the notion that the interpersonal behavior of adults can be adequately explained in terms of stable underlying traits or dispositions, e.g., oral personality. This thesis is a good deal more controversial than Demos would lead us to believe (cf. Mischel, 1968, 1973). The available evidence suggests that there is a good deal more variability in the behavior people display than trait theorists once assumed, and this variability cannot be accounted for without giving careful consideration to the role played by situational contingencies. Thus, even if Demos were correct in assuming that certain reports indicated "repressed oral conflicts," we would still know nothing about why demoniacs gave such reports in some situations and not in others, why they consistently displayed symptoms in the presence of some persons but not others, why their demonic behavior terminated when it did, and why, as in the case of Salem Village, groups of individuals began displaying similar demonic behavior within a short span of time. As we shall see, answers to these questions can be approached when demonic behaviors are viewed an enactments that were geared to the requirements of certain social contexts, rather than as symptoms that resulted automatically from diseased mental processes.

Psychiatric Formulations and Socially Defined Reality

Not only do psychiatric formulations of possession assume that the diagnostic practices of modern psychiatry are reliable and valid, they further assume that such validity is maintained when the historical figures being diagnosed lived in different cultures and shared assumptions about the nature of reality that were often quite different from those taken for granted in our own society. There is nothing in the work of psychiatric historians to suggest that this assumption has been met or, for that matter, even seriously considered. The problem here can be illustrated by examining the testimony of John Walsh, a sixteenth century village wizard. When asked by an ecclesiastical court how he knew that someone was bewitched, he answered that: "he knew it partly by the fairies, and saith that there be 3 kinds of fairies, white, green and black, which when he is disposed to use he speaketh with them upon hills" *(The examination of John Walsh . . . ,* 1566/ 1972, p. 68).

From a traditional psychiatric perspective, John Walsh was obviously deluded and hallucinating and therefore was probably schizophrenic. By and large, however, testimony of this type is taken to reflect "sickness" simply because it contradicts the largely mechanistic, technologically oriented world view that literate, industrialized modern man has come to take for granted as real and, therefore, as normal. From a psychiatric perspecitve, behavior is deemed to be symptomatic of some mental aberration to the extent that it is not readily understandable in terms of this socially constructed reality (Coulter, 1973). However, the world view common to the sixteenth and seventeenth century European was quite different from our own. During those centuries, the occurrence of harmful magic and the existence of spirits and demons were, for the vast majority, unquestioned realities (Tillyard, 1948). Moreover, certain classes of experience that are consistent with a supernatural frame of reference, e.g., imagining a ghost or demon, were undoubtedly more common, more elaborate, and much more likely to be classified as actual external occurrences than they are today (Thomas, 1971). In short, the testimony of John Walsh, when viewed in terms of his status as a village wizard, may tell us something about the implicit assumptions he (as well as his interrogators and his neighbor-customers) held about the nature of reality. It is less clear that such testimony can tell us anything about hysteria, schizophrenia, or the like.

In summary, stating that demoniacs were hysterics, schizophrenics, or whatever, does little more than restate the fact that these individuals behaved in ways that, to us, appear unusual. Diagnoses of this sort tell us nothing about the variables that produced or maintained the unusual behavior. Moreover, in diagnosing these behaviors we have a strong tendency to wrench them from their historical context and interpret them within our own contemporary frame of reference. Thus, reports by demoniacs of seeing witches' specters—events that make a great deal of sense within the world view of seventeenth century Puritans—are diagnosed as hallucinations because they call up in us "specters" of mental patients. Witches' specters, previously not understandable, now make sense; they become the products of diseased minds and, as such, fit comfortably within our own conceptual framework. Unfortunately, superimposing our own implicit world view on historical events can lead us to seriously distort the meaning to those events. As a result, we may end up believing that we have explained events that we have not yet begun to understand.

A Social Psychological Interpretation

The social psychological perspective that is elaborated in the remainder of this paper rejects mental illness interpretations of possession. It suggests instead that the pattern of behaviors enacted by the demonically possessed can be usefully conceptualized as reflecting a social role; a learned pattern of interpersonal responding that was shaped and maintained by elements of the social context in which it occurred. From this perspective, demonic possession can only be understood when viewed in terms of its historical context and when the social and political functions that it served in that context are appreciated.

Before proceeding, I will attempt to clarify a potentially troublesome issue associated with the theoretical notion of social role behavior. The term *role enactment* refers to patterns of activity that are linked to and identifed with a particular social status, e.g., physician, an informally defined social position, e.g., class clown, or a particular social value, e.g., a patriot (Biddle & Thomas, 1966; Turner, 1956). Role enactment may involve prescribed patterns of subjective experience as well as overt behavior. Moreover, this notion implies neither that enactments involve a lack of personal conviction, nor that they involve a superficial performance without subjective involvement (Goffman, 1961; Sarbin & Allen, 1968). Thus, to say that individuals enacted the role of a demoniac does not imply that they were faking or that they did not actually believe themselves to be possessed (Spanos & Gottlieb, 1979). On the other hand, a role-playing perspective does not preclude analyses of such phenomena as faking or disinterested enactment. For instance, several reports (e.g., *The Boy of Bilson* ... 1622; Harsnett, 1599; Hutchinson, 1718) indicate that some demoniacs were faking at least part of the time. These individuals confessed to enacting fits and other behaviors in order to obtain various rewards, and without believing that they were, in fact, possessed. Some went so far as to publicly reenact their supposedly involuntary symptoms in order to demonstrate how they had faked (Harsnett, 1599).

From a social psychological perspective, faking is not a quality of behavior. It refers instead to the beliefs concerning the causes of their own behavior that are held by individuals labeled as frauds, and as such, it can be analyzed in role performance terms. Thus, at one extreme, some demoniacs attributed their fits and other behaviors to voluntary actions carried out for the purpose of obtaining specified rewards, e.g., attention from others, money. Others enacted similar behaviors but attributed their actions not to themselves or to the inducements of extrinsic rewards, but to the machinations of an indwelling demon. Both the faked and the nonfaked performances are conceptualized here as role enactments. The task of the social psychologist in such cases is to delineate the variables that led to the very different causal attributions held by faking and nonfaking demoniacs who enacted similar overt behaviors.[3]

Socialization into the Demonic Role

Earlier I noted that demoniacs from different historical eras and in different places often enacted a similar constellation of behaviors, e.g., convulsions, amnesia, insensitivity to pain. This core of similarity should not be taken to mean that cultural variations in demonic role performance did not occur. In fact, such variation was common and sometimes quite dramatic. For instance, in seventeenth century France demonic nuns invariable spoke in a voice different from their usual one, and this voice was identified with an indwelling demon (Aubin, 1716; Michalis, 1613). In fact, many of these nuns spoke in several different voices and each identified itself as a different demon. These voice changes were accompanied by changes in facial expression, mood, and behavior that suggested a unique personality for each demon (Aubin, 1716; Oesterreich, 1966). A number of modern investigators have diagnosed these demonic performances as dissociation reactions and multiple personalities (Hilgard, 1977;

Huxley, 1952; Lhermitte, 1972). It is interesting to note, however, that demonic voices occurred much less frequently among English demoniacs of the same period, and they never occurred among the afflicted, i.e., demoniac girls of Salem Village (Burr, 1914; Thomas, 1971; Woodward, 1864/1969).

Cultural variation in the frequency of demonic voices can be better understood by examining the different religious practices of the French and English than by conferring psychiatric diagnoses. France was a Catholic country, and Catholic exorcism procedures were standardized and involved the priest communicating directly with the indwelling demon (as opposed to the person possessed). For instance, as a preliminary to the exorcism rite the priest was required to question the indwelling demons and obtain from them their names, number, their reasons for possessing the individual, the exact hour they entered the body, and the length of time they proposed to stay (*Manual of Exorcism*, 1720/1975; *The Roman Ritual of Exorcism*, 1614/1976; Woolley, 1932). During the exorcism, the demons were often questioned at length regarding their motives, associates, ranking in the social structure of Hell, the manner in which they fell from grace, and so on, e.g., Michalis, 1613. In short, Catholic exorcism procedures demanded demonic voices as a central feature of the demoniac's role performance. English and American Protestants rarely employed formalized exorcisms. They tended to treat possession with prayer and fasting and often shunned communication with the indwelling demon as a sinful practice (Thomas, 1971). Thus, Catholic demoniacs were exposed to a ritual that taught them to manifest demonic voices. Protestant demoniacs were much less likely to be taught this aspect of the demoniac role.

Cultural variations of this type indicate that demonic possession cannot be understood unless careful consideration is given to the social context in which it occurred. The demonic role, like other culturally prescribed roles, had to be learned. Let us look, therefore, at how it was learned.

Demonic possession was one of the causes that might be suspected when individuals suffered certain physical illnesses and/or when their behavior was socially disruptive, annoyingly idiosyncratic, and largely inexplicable within the community's frame of reference concerning what constituted normal interpersonal behavior. The demonic role was taken for granted by the culture. Its components were, at least in a general way, known to the average person in Late Medieval-Early Modern Europe (Baroja, 1964; Nauman, 1974). Moreover, the demoniac's exposure to experts (usually clerics) served to define the subtleties of the role more precisely. During initital stages of possession, the demoniac's symptoms were often quite ambiguous. For instance, the afflicted girls of Salem Village initially enacted behaviors like "getting into holes, and creeping under chairs and stools and [using] sundry odd postures and antic gestures, uttering foolish and ridiculous speeches" (Calef, 1700/1914, p. 342). One of them ran about the house flapping her arms and crying "whish" "whish" "whish." She also pulled burning wood from the fire and scattered it about (Lawson, 1693/1914).[4]

The girls' behavior began to correspond more closely to popular stereotypes concerning demonic symptoms as they gained increasing exposure to information about those stereotypes. Thus, about 2 weeks after their initial symptoms a neighbor had a "witch cake" baked in order to determine if the girls were bewitched. Only after the village minister deplored this event as one that provided the devil with access to the girls, i.e., baking the cake was a magical practice and therefore constituted a sin, did they begin convulsing and reporting specters of witches that attacked them and others (Calef, 1914). As the witchcraft examinations progressed, the girls added to their repertoire of demonic symptoms. They collapsed en masse when looked at by the accused during the first examination (Woodward, 1864/1969), but it was not until the examination of the fourth witch that they began responding to more subtle aspects of the accused's behavior. Here, they complained of being bitten whenever they observed the accused nervously bite her lip and of being pinched when she moved her hand (Upham, 1867). In later examinations they began to mimic the accused; they held their heads in the same position as that of the accused and rolled their eyes up after the accused made a similar gesture (Woodward, 1864/1969). This temporal pattern in symptomatology suggests that the demonic enactments were learned; that the girls' behavior was shaped (perhaps unwittingly) to fit the preexisting expectations for demonic behavior held by significant others in their community (Spanos & Gottlieb, 1976).

A similar pattern of exposure to experts leading to increasingly sophisticated demoniac role playing occurred in the seventeenth century possession of Elizabeth Knapp of Groton, Massachusetts. Elizabeth was the servant of Samual Willard, the local minister, who (Willard, 1683/1974) wrote a fairly extensive account of her case. The girl's initial symptoms were rather ambiguous, consisting of occasional shrieking, "immoderate and extravagant laughter (p. 176)," and several days later, "many foolish and apish gestures (p. 176)." Willard vaguely suspected the possibility of diabolical influence and frequently questioned the girl as to the true cause of her affliction. Shortly thereafter a physician "judged a main part of her distemper to be natural...." (p. 180). However, her behavior became increasingly bizarre and the physician changed his mind and "consented that the distemper was diabolical . . . ." (p. 181). Throughout this period Elizabeth was the object of much concern and curiosity by neighbors who continually questioned her about her symptoms, speculated in her presence as to their cause, and prayed for her deliverance. Finally, about a month after the initial symptoms all doubt was laid to rest concerning their cause"

> It has been a question before whether she might properly be called a demoniac ... but it was then put out of question. He [the demon] began . . . by drawing her tongue out of her mouth most frightfully to an extraordinary length and greatness, and [making] many amazing postures of her body. And then [he continued] by speaking vocally in her... .(p. 189)

In order to fully appreciate the extent to which the members of Elizabeth's community provided her with information concerning the definition of her affliction as demonic, the reader is encouraged to read Willard's (1693/1974) interesting firsthand account of the case. Suffice it to say here that Elizabeth's role performance as a demoniac was shaped by the expectations transmitted to her from her clergyman, neighbors, and physician.

As indicated earlier, among Catholics the single most extensive source of information concerning demonic role expectations was the exorcism procedure itself. In conducting the exorcism, the priest never spoke to the possessed individual. Instead, he addressed only the possessing demon and expected to be answered only by the demon. The following firsthand account from a nineteenth century Jewish exorcism in Russia demonstrates the manner in which such role expectations could be foreceably conveyed to the subject:

> "What is thy name"? the rabbi asked the sick woman in a loud, harsh voice. "Esther", replied the girl softly and faintly, trembling all over. "Silence, thou chazufe" (impudent woman) cried the rabbi. "I asked not thee but the dibbuk" (demon). (cited in Oesterreich, 1966, p. 208)

Following this interchange, the rabbi threatened to strike the girl if she did not answer. Needless to say, she answered in a voice other than her own and gave the name of her possessing spirit.

Detailed information concerning role enactments was also conveyed to the demoniac outside of the exorcism situation proper. The sources of this information sometimes included (a) explicit coaching by parties with a vested interest in the demoniac giving a convincing performance; (b) conversing in the demoniac's presence about the occurrence, timing, and termination of expected symptoms; and (c) opportunities to observe the performance of other, more practiced demoniacs (de Bergerac, 1654/1969; Harsnett, 1599, 1603; Hutchinson, 1718). In summary, the components of the demonic role were widely known throughout the period in which possession was a common occurrence. Furthermore, exposure to experts and to exorcism procedures defined the components of the role in great detail.

Persons labeled by authorities as demoniacs sometimes resisted that designation. However, once the person was labeled as a demoniac by ecclesiastical authorities, she could not escape the role of denying possession. In fact, such denials were expected and taken as indications of a wiley demon attempting to escape divine punishment at the hands of the exorcist *(A Manual of Exorcism* about 1720/1975; Oesterreich, 1966). If the individual continued in her refusal to enact the role appropriately, she could be bound and whipped into submission (Law, 1894). Usually, the only way the demoniac role could be escaped was by successfully playing it. A number of potent social psychological variables converged in leading the potential demoniac to define herself as possessed. First and most important, she shared the same cultural frame of reference as the community that labeled her and therefore, was likely to view her own illness or behavioral deviation in the same light as her neighbors. Second, she was under continual social pressure from those on whom she depended most, i.e., parish priest, family friends, to accept the demoniac definition of her situation. Third, as we shall shortly see, there were often many social advantages contingent on playing the role successfully.

The advantages incumbent on playing the demoniac role can best be understood by examining the social situations of those who frequently filled the role. For example, in France during the sixteenth and seventeenth centuries, the most celebrated cases of possession occurred among cloistered nuns (Mandrou, 1968). Usually, becoming a nun was not a chosen profession. Instead, adolescent girls were placed in convents by their families in order to avoid the financial burden involved in providing a dowry (O'Faolain & Martines, 1973). For a girl not committed to a religious career it could be a very dull life; chores, frequent prayer, proper deportment, rigid rules, perhaps some teaching, and no men. Woods (1974) describes the physical and social conditions of convents during this period as follows:

> In the sixteenth and seventeeth centuries, it has been computed, a nun could generally stand about ten years of incarceration before it killed her. By the end of that time the lack of exercise and sunlight, the gloom, the damp walls, the loneliness, the monotony and the sheer boredom of a life without any hope of change had planted in her the tuberculosis, the dysentery or one of the various fevers that carried her off. (p.210)

The unwilling nun had no socially recognized means of portesting against her predicament. However, adoption of the demoniac role (the components of which were usually quite well known by nuns) offered a relatively safe avenue of protest. The nun could express her pent-up frustrations by blaspheming against her family, her superiors, and the Church, and she could carry out provocative sexual displays towards her exorcist. In effect, she could express wishes and feelings which in any other social context were heavily sanctioned, because, within the confines of the demoniac role, responsibility for such expression was assigned not to her but to the invading demon. Other advantages associated with the demoniac role included escaping from unpleasant responsibilities, i.e., chores, and becoming the center of attention. The possessed nun gained a good deal of sympathy, concern, and solace from individuals of higher social status, e.g., priests, physicians, who, in other circumstances, paid her little attention. She gained fearful respect as well. She became a seer whose words provided hints about the supernatural and those she accused of witchcraft might well be arrested and executed. Once a nun became possessed the advantages of her situation soon became apparent to other nuns and, as a result, French convents were frequently swept by small epidemics of possession affecting a number of nuns (Oesterreich, 1966).

England had no cloistered nuns after the sixteenth century, but possession occurred among a different socially impotent group—the children of both sexes (Robbins, 1959). The advantages of adopting this role in England were similar to those in France: an opportunity to vent frustration, sympathetic concern and attention, a temporary rise in social status to that of a person who was listened to and taken into consideration, and an alleviation of burdensome chores. Small epidemics of possession also occurred in England. the contagion usually spread to siblings or other close associates of the young demoniac who had an opportunity to observe enactment of the role and its reinforcing consequences (Hole, 1947: Notestein, 1911).

In summary,the role of demoniac was usually filled by socially powerless individuals who were without access to socially approved channels for changing their situation (Oesterreich, 1966). Adoption of the role frequently led to a dramatic rise in social status. On the one hand, demoniacs were seen as helpless victims of satanic influence and thereby received sympathetic attention. On the other, they often became awesome seers, repositories of arcane knowledge, and doers of amazing feats whose performances commanded fearful attention and respect (Aubin, 1716; Glanvill, 1689; Mather, 1693/1914; Michaelis, 1613). In some cases they even became determiners of life and death. In short, adopting a demoniac role frequently catapulted an individual from a position of little power to one in which she was afforded a degree of respect and social privilege that would have been unattainable in other ways.

These descriptions suggests that possession sometimes functioned as a strategy adopted by the socially powerless to obtain privileges that were not otherwise forthcoming. It is important, however, to keep the limitations of this strategy in mind. The demonically possessed, despite their cursing aginst God and their Church, were more the unwitting servants of social authority than rebels against it. As Lewis (1971) pointed out:

> The possessed person manipulates his superior without radically questioning his superiority. He ventilates his pent-up animosity without questioning the ultimate legitimacy of the status differences enshirined within the established hierarchical order. (p. 33)

A Case Illustration The importance of the variables described previously in socializing demoniacs into their role and, particularly, in imbuing them with the notion that their own behavior resulted from the activities of an indwelling demon, can be illustrated by examining a set of late sixteenth century cases of demonic possession described in detail in a long pamplet written by Samual Harsnett (1603). Harsnett was an Anglican churchman involved in the apprehension of Catholic missionaries who operated illegally in England and carried out semipublic exorcisms. His pamphlet was based primarily on various documents written by the missionaries and captured with them and on the statements provided by the demoniacs whom the missionaries exorcised.

Public exorcisms, of course, required demoniacs. The missionaries brought none with them and therefore recruited most of their demoniacs from among the servants of the Catholic sympathizers with whom they resided. These servants did not initially believe themselves to be possessed. They learned to construe their behavior in that manner as they became involved in performing the demoniac role.

The missionaries began their recruitment by choosing a suitable location—a house that was rumored to be haunted. They reinforced these rumors, and soon members of the household frightened one another with stores of demons lurking everywhere. Having been primed in this manner, individual servants were then exposed to a series of experiences aimed at fostering a selfdefinition of being demonically possessed. For instance, one adolescent maidservant, startled by a missionary while she did the laundry, fell and badly bruised herself. The missionary was very solicitous and explained that a devil had tripped her because she was washing his holy garment. He also informed her that she was possessed by a demon. The girl's protests were reinterpreted as a subterfuge of the demon. As she recovered from her injury over several weeks, the missionaries remained friendly, but talked continuously of her possession, the horrible consequences that might ensue as a result, and of conversion to Catholicism as a necessary precondition to successful exorcism and the saving of her soul.

Similar procedures were carried out with other potential demoniacs. They were continually informed of their grave plight and then sympathetically and earnestly offered conversion and exorcism as a cure. They were not allowed to leave the house and were isolated from anyone who might offer a nondemonic interpretation of their situation. Their protests were reinterpreted in a manner consistent with the notion of being possessed. Attempts to run away or changes in mood or behavior were quickly and consistently interpreted as produced by an indwelling demon. For instance, one demoniac complained to a missionary about harsh treatment and denied that she was really possessed. She was answered as follows:

> .... she began to complain unto him of her hard usage, and told him, that she verilie thought they did her injury, and that she was not troubled with any wicked spirits in her. ... Whereupon he cast his head aside, and looking fullie upon her face under her hat, What (quoth he) is this Sara, or the

devill that speaketh these words? No, no, it is not Sara, but the devil. And [Sara] perceiving she could have no other reliefe at his hands, fell a weeping, which weeping also he said was the weeping of the evill spirit. (Harsnett, 1603, pp. 186–187)

The missionaries continually described the behavior of previous demoniacs they had dealt with within earshot of those they were recruiting into that role. The potential demoniacs were never directly instructed to behave in any particular way. Nevertheless, in their everyday conversation the missionaries repeatedly described the components of the demoniac role in great detail. As one of the demoniacs eventually pointed out to an English tribunal:

> It was the ordinary custome of the Priestes to be talking of such, as had been possessed beyond the seas, and to tell the manner of theyr fits, and what they spake in them: also of what uglie sights they saw sometimes . . . . and how when reliques were applyed unto them, the parties would roare: how they could not abide holy water, not the sight of the sacrament, nor the annointed Priests of the Catholique church, nor any good thing . . . how the devills would complaine, when the Priests touched the parties, that they burned them . . . (Harsnett, 1603, p.36)

The demoniacs were not recruited simultaneously and those who had learned the role most proficiently served as role models for the others. For instance: ". . . . they permitted mee to have accesse unto Sara Williams when she was in her fits, and informed me likewise of the manner, how she and others had beene troubled" (Harsnett, 1603, p. 265).

Thus, the novice had repeated firsthand opportunities to observe both demonic role enactments and the rewards contingent upon these enactments.

One source of reinforcement for appropriate demonic role enactment was solicitous attention from those higher-status individuals who appeared to have such unlimited control over the demoniacs' lives—the missionary—exorcists themselves. Also gratifying to the demoniacs was a sense of power gained from observing the awe and admiration they created in the crowds who attended the exorcisms. They were, after all, the star attractions in what the audience considered a deadly serious combat between the forces of heaven and hell. Thus, one demoniac described some of his motives as follows: "[it may have been] to gaine to my selfe a little foolish commendation, or admiration, because I saw how . . . . [the observers who] were present at many of my fond speeches, did seem to wonder at me" (Harsnett, 1603, p. 275).

Harsh measures were sometimes used on demoniacs who resisted appropriate role enactments. For instance, one was tied to a chair, forced to drink a concoction that produced nausea, and then forced to breath the fumes of burning brimstone. All of this was, of course, interpreted as punishment given to the indwelling demon, rather than the person possessed.

The missionaries strived to reinterprest the demoniacs' current behavior and their previous life experiences as consistent with their status as demonically possessed. Thus, they questioned the demoniacs at length about their previous failings, sins, and character flaws and interpreted these as evidence that they had really been possessed all along.

In summary, Harsnett's (1603) report illustrates the extremely important role of the social context in shaping manifestations of demonic possession. The missionary-exorcists held enough social power to control the official definition of the situation as one involving demonic possession. Alternative construals were not legitimated. Potential demoniacs were isolated from anyone who might support an alternative definition of their behavior, and the demoniacs' own attempts to define themselves as "not possessed" were reinterpreted as signs of possession. The components of the demoniac role were transmitted to novice demoniacs indirectly, through overheard conversation and the observation of role models. Appropriate role enactments were met with solicitous attention and the admiration of audiences. Nevertheless, the exorcists never explicitly instructed demoniacs to do anything and never rewarded appropriate enactments with tangible or explicit rewards like money or praise. To have done any of these would have allowed the demoniacs to attribute their enactments to external inducement rather than to an indwelling demon. For similar reasons, punishment for inadequate role performance was always defined as punishing the demon in an attempt to help the person possessed. Finally, demoniacs were encouraged to reinterpret their previous experiences in a manner consistent with the idea that they were now possessed.

It is interesting to note that procedures described by Harsnett (1603) for inducing demonic enactments share a good deal in commmon with the techniques of coersive persuasion used in modern times by the Chinese Communists to elicit false confessions and attitude change from political prisoners and prisoners of war (Biderman, 1960; Schein, 1956; Schein, Schneier, & Barker, 1961). In both the Harsnett and the Communist cases the social situation was manipulated by authorities to produce changes in personal identity. The persons to be changed were made dependent on the authorities for satisfaction of their physical and social needs. Others who modeled role-appropriate behavior were available. Rewards and punishments were administered subtly and indirectly and attempts were made to relate the individual's current predicament to previous personal errors and failings. Moreover, there is evidence from both the Harsnett (1603) and the Communist (Schein et al., 1961) cases that these procedures, when used consistently, were successful in producing varying degrees of identity change. However, the individual's new identity, like their old one, was grounded in and validated by their current social situation. When the validating context for their new identity changed radically, e.g., when prisoners were repatriated and when demoniacs were separated from the control of the missionaries, then individuals once again redefined themselves and their past experiences, e.g., they never really believed the confessions they signed and they never really believed they had been possessed.

The cases described by Harsnett (1603) along with the material reviewed earlier indicates that manifestations of possession were frequently shaped by social authorities. But shaped for what purpose? It is to this question that we now turn.

Social Functions of Demonic Possession

As we have seen, the demonic role was multifaceted and was shaped to fit Judeo-Christian conceptions of demons and demonic activity. The role was maintained over a number of centuries because the status of demoniac became associated with a number of important social functions. The demoniac notion provided a culturally consistent explanation for various physical disorders and for otherwise inexplicable propriety norm violations. When coupled with exorcism procedures, the role provided a means of reintegrating deviants into the social community, served as a proselytizing device, and in various ways supported the religious and moral values of the community. The role also provided a channel for allowing, while simultaneously controlling, some expressions of social and personal dissatisfaction. Finally, from the fifteenth to the eighteenth century the role was increasingly exploited as a means for controlling personal, political, or ideological enemies by having the demoniac label them as witches (Spanos & Gottlieb, 1979). We shall examine two of these social functions in somewhat more detail.

Witchcraft accusations and possession. Earlier I described the 1683 possession of Elizabeth Knapp of Groton, Massachusetts. During her possession, Elizabeth accused a neighbor of witchcraft. Her minister, however, refused to believe her. He informed her and the rest of his parish that the devil's word could not be trusted, i.e., the Devil is the Father of lies, and the accusation was pursued no further (Willard, 1683/1974). A similar event occurred in Boston in 1693 during the demonic possession of seventeen-year-old Margaret Rule. Margaret, like Elizabeth, provided her minister with the names of people she accused of witchcraft. She claimed to have seen the specters of the accused engaged in various nefarious activities. The minister, however, refused to proceed with accusations based only on such spectral evidence (Calef, 1700/1914). Thus, in neither of these cases did the accusations of demoniacs lead to formal legal proceedings or to a local panic about witchery.

The behavior of the Salem Village demoniacs was very similar to that displayed by Elizabeth Knapp and Margaret Rule. The Salem girls also reported seeing the specters of witches. In this case, however, the local minister believed the accusations and legal proceedings were initiated against the accused (Upham, 1867/1959). The result, of course, was the famous Salem witch panic of 1692. Before the witch trails, Salem Village had been torn by economic and political factionalism. The minister and the families of many of the afflicted girls were aligned with one economic faction, and the accusations of witchcraft made by the girls and legitimated by the religious and legal authorities were against family members of the competing faction (Boyer & Nissenbaum, 1974).

When combined, these cases begin to illustrate the important social and political functions that could be served by demonic possession. Accusations of witchcraft by the possessed were not necessarily believed and automatically acted upon. Instead, they required the legitimation of social authority. However, the formal rules for granting such legitimation were ambiguous, e.g., spectral evidence could be believed, or it could be dismissed as the product of "the Father of lies." Precisely because they were ambiguous, these rules could be interpreted to suit the vested interests of those who held social power.

The importance of legitimation by authority in witchcraft accusations by the possessed was illustrated in Continental as well as in colonial American cases. For example, in what is probably the most famous European witchcraft case involving possession, a group of seventeenth century French nuns accused a priest named Urban Grandier of bewitching them. Grandier was eventually tortured, found guilty of sorcery, and burned alive. However, this train of events did not occur simply because Grandier was accused of witchcraft by a group of lowly nuns. Grandier had made numerous powerful enemies both inside and outside the Church. It was they who legitimated (and perhaps even initially suggested) the accusations of witchcraft made by the demoniacs. In fact, the principle demoniac in the case confessed to an ecclesiastical court that Grandier had not bewitched her. She was informed by the court that it was not she but a demon that made the statement, and Grandier's trial continued (Aubin,

1716; Huxley, 1952; Robbins, 1959). In short, accusations of witchery by the possessed cannot be adequately understood until they are placed in a social nexus, in relation to vested social and political interests. It is important to keep in mind that accusations of witchcraft by the possessed became an important aspect of their role enactment only after the fifteenth century. Other, more basic social functions of this role become manifest when possession phenomena are seen in relation to exorcism procedures.

Exorcism and religious proselytizing. The practice of exorcising demoniacs appears to have been widespread from the earliest Christian centuries through the seventeenth century (Keller, 1974; Oesterreich, 1966). Initially, exorcisms tended to be relatively unstructured and unelaborate affairs that consisted mainly of "laying on of hands" and commanding the demon to depart in the name of Jesus. In time, the procedure became both more standardized and more complex. Prayers were added, the demon was addressed in order to gain certain information, and the use of holy water and consecrated objects became common. By the Middle Ages the procedure was quite elaborate, involving many prayers and adjurations, and sometimes even violent cursing of the demon by the exorcists. Exorcisms sometimes lasted months or even years. They were often performed publicly, sometimes with groups of demoniacs at once (Keller, 1974; Oesterreich, 1966). For example, it has been estimated that on one day as many as 7,000 people attended a public exorcism in Loudun during the seventeenth century (Baskin, 1974). Every exorcism represented a dramatic moral confrontation between the power of God and that of the Devil. Thus, successful exorcism served to illustrate the power of the church, and in that manner to affirm its values and maintain its authority.

The successful exorcism of demoniacs was a powerful tool for converting unbelievers and redoubling the faith of believers. For instance, the New Testament stories of Jesus casting out demons and of the demons recognizing him as the son of God and acknowledging their submission to his greater power can be seen as the propaganda vignettes of a young religion competing for converts against more established belief systems. Along the same lines, many early Christians contended that demons could be driven out only in the name of Jesus and used their success at exorcism as proof for the validity of their doctrines (Kelly, 1974; Oesterreich, 1966). Such an attitude is evident in the writings of Justin Martyr, a second century propagandist for Christianity:

> For every demon when exorcised in the name of this very Son of God ... is overcome and subdued. But though you exorcise any demon in the name of any [others] ... it will not be subject to you.
> For numberless demoniacs throughout the whole world [Christian exorcists] have healed and do heal, rendering helpless and driving the possessing demons out of men, though they could not be cured by all the other exorcists, and those who used incantations and drugs. (Cited in Kelly, 1974, p. 72)

After Christianity became firmly established in Western Europe, tales of possession and exorcism continued to funtion as pedagogical devices. Instructional tracts used in the training of clerics were filled with stories of Christian saints casting out demons who had been impervious to the techniques of non-Christian exorcists. These same tracts often defined possession as just punishment for the sin of pride (Keller, 1974). With the reformation and counterreformation movements of the sixteenth and seventeenth centuries, possession and exorcism once again became important tools for facilitating religious conversion. In an age where distinctions between church and state were not drawn in the same manner as today, religious conversion often meant political conversion as well. The use of possession and exorcism to serve political ends can be illustrated with an example from sixteenth century England.

During the latter part of the sixteenth century England was Protestant and the head of the English (Anglican) church was the the monarch, Elizabeth I. England, of course, had been Catholic until Elizabeth's father (Henry VIII) had severed connections with Rome earlier in the century. Many Englishmen, some who were wealthy and powerful, continued to abide by Catholicism in private, and hoped for an eventual restoration of their religion in England (Thomas, 1971).

The Anglican Church attempted to adopt a middle of the road position between what it considered the abuses of Catholicism, on the one hand, and radical Puritanism, on the other. Thus, the Anglicans deemphasized the marvelous, eliminated indulgences, discouraged the veneration of saints, and all but eliminated the practice of exorcism. Demonic possession and exorcism were considered to be Catholic or Puritan tricks aimed at beguiling the ignorant. Possession by demons was not denied as a theoretical possibility, but specific instances of possession were regularly interpreted in terms of deliberate fakery (Notestein, 1911; Thomas, 1971). The propaganda value of exorcism was clearly appreciated by the Anglicians who did their best to track down and punish Catholic or Puritan exorcists who operated illegally in England.

England's most serious military threat at this time was from Spain, and a Spanish invasion was expected imminently.(It was attempted in 1588 and led to the destruction of the Spanish Armada.) England's enemies hoped to aid the coming invasion by enhancing pro-Catholic sentiments among the English populus. If such sentiment grew strong enough, an invasion might set off popular rebellions within England and, thereby, aid the Catholic cause. To this end, Catholic missionaries were landed in England with the aim of converting as much of the populace as possible. The missionaries were housed and plied their trade in the homes of wealthy Catholic sympathizers in the areas of Buckinghamshire and Middlesex in 1585 to 1586 (Notestein, 1911; Law, 1894). Their major tool of conversion was semipublic displays of successful exorcism. These were the missionaries described by Harsnett (1603) and whose practices were outlined earlier. The Catholics capitalized on the Anglican policy of disallowing exorcisms by declaring that the Anglicans had fallen away from the true faith and, therefore, had no power to cast out demons. Thus, the missionaries used successful exorcism to demonstrate the truth of their doctrines.

The demoniacs recruited by the missionaries did not simply howl and convulse. Their enactments were clearly geared toward supporting the religious values of the Catholic church. Thus, as representatives of Satan they claimed to hate the Catholic church but to love Protestants. They were unaffected by Anglican prayerbooks but screamed as if burned when touched by the relics of Catholic saints. The missionaries contended that demons were forced to speak the truth when confronted by representatives of the true faith. Following this, the demoniacs affirmed the truth of transubstantiation and the falsity of Protestant doctrines (Harsnett, 1603).

Possession and exorcism were used as propaganda devices in France as well as England and by Puritans as well as Catholics. For instance, French demoniacs frequently affirmed the truths of Catholicism and spoke of loving Calvin and Huguenots (Michaelis, 1613). On the other hand, Puritan demoniacs in England and colonial America ranted against Calvin and indicated an affinity for the Pope, Quakers, and Anglicans (Harsnett, 1599; Mather, 1684). In short, exorcism was not simply a primitive or misguided psychotherapy aimed solely at treating certain social deviates. It was an ideological tool used to affirm particular values and win conversions while denegrating the values of religious competitiors. Similarly, to classify demonic enactments in cases such as these as psychotic or hysterical manifestations is to miss their political import. These enactments were strategic. They were orchestrated (probably with varying degrees of conscious intent) by those who held power over the demoniacs for the purpose of affecting the attitudes and beliefs of potential converts. To view such enactments in terms of individual psychopathology is to seriously distort their meaning.

From Possession to Hysteria

Demonic possession remained a fairly common occurrence throughout the eighteenth century. Even during the early nineteenth century such cases were common enough for Esquirol (1838/1965) to classify them as a type of demonomania and devote a chapter to them in his famour *Des Malades Mentales.* Interpretations of this phenomenon were, however, changing. During the eighteenth century, religious interpretations were still considered seriously in many intellectual circles (Leventhal,

1976; Wilkins, 1974), and as late as 1749 a German nun was burned as a witch for causing the possession of her sister nuns (Gaar, 1749; Robbins, 1959). Nevertheless, purely medical explanations for possession became increasingly prominent as the eighteenth century progressed (Diethelm, 1970; Tourney, 1972), and this view gained general acceptance in intellectual circles by the middle of the nineteenth century (Richet, 1887).

The gradual conceptual shift from possession to disease that occurred from the sixteenth through part of the nineteenth centuries was associated with delimited changes in patients' role performance. As patients, as well as physicians, began defining behavioral deviance as a purely medical issue, role behaviors that were incompatable with notions of natural disease became less prominent, e.g., speaking in a demonic voice, defining oneself as possessed, vomiting pins. Role behaviors that could be more easily conceptualized in terms of natural disease, e.g., convulsions, analgesia, temporary sensory and motor disturbances, vague physical complaints, continued to be enacted as a more or less recognizable syndrome throughout the nineteenth century and came to be recognized as classic symptoms of the "disease" hysteria (Janet, 1925).[5]

In many respects, individuals labeled as hysterics during the nineteenth century shared a number of characteristics with earlier demoniacs. They tended to be unhappy women who were socialized into viewing themselves as weak and passive. They were dissatisfied with their lives, socially and economically powerless, and without access to means of voicing their dissatisfactions or improving their lot outside of adopting the role of a sick person (Smith-Rosenberg 1972). When individuals were hospitalized with a diagnosis of hysteria, the social structure of these institutions often functioned to reward and thereby maintain skillful enactments of the hysterical role. For example, a number of investigators have described the manner in which the social organization of the Salpetrièrè and other midnineteenth century French hospitals led patients to enact the constellation of symptoms deemed by Charcot and his disciples to be characteristic of hysteria. These accounts indicate that the lower-level staff and students at these institutions were afraid of displeasing or contradicting their supervisors. Therefore, with varying degrees of subtlety, they shaped patients to display the constellation of symptoms that they believed their supervisors wanted to see. The patients, often anxious to please and desirous of being at the center of attention, guided their role enactments on the basis of the cues provided by the staff. Ellenberger (1970) described the situation at the Salpetrièrè as follows:

> This closed community sheltered not only crowds of old women, but comprised also special wards for hysterical patients, some of them young, pretty, and cunning: nothing could be more eminently propitious to the development of mental contagion. These women were the star attractions, utilized to demonstrate clinical cases to the students. . . . Because of Charcot's paternalistic attitude and his despotic treatment of students, his staff never dared contradict him; they therefore showed him what they believed he wanted to see. After rehearsing the demonstrations, they showed the subjects to Charcot, who was careless enough to discuss their cases in the patients' presence. A peculiar atmosphere of mutual suggestion developed between Charcot, his collaborators and his patients. . . . (p. 98)

In short, unbeknown to Charcot patients were being taught to display the behaviors which he believed to be uniquely characteristic of hysteria, in the same way that earlier demoniacs had been taught to display the symptoms of possession. Years after Charcot's death, Guillain (1955) observed that the results of his teaching were still evident:

> . . . . I saw as a young intern at the Salpetriere the old patients of Charcot who were still hospitalized. Many of the women, who were excellent comedians, when they were offered a slight pecuniary remuneration imitated perfectly the major hysteric crises of former times.(p. 434)

I indicated earlier that hysteria is often conceptualized by historians of psychiatry as a mental disease the symptoms of which have remained fairly constant down through the centuries

(Veith, 1965). From this perspective, the similarities in behavior exhibited by demoniacs and hysterics occurred because demoniacs were really misdiagnosed hysterics all along. The argument I have advanceed in this chapter suggests instead, that the social role of hysteria in the nineteenth century included many of the behaviors earlier associated with demonic possession, at least in part, because it invoved a secularization of the demoniac role. In this sense, hysteria did not cause demonic possession but, instead, notions about possession shaped the constellation of behaviors that came to be called hysteria.[6]

IMPLICATIONS

A number of investigators (Jones, 1979; Nisbett & Ross, 1980; Ross, 1977) have stressed that, in our everyday life, we usually function as implicit trait theorists. We tend to explain the behavior of others by attributing stable, internal dispositions to them. In so doing, we frequently minimize potent (and seemingly obvious) situational determinants of behavior. For instance, observers who are aware that a member of a debating team made a speech in favor of racial segregation tend to rate the debater as possessing relatively strong prosegregationist sympathies even when they know that the debating team advisor required the debater to prepare the prosegregationist speech (Jones & Harris, 1967). In making such ratings, observers ignored the potent situational demands, e.g., imposed speech requirements that led the debater to express segregationist views.

Dispositional attributions are particularly likely when the behavior being observed is deviant or unusual. If observers note that almost everyone behaves in a particular manner in situation X, they will tend to attribute the common behavior to the situation. The behavior of the few nonconformists will tend to be explained in terms of nonconforming stable dispositions (Jones, 1979). Along similar lines, observers often account for the behavior common to a deviant group by attributing the unusual behavior to stable dispositions of individual group members. We have already seen, for example, that the behavior common to the "afflicted girls" of Salem Village has been explained by hypothesizing that all of them possessed "hysterical" character traits (Hansen, 1969).

Many traditional approaches to the study of personality and traditional psychiatric nosologies involve a codification of the common-sense view that behavior (and especially deviant behavior) is a function of longstanding personal dispositions. It surprises no one, for example, when psychiatrists "explain" the behavior of famous contemporaries like Patti Hearst, "Son of Sam," Charles Manson, and the "Hillside Strangler" by applying dispositional labels like "schizophrenia," "multiple personality," and "psychopath" to these individuals. Similar dispositional labels are also commonly used to "explain" the deviant behaviors common to the members of discredited or socially marginal groups. Thus, "mental illness" labels have been applied frequently in accounting for the glossolalia of Pentacostolists (e.g., Cutten, 1927; Hoekema, 1966; Stagg, Hinson, & Oates, 1967) or the systematic cruelty of Nazi concentration camp officials (e.g., Dicks, 1972). (For an alternative view of glossolalia see Samarin, 1972 amd Spanos & Hewitt, 1979; for concentration camp officials see Kogon, 1974 and Rubenstein, 1975).

In this chapter I argued that the application of modern psychiatric diagnoses has been of little value in understanding historical manifestations of demonic possession. I also argued that these manifestations can be more adequately understood when viewed in terms of the socially shared understandings of those who participated in these historical dramas. I now wish to suggest that such a social psychological perspective provides a useful framework for understanding some of the modern phenomena that are routinely explained in terms of "mental illness." This suggestion is certainly not new. For example, a number of investigators (Coulter, 1973: Sarbin & Mancuso, 1980) have provided useful contextual accounts of the deviant behaviors commonly diagnosed in our culture as resulting from "schizophrenia." My comments, however, will be restricted to a modern example of "group psychopathology." More specifically I will apply the social psychological framework used to conceptualize demonic possession to the mass suicides that occurred a few years ago in Jonestown, Guyana.

As is well known, in November 1978 over 900 members of

the Peoples Temple, a utopian religious sect that had migrated from San Francisco to Guyana, were victims of mass murder/suicide. The killings were orchestrated by the group's charismatic leader, the Rev. Jim Jones. Popular accounts of these events are often phrased in terms of psychopathology on the part of Rev. Jones, his followers, or both. For instance, the victims are sometimes characterized as "mentally unstable" and, therefore, easily "brainwashed," and Jones is frequently characterized as an insane master of "mind control" techniques (see Richardson, 1980, for a description of popular accounts). A social psychological perspective suggests instead that these events will be better understood by examining the social organization of Jonestown, and its members' construals concerning their relationship to salvation, the "hostile" outside world, and their roles as religious martyrs.

Jonestown and the Apocalyptic World View

The People's Temple community at Jonestown was characterized by Hall (1979) as an apocalyptic sect; one that viewed the world at large as basically evil and soon to be replaced by a community of the elect. Socialization practices of the People's Temple, like those of most apocalyptic groups, were aimed at inculcating a strong distinction between ingroup and outgroup and in fostering the view of the community as a "heaven on earth" (Hall, 1979; Richardson, 1980). Converts to apocalyptic sects are typically required to renounce their "old" identity and develop a new one that derives its meaning from the apocalyptic mythology of the community (Cohn, 1970). The convert's newly found identity and world view are reinforced by a variety of institutionalized practices aimed at engendering and maintaining "right thinking" and preventing or correcting lapses into error, e.g., confession, "study groups," mutual surveillance. All of these procedures characterized the socialization practices of the People's Temple (Hall, 1979; Johnson, 1979). Dependence upon the community and its norms was fostered by requiring members to sever social ties with the outside world and to contribute their financial as well as emotional resources to the community (Johnson, 1979). The severing of social ties and consequent increased dependence on the community for the satisfaction of emotional and physical needs was, of course, augmented with the establishment of Jonestown in the Guyanese jungle.

The sect's world view as a righteous minority persecuted by the forces of evil also became more pronounced with the move to Guyana. The Jonestown community, according to its own view, offered the world an example of a racially integrated socialist utopia. Evil capitalist forces were unable to tolerate this reality and, thereby, used their various agencies, e.g., newspapers, CIA, to persecute the sect (Hall, 1979). This perspective was reinforced by "horror stories" circulated within the community about the consequences of capture or military defeat by the various "enemy" groups. It was reinforced still further by the presence of armed guards against imminent CIA or Guyanese army attack, mock CIA attacks staged by the community itself, and "white night" suicide drills in which the members drank what they had been told was poison (Kilduff & Javers, 1978).

The sucide drills served a number of important social functions. They allowed members to simultaneously express their solidarity to the community and their fear of its disruption by external forces; death was preferable to the loss of communal solidarity. These rituals also served in a dramatic way to symbolize and thereby validate the social stratification system of the community. The social organization of Jonestown, like that of many charismatic groups, was relatively simple. It was authoritarian, involved only a few hierarchically organized status levels, and centralized power in the hands of the leader. The large majority of members were at the lowest status level (Richardson, 1980). The drills served to dramatically illustrate the relationship of dominance and subordination between leaders and members that was taken for granted by the community (Johnson, 1979).

The mass suicides that occurred at Jonestown were consistent with the community's apocalyptic world view. In contrast to most of his contemporary religious leaders, Jones advocated collective suicide (revolutionary suicide he called it) as a reasonable alternative to the extermination of the community by external forces (Richardson, 1980). The investigative visit of Congressman Ryan and his cortege of "concerned relatives," the defection of those group members who chose to leave with Ryan, and, finally, the murder of the Congressman and his party, were interpreted as portents of Jonestown's imminent destruction and the dissolution of the group's collective identity. Provided with this interpretation of the situation the members of the community did as they were told. They followed the orders of legitimate authority—orders that were consistent with their apocalyptic world view, the turn of external events, the authority structure of their community, and their previous training concerning such an emergency—and drank poison. As Richardson (1980) suggested, "The mass suicide at Jonestown was 'dying for a cause' for the more politically oriented [sect members], and it was achieving 'other worldly salvation' for the more religious" (p. 249).

Implicit in many psychological accounts of deviant behavior is the notion that the occurrence of the unusual or dramatic behavior necessitates that there be unusual and dramatic explanatory causes (Nisbett & Ross, 1980). Contextual accounts of deviant behavior suggest, instead, that the causes of such behavior are frequently mundane and similar to the causes of every-day social behavior (Becker, 1963; Nisbett & Ross, 1980). For instance, seventeenth century nuns learned to enact the role of being demonically possessed in the same way that people now learn to enact the role of army recruit, boy scout, mental patient, or experimental subject. Demonic enactments were deviant because of what the actor learned (and performed), not because the manner in which the enactments were learned, i.e., their causes, was unusual. To take another example, S.S. officers signed orders for the arrest and extermination of Jews for the same basic reasons that college professors sign grade change forms, nurses administer prescribed medication, postmen deliver mail, and social workers administer welfare checks. The behavior was prescribed by the authority structure of the bureaucracy in which these individuals operated, and legitimated by the value system and ideology of the social system at large (or at least those aspects of the social system in which they functioned; for more along these lines see Milgram, 1974; Rubenstein, 1975).

In summary, an adequate theoretical account of deviant social behaviors is unlikely to be facilitated by the straightforward application of dispositional concepts or by the invention of dramatic causes to explain dramatic consequences. Instead, such accounts require scrutiny of the social context in which the behavior occurs and examination of the understandings held by the participants in the social interaction. In order to understand social behavior, we must study the intimate and continuous interplay of context and cognition.

REFERENCES

Abse, D. W. Hysteria. In S. Arieti, (Ed.) *American handbook of psychiatry. (Vol. 1).* New York: Basic Books, 1959, 272–292.

Alexander, F. G., & Selesnick, S. T. *The history of psychiatry.* New York: Harper & Row, 1966.

Aubin, N. *Cruels effets de la vengeance du Cardinal de Richelieu ou histoire des diables de Loudun.* Amsterdam, 1716.

Baroja, J. C. *The world of the witches.* London: Weidenfeld & Nicholson, 1964.

Baskin, W. The devils of Loudun. In. E. Nauman (Ed.), *Exorcism through the ages.* Secaucus, N. J., Citadel Press, 1974 15–20

Becker, H. S. *Outsiders.* New York: Free Press, 1963.

de Bergerac, C. A letter against witches (1654). In E. W. Monter (Ed.), *European witchcraft.* New York: Wiley, 1969.

Biddle, B. J., & Thomas, E. J. (Eds.) *Role theory: Concepts and research.* New York: Wiley, 1966.

Biderman, A. D. Social-psychological needs and "involuntary" behavior as illustrated by compliance in interrogation. *Sociomety,* 1960, *23*:120–147.

Boguet, H. *An examen of witches* (Orig. Pub., 1603). Translated and edited by Montague Summers, London, 1929.

The boy of Bilson, or the true discovery of the late impostures, London, 1622.

Boyd, J. W. *Satan and Mara: Christian and Buddhist symbols of evil.* Leiden: E. J. Brill, 1975.

Burr, G. L. (Ed) *Narratives of the witchcraft cases.* 1648–1706. New York: Scribners, 1914.

Bodin, J. *De la demonomainie des Soeciers.* Lyons A Choquemin, 1593.

Boyer, P., & Nissenbaum, S. *Salem possessed.* Cambridge, Mass.: Havard University Press, 1974.

Brattle, T. Letter, In G. L. Burr (Ed.), *Narratives of the witchcraft cases 1648–1706*. New York: Scribner's 1914, reprinted in 1972.

Brown, P. Sorcery, demons and the rise of Christianity from late antiquity into the middle ages. In M. Douglas (Ed.), *Withchcraft confessions and accusations*. London: Tavistock, 1970

Calef, R. More wonders from the invisible world. London, 1700. Reprinted in G. L. Burr, (Ed.), *Narratives of the witchcraft cases*. New York: Scribner's, 1914, 289–393.

Cartwright, F. F. and Biddis, M. D. *Disease and History* New York: Crowell, 1972.

Catherinet, F. M. Demoniacs in the Gospel. In F. J. Sheed (Ed.), *Soundings in satanism*. New York: Sheed & Ward, 1972, 121–137.

Caulfield, E. Pediatric aspects of the Salem witchcraft tragedy. *American Journal of Diseases of Children, 1943, 65, 788–802*

Cesbron, H. *Histoire critique de l'hystere*. Paris: Asselin et Houzeau, 1909.

Charcot, J. M. *Clinical lectures on the diseases of the nervous system, III*. London: New Sudenham Society, 1889.

Charcot, J. M. & Marie, P. Hysteria. In D. Hack Tuke (Ed.), *Dictionary of psychological medicine*. London: Churchill, 1892.

Charcot, J. M. & Richer, P. *Les demoniaques dans l'art (1887)*. Amsterdam: B. M. Israel, 1972.

Chodoff, P., & Lyons, H. Hysteria, the hysterical personality and "hysterical" conversion. *American Journal of Psychiatry*, 1958, *114*: 734–740.

Cohn, N. *The pursuit of the millennium*. New York: Oxford University Press, 1970.

Coulter, J. *Approaches to insanity*. New York: Halstead Press, 1973.

Cutten, G. B. *Speaking in tongues: Historically and psychologically considered*. New Haven, Conn.: Yale University Press, 1927.

Demos, J. Underlying themes in the witchcraft of seventeenth-century New England. *American Historical Review*, 1969–70, *75*: 1311–1326.

Dicks, H. V. *Licensed mass murder: A socio-psychological study of some S.S. killers*. New York: Basic Books, 1972.

Diethelm, O. The medical teaching of demonology in the seventeeth and eighteenth centuries. *Journal of the History of the Behavioral Sciences*, 1970, 7: 3–15.

Ellenberger, H. *The discovery of the unconscious*. New York: Basic Books, 1970.

Esquirol, J. E. D. *Mental maladies* (Orig. pub., 1838). New York: Hafner, 1965.

The examaination of John Walsh before Maister Thomas Williams, Commissary to the Reverend Father in God William Bishop of Excester, upon certayne interrogatories touchying wytchcrafte and sorcerye, in the presence of divers gentlemen and others, the XX of August, 1566, In B. Rose. (Ed.), *Witchcraft* (Orig. pub. 1566) New York: Taplinger, 1969.

Fenichel, O. *The psychoanalytic theory of neurosis.* New York: Norton, 1945.

Gaar, Georgius. *Christliche anred nachst dem schieterhauffen worauff der leichnam Mariae Renata.* Wurzburg, 1749.

Gaster, T. H. (Ed.). *The Dead Sea scriptures.* Garden City, N.Y.: Anchor Books, 1956, 1964.

Glanvill, J. *Saducimus triumphatus.* London: 1689.

Goffman, E. *Encounters: Two studies in the sociology of interaction.* Indianapolis, Ind.: Bobbs-Merrill, 1961.

Guazzo, F. M. *Compendium maleficarum* (Orig. pub., 1608). Republished New York: Barnes & Noble, 1970.

Guillain, C. J. M. Charcot, his life—his work. New York: Harper & Row, 1955. Chapter entitled Hypnotism reprinted in M. Tintterow (Ed.), *Foundations of Hypnosis.* Springfield: Thomas, 1970, 425–437.

Guze, S. B. The diagnosis of hysteria: What are we trying to do? *American Journal of Psychiatry,* 1967, *124*: 491–498.

Hall, J. R. Apocalypse at Jonestown. *Society,* 1947 (Sept/Oct.) 52–61.

Hall, M. *Commentaries on some of the more important of the diseases of the female.* London, 1827.

Hansen, C. *Witchcraft at Salem.* New York: Mentor, 1969.

Harsnett, S. *A declaration of egregious popish impostures . . . . under the pretense of casting out devils.* I. Roberts: London, 1603.

———.*Discovery of the fraudulent practices of John Darrel.* John Wolfe: London, 1599.

Hartwell, A. *A true discourse upon the matter of Martha Brossier of Romorantin, pretended to be possessed by a devil.* John Wolfe: London, 1599.

Hilgard, E. R. *Divided consciousness.* New York: Wiley, 1977.

Hoekema, A. A. *What about speaking in tongues?* Grand Rapids, Mich.: Eerdmans, 1966.

Holcombe, W. H. *The sexes here and hereafter.* Philadelphia, 1869.

Hole, C. *Witchcraft in England.* New York: Schribner's, 1947.

Hutchinson, F. *An historical essay concerning witchcraft.* London: R. Knaplock, 1718.

Hutchinson, T. *The history of the province of Mass-Bay colony* (Boston, 1718). New York: Orno Press, 1972.
Huxley, A. *The devils of Loudun.* New York: Harper & Row, 1952.
Jacoby, G. W. *Suggestion and psychotherapy.* New York: Scribner's, 1912.
Janet, P. *Psychological healing* (2 Vols.). New York: MacMillan, 1925.
Johnson, D. P. Dilemmas of charismatic leadership: The case of the People's Temple. *Sociological Analysis,* 1979, *40:* 315–323.
Jones, E. E. The rocky road from acts to dispositions. *American Psychologist,* 1979, *34:* 107–117.
Jones, E. E., Harris, V. A. The attribution of attitudes. *Journal of Experimental Social Psychology,* 1967, *3:* 1–24.
Jorden, E. *A brief discourse of a disease called the suffocation of the mother,* 1603.
Kelly, H. A. *The devil, demonology and witchcraft.* New York: Doubleday, 1974.
Kilduff, M., & Javers, R. *The suicide cult.* New York: Bantam, 1978.
Kocher, P. H. *Science and religion in elizabethan England.* San Martino, Calif.: Huntington, Library, 1953.
Kogon, E. *The theory and practice of hell: The German concentration camps and the system behind them.* New York: Harper & Row, 1974.
Kramer, H., & Sprenger, J. *Malleus maleficarum* (Orig. pub. 1489). Republished, New York: Dover, 1971.
Krohn, A. *Hysteria: The elusive neurosis.* New York: International Universitites Press, 1978.
Kroll, J. A reappraisal of psychiatry in the Middle Ages. *Archives of General Psychiatry,* 1973, *29:* 276–283.
Law, T. G. Devil-hunting in elizabethan England. *Nineteenth Century,* 1894, *35:* 397–411.
Lawson, D. A brief and true narrative of witchcraft at Salem Village (Orig. pub. 1693). In G. L. Burr (Ed.), *Narratives of the witchcraft cases 1648–1706.* New York: Scribner's, 1914, 145–164.
Lea, H. C. *Materials toward a history of witchcraft* (3 vols.) New York: Thomas Yoseloff, 1957.
Leventhal, H. *In the shadow of enlightenment: Occultism and renaissance science in 18th century America.* New York: New York University Press, 1976.
Lewis, I. M. *Ecstatic religion: An anthropological study of spirit possession and shamanism.* Middlesex, England: Penguin Books, 1971.

Lhermitte, J. Pseudo-possession. In F. J. Sheed (Ed.), *Soundings in satanism*. New York: Sheed and Ward, 1972, 12–35.

Mandrou, R. *Magistrats et corciers en France au XVIIe siecle: Une analyse de psychologique historique*. Paris: Plan, 1968. *A Manual of Exorcism* (Originally prepared about 1720). Tr. by E. Beyersdorf & J Brady. New York: The Hispanic Society of America, 1975.

Mather, C. A brand pluck't out of the burning (Orig. pub., 1693). In G. L. Burr (Ed.), *Narratives of the witchcraft cases 1648–1706*. Schriber's: New York, 1914, 203–287

McCasland, S. V. *By the finger of god*. New York: MacMillan, 1951.

Merskey, H. and Buhrich, N. A. Hysteria and organic brain disease. *British Journal of Medial Psychology*, 1975, 48, 359–366.

Michaelis, S. *The admirable history of the possession and conversion of a penitent woman*. London: W. Aspley 1613.

Milgram, S. *Obedience to authority*. New York: Harper & Row, 1974.

Mischel, W. *Personality and assessment*. New York: Wiley, 1968.

———Toward a cognitive social learning reconceptualization of personality. *Psychological Review*, 1973, *80*: 252–283.

More, G. *A true discourse concerning the certain possession and dispossession of 7 persons in one family in Lancashire* London, 1600.

The most strange and admirable discovery of the Witches of Warboys.... (1593). In B. Rosen (Ed.), *Witchcraft*. Taplinger: New York, 1972, 239–297.

Nauman, E. Exorcism and satanism in medieval Germany. In E. Nauman (Ed.), *Exorcism through the ages*. Secaucus, N. J.: Citadel Press, 1974, 73–86.

Neaman, J. S. *Suggestion of the Devil*. New York: Anchor Press, 1975.

Neugebaur, R. Treatment of the mentally ill in medieval and early modern England: a reappraisal. *Journal of the history of the Behavioral Sciences*, 1978, 14, 158–169.

Nisbitt, R., & Ross, L. *Human inference: Strategies and shortcomings of social judgment*. Englewood Cliffs, N. J.: Prentice Hall, 1980.

Notestein, W. *A History of witchcraft in England*. New York: Crowell, 1911.

O'Connor, N., & Franks, C. Childhood upbringing and other environmental factors. In J. H. Eysenck (Ed.), *Handbook of abnormal psychology*. New York: Basic Books 1960.

Oesterreich, T. K. *Possession: Demonical and other*. Secaucus, N. J.: Citadel, 1966.

O'Faolain, J., & Martines, L. (Eds) *Not in God's image* New York: Harper & Row, 1973.

Pickett, R. *Mental afflication and church law.* Ottawa: University of Ottawa Press, 1959.

Richardson, J. T. People's Temple and Jonestown: A corrective comparison and critique. *Journal For The Scientific Study of Religion,* 1980, *19*: 239–255.

Richet, C. *L'homme et l'intelligence. Fragments de physiologie et de psychologie.* Paris: Alcan, 1887.

Richter, A. (Ed.). *Corpus iuris canonici* (2 Vols.). Graz. Austria: Akademische Druck and Verlagsanstalt, 1959.

Roback, A. A. *History of psychology and psychiatry.* New York: Citadel Press, 1962.

Roberts, A. *A treatise of witchcraft.* In A. E. Green, (Ed) *Witches and witch–hunters.* Yorkshire, England: S. R. Publishers, 1971, (orig. pub., 1616).

Robbins, R. H. *The encyclopedia of witchcraft and demonlogy.* New York: Crown Publishers, 1959.

The Roman Ritual of Exorcism (Rituale Romanum, Orig. pub. 1614). Tr. and reprinted as an appendix in M. Malachi, *Hostage to the Devil.* New York: Reader's Digest Press, 1976, 459–472.

Ross, L. The intuitive psychologist and his shortcomings. In L. Berkowitz (Ed.). *Advances in experimental social psychology.* New York: Academic Press, 1977.

Rosen, B. (Ed) *Witchcraft.* New York: Toplinger, 1869.

Rubenstein, R. L. *The cunning of history: The holocost and the American future.* New York: Harper & Row, 1975.

Russel, D. S. *Between the testaments.* Philadelphia Fortress Press, 1960.

Samarin, W. J. *Tongues of men and angels: The religious language of Pentecostalism.* New York, Macmillan, 1972.

Sarbin, T. R., & Allen, V. L. Role theory. In G. Lindzey & E. Aronson (Eds.), *Handbook of social psychology* (Vol. 1). Reading, Mass.: Addison-Wesley, 1968.

Sarbin, T. R., & Mancuso, J. C. *Schizophrenia: Medical diagnosis or moral verdict?* New York: Pergamon, 1980.

Schein, E. H. The Chinese indoctrination program for prisoners of war. *Psychiatry,* 1956, *19*: 149–172.

Schein, E. H., Schneier, I., & Barker, E. C. H. *Coercive persuasion.* New York: W. W. Norton, 1961.

Shryock, R. H. The beginnings: From colonial days to the foundation of the American psychiatric association. In J. K. Hall (Ed.), *One hundred years of American psychiatry.* New York: Columbia University Press, 1944.

Slater, E. Diagnosis of "hysteria." *British Medical Journal,* 1965, *29*: 1395–1399.

Smith, W. D. So called possession in pre-Christian Greece. *Transactions and proceedings of the American philogical association,* 1965, *95*: 403–426.

Smith-Rosenberg, C. The hysterical woman: Some reflections on sex roles and role conflict in 19th century America. *Social Research,* 1972, *39*: 652–678.

Spanos, N. P. Witchcraft in histories of psychiatry: A critique and an alternative conceptualization. *Psychological Bulletin,* 1978, *85*: 417–439.

Spanos, N. P., & Gottlieb, J. Demonic possession, mesmerism and hysteria: A social psychological perspective on their historical interrelations. *Journal of Abnormal Psychology,* 1979, *88*: 527–546.

———.Ergotism and Salem Village witchcraft: A critical appraisal. *Science,* 1976, *194*: 1390–1394.

Spanos, N. P., & Hewitt, E. C. Glossolalia: A test of the "trance" and psychopathology hypotheses. *Journal of Abnormal Psychology,* 1979, 427–434.

Stagg, F., Hinson, E. G., & Oates, W. E. *Glossolalia: Tongue speaking in biblical, historical, and psychological perspective.* Nashville, Tenn.: Abington Press, 1967.

Summers, M. *The History of witchcraft.* N.J.: University Books, 1956.

Temkin, O. *The falling sickness.* Baltimore: John Hopkins, 1971.

Thomas, K. *Religion and the decline of magic.* New York: Scribners, 1971.

Thompson, R. Salem revisited. *Journal of American Studies.* 1972, *6*: 317–336.

Tillyard, E. M. W. *The elizabethan world picture.* London: Chatto and Windsor, 1948.

Toner, P. J. Exorcism and the Catholic faith. In St. Elmo Nauman Jr. (Ed.), *Exorcism through the ages.* Secaucus, N.J.: Citadel Press, 1974.

Tourney, G. The physician and witchcraft in restoration England. *Medical History,* 1972, *16*: 143–155.

Turner, R. H. Role taking, role standpoint, and reference-group behavior. *American Journal of Sociology*, 1956, *61*: 316–328.
Upham, C. D. *Salem witchcraft* (2 Vols.). Boston: Wiggins & Lunt, 1867.
Valenstein, E. S. *Brain control*. New York: Wiley, 1973.
Veith, I. Four thousand years of hysteria. In M. J. Horowitz (Ed.), *Hysterical personality*. New York: Aronson, 1977.
———.*Hysteria*. Chicago: University of Chicago Press, 1965.
Wilkins, K. Attitudes to witchcraft and demonical possession in France during the 18th century. *Journal of European Studies*, 1974, 3: 349–362.
Willard, S. A brief account of a strange and unusual providence of God befallen to Elizabeth Knapp of Groton (Orig. pub. 1683). In E. Nauman (Ed.), *Exorcism through the ages*. Secaucus, N.J.: Citadel Press, 1974, 175–194.
Wilson, E. *The scrolls from the Dead Sea*. New York: Oxford University Press, 1955.
Woods, W. *A History of the Devil*. New York: Berkley, 1974.
Woodward, W. E. *Records of Salem witchcraft* (2 Vols.). New York: Da Capo Press, 1864–1865; reprinted, 1969.
Wooley, R. M. *Exorcism and the healing of the sick*. London: Society for Promoting Christian Knowledge, 1932.
Zilboorg, G., & Henry, G. W. *A history of medical psychology*. New York: W. W. Norton, 1941.

Footnotes

Thanks to J. Gottlieb for help in formulating many of the ideas that underlie this paper, and to D. Addey, D. Dubreuil, P. Golding, H. L. Radtke, and H. J. Stam for critically reading earlier drafts.

1. It appears doubtful that pre-Christian Greeks and Romans believed in demonic possession (McCasland, 1951; Smith, 1956; Temkin, 1971). The most important precursor of Christian beliefs in possession was Jewish demonology. Although Judaism had not organized demonology during the Old Testament period, an extensive demonology developed in the period between the testaments (Boyd, 1975; Gaster, 1956; Kelly, 1974; Wilson, 1955). During the second

and first centuries B.C., the Babylonian and Assyrian notion that demons could invade the human body became common among the Jews, as did the practice of exorcism (Russell, 1960; Toner, 1974). The authors of the New Testaments were strongly influenced by the beliefs of sects on the fringe of Judaism that were immersed in dualistic and escatological thinking (Boyd, 1975; Kelly, 1974). As a result, the New Testament is permeated with those themes expressed through the medium of demonological imagery.

2. The fact that transcendent phenomena like clairvoyance were part of the demoniac role does not, of course, mean that they occurred. As the last quotation illustrates, the tests for these phenomena, when conducted at all, were often lax, informal, and carried out by individuals with a strong vested interest in validating their occurrence, e.g., Harsnett, 1599.

3. For instance, modern work on the social psychology of causal attribution (e.g., Jones, 1979; Ross, 1977) suggests that demoniacs would have been likely to define their behavior as faked when (a) tangible rewards and punishments were explicitly made contingent on their performing (or failing to perform) this behavior; (b) they made an explicit agreement to adopt the role in order to secure tangible objectives, e.g., money; and (c) role behaviors were taught to them through explicit coaching and instruction. On the other hand, demoniacs would have been likely to define themselves as possessed when (a) they perceived their behavior as deviating from social norms and were unable to attribute these deviations to external inducements; (b) possession was a salient conceptual category for classifying their deviant behavior and significant others validated this self-classification; and (c) the demonic role was learned through exposure to implicit cues and the observation of convincing role models rather than through direct instruction

4. The regularity with which psychological disturbances were explained in terms of demonic influence has been greatly exaggerated by some psychiatric historians (Alexander, & Selenick, 1966; Zilboorg & Henry, 1941). Naturalistic explanations for such disturbances were regularly employed by both physicians and nonphysicians throughout the Medieval-Early Modern Period (Kocher, 1953; Kroll, 1973; Neugebauer, 1978; Temkin, 1971). For example, Neugebauer studied the extant records of the English court that made mental competency determinations. He found a demonic

explanation for insanity proffered in only a single case between the thirteenth and seventeenth centuries. The majority of lunacy cases were explained in naturalistic terms: grief, fever, head injury, and so on. The circumstances that led to demonic rather than naturalistic explanations for deviance are not altogether clear, and their determination remains an interesting problem for historical research. In many cases, however, these circumstances probably had much less to do with the characteristics of the behavior being labeled than with the attitudes of the labelers and the vested interests served by positing demonic explanations (Boyer & Nissenbaum, 1974).

5. A social role formulation does not exclude the possibility that some of the symptoms displayed by some hysterics may be related to physiological dysfunctions. For instance, temporal lobe dysfunctions may sometimes be associated with unusual sensory and perceptual experiences (Valenstein, 1973). According to a social role perspective, however, whether or not a person with such experiences becomes labeled a hysteric would depend on a host of psychosocial variables such as the manner in which (a) the experiences were defined to the self and described to others; (b) significant others reacted to the descriptions (e.g., dismissed them as unimportant, viewed them as interesting and nonpathological, or called a physician in alarm); (c) manifestations or descriptions of the experiences became incorporated into an interpersonal strategy designed to communicate a particular self-presentation and/or elicit particular reactions from others (e.g., "I'm sick and helpless save me" versus "I feel like I lose my sense of self and become one with the universe—its a beautiful experience"); and (d) exposure to experts (physicians) shaped such rather diffuse experiences into one component of a complex social role.

A social role theory also does not exclude the possibility that certain personal attributes may have enabled some individuals to enact the hysterical role more effectively than others. Nineteenth century investigators regularly described hysterics as highly imaginative, attention-seeking, suggestible females with a strong flair for the dramatic (Hall, 1827; Holcombe, 1869; Jane 1925). When stripped of pejorative connotations, such a description seems to refer to individuals who enjoy and are highly skilled at becoming absorbed in a variety of make-believe role-playing endeavors. Given the appropriate definition of the situation along with requisite interpersonal cuing and reinforement, it is not surprising that such individuals would be particularly adept at enacting the hysterical role. However, labeling people as sick because they possess and utilize flexible and convincing role-playing skills does little to advance our understanding of behavior.

6. I have referred to domoniacs and hysterics as "she" rather than as "he/she" throughout this paper to emphasize that these roles were usually filled by women, and that at the time, women were conceptualized as possessing innate deficiencies that predisposed them to these disorders (Smith-Rosenberg, 1972). It is certainly true, however, that some demoniacs were male and that some nineteenth century physicians spoke of male hysteria (Ellenberger, 1970; Oesterreich, 1966).

Chapter 7

THE CONTROL OF CONDUCT

Authority vs. Autonomy

Thomas S. Szasz*

There is only one political sin: independence; and only one political virtue: obedience. To put it differently, there is only one offense against authority: self-control; and only one obeisance to it: submission to control by authority.

Why is self-control, autonomy, such a threat to authority? Because the person who controls himself, who is his own master, has no need for an authority to be his master. This, then, renders authority unemployed. What is he to do if he cannot control others? To be sure, he could mind his own business. But this is a fatuous answer, for those who are satisfied to mind their own business do not aspire to become authorities. In short, authority needs subjects, persons not in command of themselves—just as parents need children and physicians need patients. Hence, too, the paradox that self-control may be defined as precisely that capacity which, the less of it a person possesses, the more of it the authorities want him to have, and the more of it he possesses, the less of it they want him to have.

*Reprinted by permission from the *Criminal Law Bulletin,* Vol. 11, No. 5, September-October 1975, Copyright, 1975 Warren, Gorham, and Lamont, Inc., 210 South Street, Boston, Mass. All rights reserved.

Autonomy is the death knell of authority, and authority knows it: hence, the ceaseless warfare of authority against the exercise, both real and symbolic, of autonomy—that is, against suicide, against masturbation, against self-medication, against the proper use of language itself.[1]

Control

The parable of the Fall illustrates this fight to the death between control and self-control. Did Eve, tempted by the Serpent, seduce Adam, who then lost control of himself and succumbed to evil? Or did Adam, facing a choice between obedience to the authority of God and his own destiny, choose self-control?

How, then, shall we view the situation of all those countless persons who are now considered to be "mentally ill" and are called "mental patients"? For example, how shall we view the so-called neurotic, who may be fearful, depressed, obsessive, compulsive, and so forth; or the so-called psychotic, who may feel too important or not important enough, may refuse to eat or speak or sleep, be depressed and suicidal, and so forth; or the so-called pervert, who may engage in sexual practices disapproved by ecclesiastic, legal, and psychiatric authorities; or the so-called drug abuser or drug addict, who may ingest chemicals forbidden by legal and medical authorities?

Should we think of these persons (the list is, of course, virtually inexhaustible) as stupid, sick, and helpless children—lured by forbidden impulses or unconscious drives, pressured by hormones or peers, tempted by the pleasures of caresses or chemicals—succumbing to "irresistible impulses" and thus losing control of themselves? Or should we think of them as persons in control of themselves, choosing, like Adam, the forbidden fruit as the elemental and elementary way of affirming their identity by pitting themselves against authority?

There is, as a rule, no empirical or scientific way of choosing between these two answers, of deciding which is right and which is wrong. The questions frame two different moral perspectives, and the answers define two different moral strategies.

If we side with authority and wish to repress the individual, we shall treat him *as if* he were helpless, the innocent victim of overwhelming temptation. We shall then "protect" him from further temptation by treating him as a child, a slave, or a madman. The so-called mental patient is thus typically viewed as someone who has, or is alleged to have, lost control of himself. Psychiatry and behavioral science supply the ideology and the justification, and the courts and the police supply the authority and the power, for controlling him.

If we side with the individual and wish to refute the legitimacy and reject the power of authority to infantilize him, we shall treat him *as if* he were in command of himself, the executor of responsible decisions. We shall then demand that he respect others as he respects himself by treating him as an adult, a free individual, or a "rational" person. However, the person securely in control of himself frustrates others from controlling him; hence, he is the object of both admiration and envy, awe and hate.

Either of these positions and policies makes sense. What makes less sense—what is confusing in principle and chaotic in practice—is to treat people as both adults and children, as both free and unfree, as both sane and insane.

Nevertheless, this is just what social authorities throughout history have done: In ancient Greece, in medieval Europe, in the contemporary world, we find various mixtures in the attitudes of the authorities toward the people. In some societies, the individual is treated as more free than unfree, and we call these societies "free"; in others, he is treated as more determined than self-determining, and we call these societies "totalitarian." In none is the individual treated as completely free. Perhaps this would be impossible: Many persons insist that no society could survive on such a premise consistently carried through. Perhaps this is something that lies in the future of mankind. In any case, we should take satisfaction in the evident impossibility of the opposite situation: No society has ever treated the individual, nor perhaps could it treat him, as completely determined. The apparent freedom of the authority, controlling both himself and subject, provides an irresistible model: If God can control, if Pope and prince can control, if politician and psychiatrist can control—then perhaps the person can also control, at least himself.

Power

The conflicts between those who have power and those who want to take it away from them fall into three distinct categories. In moral, political, and social affairs (and I, of course, include psychiatric affairs among these), these categories must be clearly distinguished. If we do not distinguish among them, we are likely to mistake opposition to absolute or arbitrary power with what may, actually, be an attempt to gain such power for oneself or for the groups or leaders one admires.

First, there are those who want to take power away from the oppressor and give it to the oppressed as a class—as exemplified by Marx, Lenin, and the Communists. Revealingly, they dream of the "dictatorship" of the proletariat or some other group.

Second, there are those who want to take power away from the oppressor and give it to themselves as the protectors of the oppressed—as exemplified by Robespierre in politics; Rush in medicine; and by their liberal, radical, and medical followers. Revealingly, they dream of the incorruptible honest or incontrovertibly sane ruler leading his happy or healthy flock.

And third, there are those who want to take power away from the oppressor and give it to the oppressed as individuals, for each to do with as he pleases, but hopefully for his own self-control—as exemplified by Mill, von Mises, the free-market economists, and their libertarian followers. Revealingly, they dream of people so self-governing that their need for and tolerance of rulers is minimal or nil.

While countless men say they love liberty, clearly only those who, by virtue of their actions, fall into the third category, mean it.[2] The others merely want to replace a hated oppressor by a loved one—having usually themselves in mind for the job.

Psychiatrists, psychologists, and other so-called mental health professionals have traditionally opted for "reforms" of the second type; that is, their opposition to existing powers, ecclesiastic or secular, has had as its conscious and avowed aim the paternalistic care of the citizen-patient, and not the freedom of the autonomous individual. Hence, medical methods of social control tended not only to replace religious methods, but sometimes to exceed them in stringency and severity. In short, the usual response of medical authority to the controls exercised by nonmedical authority has been to try to take over and then escalate the controls, rather than to endorse the principle and promote the practice of removing the controls by which the oppressed are victimized.

As a result, until recently, most psychiatrists, psychologists, and other behavioral scientists had nothing but praise for the "behavioral controls" of medicine and psychiatry. We are now beginning to witness, however, a seeming backlash against this position. Many behavioral scientists are jumping on what they evidently consider to be the next "correct" and "liberal" position, namely, a criticism of behavioral controls. But since most of these "scientists" remain as hostile as they have always been to individual freedom and responsibility, to choice and dignity, their criticism conforms to the pattern I have described earlier: They demand more "controls"—that is, professional and governmental controls—over "behavior controls." This is like first urging a person to drive over icy roads at breakneck speed to get over them as fast as possible, and then, when his car goes into a skid, advising him to apply his brakes. Whether because they are stupid or wicked or both, such persons invariably recommend fewer controls where more are needed, for example in relation to punishing offenders—and more controls where fewer are needed, for example in relation to contracts between consenting adults.

The supporters of the Therapeutic State are tireless: Now they are proposing more therapeutic controls in the name of "controlling behavior controls." Typical of this trend is the view, and the policy it engenders and justifies, that there is a class of human beings whose members, although innocent of crime, may justly be deprived of liberty in psychiatric institutions, but who, while so deprived of liberty, are alleged to possess a "constitutional right to treatment." This position is now officially endorsed not only by the American Psychiatric Association and the United States Department of Justice, but, characteristically, also by the American Civil Liberties Union.[3]

Clearly, the seeds of this fundamental human propensity— to react to the loss of control, or to the threat of such loss, with an intensification of control, thus generating a spiraling symbiosis of escalating controls and countercontrols—have fallen on fertile soil in contemporary medicine and psychiatry and have yielded a luxuriant harvest of "therapeutic" coercions. Our attitude toward these practices—that is, whether we approach them with a favorable or unfavorable prejudice—will depend largely on our attitude toward the two fundamental methods of regulating social relations.

Principles for Regulating Social Relations

There are two basic principles and procedures for regulating social relations, and two only: contracts, or agreements reached willingly and voluntarily between consenting parties; and commands, or codes of conduct imposed by stronger parties on weaker ones.

Free societies are characterized by the fact that—or are free because—the scope for contracting in them is large, while the scope for being commanded is relatively small. That is, the relations between the rulers and the ruled are hedged in by contractual guarantees—constitutions, the common law, the "rule of law" itself; and relations among the ruled themselves are largely governed by contracts. Despotic or totalitarian societies, on the other hand, are characterized by the fact that—or perhaps are unfree because—the scope for being commanded in them is large, while the scope for contracting is negligible. The relations between the rulers and the ruled are here unfettered by constitutional or other enforceable limits; and the relations among the ruled themselves are almost wholly bureaucratic rather than contractual.

It has been well established—indeed, no one disagrees with the contention—that in the case of psychiatric sanctions, coercion flows from the judgment of authorities, not from the breaking of contracts. In the Therapeutic State toward which we are marching under the banner of Health and Medicine, law is replaced by psychiatry, crime by insanity, and justice by therapy.[4] Those, then, who want to preserve or enlarge our traditional liberties must view any reduction in the scope of contracting with caution; and must view any such reduction justified by psychiatric considerations and replaced by psychiatric methods of control with positive alarm.

Footnotes

1. See Szasz, *The Second Sin* (Doubleday, Inc. 1973), and *Ceremonial Chemistry* (Doubleday, Inc. 1974).
2. See especially von Mises, *Human Action* (Yale University Press 1949).
3. See, for example, Szasz, "The ACLU's 'Mental Illness' Cop-Out," 5 Reason, 4–9 (Jan 1974); Shapiro, "Legislating the Control of Behavior Control," So. 47 Cal. L. Rev., 237–356 (Feb. 1974); and Ballantine, Jr., "Who Should Control the Scalpel?" Prism 42–43, 50–51 (Jan. 1975).
4. See Szasz, *Law Liberty, and Psychiatry* (Macmillan Co., Inc. 1963); *Psychiatric Justice* (Macmillan Co., Inc. 1965); and *Ideology and Insanity* (Doubleday Anchor 1970).

Chapter 8

SUMMARY OF REMARKS BY JOHN DEAN

October 29, 1977, Waldorf-Astoria Hotel, New York City

Max Rosenbaum

In his remarks at the Waldorf-Astoria, a few years ago, John Dean spoke about the ethical issues raised during his tenure at the White House, and about the compunction he felt to conform to the wishes of his superiors.

Dean began his work as counsel to the president with a great deal of respect for the Office of the President, but with little idea of what his own job would entail. He was to quickly learn. On his first day at work, he found a confidential memo from President Nixon waiting, about a recent press report on Vice-President Agnew. *Scanlon's Monthly*, a muckraking magazine, had just published an article that accused Agnew of planning to cancel the 1972 elections and repealing the Bill of Rights. Nixon, outraged by the accusations, wanted Dean to bring a lawsuit against *Scanlon's Monthly*. Dean's initial reaction was to dismiss this as a fanciful suggestion. But when he realized that Nixon considered it to be a serious matter, Dean responded seriously, and recommended that he drop the idea. Dean reasoned that the public would quickly learn of the White House's action, and the move would only help publicize the magazine.

Nixon was dissatisfied with this response, and suggested that Dean take another tack. He wanted him to intimidate *Scanlon's* by having the Internal Revenue Service (IRS) audit the magazine's returns. Dean, realizing that there was no legal basis for an audit, was hesitant to contact the IRS and sought the advice of Murray Chotiner, another White House lawyer. Chotiner argued that Nixon could legally instigate an investigation of the magazine, since the IRS was part of the executive branch of government, and the president was Chief Executive. Dean remained unconvinced and knew that this opinion conflicted with federal tax law. Chotiner's final response was more to the point. If Dean did not do what the president demanded, he would replace Dean with someone who would.

Dean remained troubled by Nixon's request. He considered the assignment illegal, but he was concerned about jeopardizing his position. He was pleased with his position as counsel to the president, and proud that he had reached such a position at the age of thirty-one. He also knew of other men who had served unsuccessfully at the White House and, as a result, found themselves blackballed from positions in government and private industry. Dean's dilemma was solved shortly thereafter, almost by accident. While ruminating over his decision, Dean met with Jack Caufield, another White House employee, who had worked for John Erlichman, Dean's predecessor as counsel. Caufield said that he would take care of the problem, through his contacts at the IRS. A few days later, he informed Dean that Nixon's wishes had been carried out.

In retrospect, Dean viewed this incident as a turning point in his life and career. By acquiescing in an illegal action, he had crossed an ethical boundary. At the time, he rationalized it as the sort of compromise one must inevitably make to advance in any job. But later, he realized that the IRS incident was the first step toward his involvement in Watergate.

Some of the deceptions that Dean was asked to partake in were petty—some might think even somewhat humorous. One morning, for example, he was summoned for an urgent conference with the president. It appears that Mr. Nixon was meeting with a group of college newspaper editors that morning, and wanted Dean to be present in the office when they entered, ostensibly to discuss budget matters with Nixon. Dean knew nothing about the budget, and had never discussed the matter with the president, so he was naturally somewhat bewildered by the request. Only later, when he discussed the event with Nixon's assistant, Robert Haldeman, did the reason become clear. Nixon apparently considered Dean to be the "White House hippie," because of his young age and supposedly irreverent behavior. As a result, Dean was to be present at any White House meetings with young people or "longhairs," as a kind of public relations symbol to American youth.

Increasingly, however, the White House activities became more serious and their effects on Dean's ethical judgments more profound. Through conversation with Jack Caufield, Dean learned that Charles Colson, Nixon's assistant, had devised a plan to firebomb the Brookings Institute, a liberal Washington think tank. Colson's scheme called for a break-in of the institute in order to see whether it contained copies of the infamous Pentagon Papers. He wanted Caufield to research whether the burglary was feasible, and Caufield was frightened.

As in the past, Dean's first reaction was disbelief at the absurdity of such an idea. As he realized that Caufield was serious, he too became frightened. He immediately flew to the presidential retreat in San Clemente, California to speak with John Ehrlichman and explain the situation. Dean recalls taking pains to describe the plan to Ehrlichman carefully, without embarrassing or offending him. It is indicative of the tenor of the Nixon administration, and of Dean's moral ambiguity, that he knew it was fruitless to argue against the break-in on ethical or legal grounds. As he recalled later, the Nixon administration never discussed the legality or ethics of its action. Instead, Dean argued against the plan on a cost-benefit analysis: the risk, he said, was not worth the possible gain. Ehrlichman listened to Dean's argument and, at its conclusion, telephoned Colson and told him to cancel the plan.

Instead of being pleased that he had been listened to, however, Dean was bothered by the aftermath of the incident. When he returned to the White House, he learned that he was considered a "little old lady" for his lack of enthusiasm for the burglary plan.

Dean resolved to be as tough as his White House superiors and recalls sending a harshly worded memo around in order to regain the good graces of the White House team. But the longer Dean remained at the White House, the more he questioned the ethics of his job, and the more he was convinced that the rewards were not worth the distress it caused him. By September 1971, he had decided to resign and take another job he had been considering. He felt that his resignation would be of minor concern to the White House since he considered his role to be nonessential. He went to see Haldeman and tell him of his decision.

Haldeman relied on the "carrot and the stick" approach in convincing Dean to stay. First, he appealed to Dean's sense of loyalty, and to his guilt, by reminding him that he would not have received any job offers had it not been for his experience as the President's counsel. Later, when Dean still hesitated, Haldeman assured him that he would be given better job offers if he continued at the White House. Haldeman's arguments were evidently convincing, because Dean remained as Nixon's counsel, only to become involved in the morass of the Watergate conspiracy.

It was around that time, in the spring of 1971, that the events leading to the Watergate break-in began. Always wary of his continued political success, Nixon had begun planning strategy for the 1972 reelection campaign. In studying campaign task force reports, Nixon noted the absence of any report dealing with political intelligence. That evening, he dictated a memo to Haldeman requesting that he begin working on an intelligence system. In accordance with the administration's office procedures, the request was placed in the "tickler" file, where staff members were consistently reminded of requests Nixon considered to be important. Eventually, Gordon Liddy was selected to head the intelligence operation.

When Liddy presented his plans for campaign intelligence operations, Dean responded as he had to the plans for the Brookings burglaries. He considered that Liddy's elaborate spy-novel plots for bugging squads, aircraft to intercept Democratic campaign communication, and prostitution teams to compromise his opponents as absurd, dangerous, and wrong. This time, however, Dean vowed that he would have no involvement in the action and met with Haldeman to tell him this. Again, he refrained from arguing the right or wrong of the situation, but only told him that he thought the White House staff should not be involved. Haldeman convinced Dean that he would not have to become involved. But, as we now know, the plans were still implemented.

Although Dean did manage to be in Manila when the actual Wagergate break-in occurred on June 17, 1972, he was still to become involved in its aftermath. When he returned to Washington that following week, he learned of the incidents and became increasingly uncomfortable with this knowledge. But as he had in the past, Dean rationalized his complicity in Watergate. He assumed the role of middleman, passing messages about bribes to be paid so that witnesses would remain silent, communicating information about the conspiracy to other people involved. But, he argued to himself, he was not actually doing the "dirty work"; he was just transmitting messages. Besides, he reasoned, if he did not do it, the White House would find someone else to do his job. As much as he could, Dean tried to deny to himself what he was doing. Sometimes, he was remarkably effective. Prosecutors and investigators would later be surprised that Dean could honestly not remember the amounts of the bribes that were paid.

But despite the emotional pressures that his complicity created, Dean felt that there were rewards for his work. It was still important to him that he be liked and respected by his superiors, and he was beginning to garner that esteem. By being the "linch pin" of the conspiracy, Dean was becoming an important person at the White House. he began to routinely telephone Haldeman on his private line, and routinely spoke with Nixon. For years, he had addressed Attorney General John Mitchell as "General" or "Mr. Mitchell," but now he was on a first-name basis.

The rewards of status and power soon began to fade. Dean still realized that he was being used by his superiors, that they found the deceptions and bribes as distasteful as he did, but were reluctant to carry them out themselves. Increasingly, Dean found it impossible to reconcile his actions with his ethical sense. He began drinking heavily every day after work.

Dean also began to realize that the loyalty he gave to Nixon and his administration was not being reciprocated. This became evident when, during the height of the 1972 campaign, Nixon announced that neither he, nor anyone at the White House, was involved in Watergate. Nixon knew this, he said, because his counsel, John Dean, had thoroughly investigated the matter.

Of course, John Dean had written no such report, and Nixon's announcement was the first that he had heard of it. It was not to be the last. Soon after the announcement, Haldeman, and then Ehrlichman, began pressuring Dean to write a bogus report to substantiate that the alleged investigation had occurred. Dean realized from the beginning that he was being used as a pawn in the administration's ploy. If Dean wrote the report they wanted, and if the White House role in the Watergate conspiracy was discovered, Nixon would have an excuse for his ignorance of the break-in. He could argue that his only knowledge of Watergate came from his counsel's report, and that Dean had misled him.

Dean's ethical quandary increased both during and after the successful 1972 campaign. He did not want to author a lie, and felt somewhat betrayed by Nixon and his staff. Yet, he still felt some need to satisfy his superiors. Haldeman continued to press Dean for the report, and in December 1972, Dean finally responded that he could only write an honest report, a report that would lead to all their indictments. Haldeman, apparently convinced that Dean meant what he said, refrained from further discussion of the matter. But Ehrlichman still thought Dean should write the bogus report. When his request was also unheeded, Dean was told to discuss the matter directly with Nixon.

Denying a request by the president did not come easily to Dean. First, Dean felt embarrassed to raise the issue. He felt unable to tell Nixon directly how severe the Watergate issue had become and how it could mean the end of his presidency. Also, Nixon was no novice at politics, and knew how to flatter his subordinates so that they would do as he liked. At previous meetings, for example, Nixon had asked Dean to brief the Cabinet, and hinted that Dean might one day hold such a post. Dean also felt that Nixon would not pay attention to messages from his subordinates, and would often pay closer attention to the style of their presentation than to the contents of their messages. After weeks of such meetings, however, Dean was exasperated. In March 1973, Dean again met with Nixon. This time, he spared no words, explaining the severity of the situation, and telling the president that Watergate might mean the end of his presidency. This time Nixon listened.

Dean, however, still seemed to underestimate Nixon's political savvy and skill at parrying questions. To every objection Dean raised, Nixon had an answer. When Dean argued that it would cost $1 million dollars to silence witnesses, Nixon responded that the money could be gotten. When Dean raised the question of perjury, Nixon countered that perjury was a difficult charge to prove, since it necessitated two witnesses. It became a battle between a master and a novice, with Nixon artfully countering all Dean's objections. As Dean recalls it, it was similar to asking the boss for a raise in pay, and then thanking him when he denies it.

John Dean's patience and endurance, however, were wearing thin. Increasingly, he felt that he had no choice but to expose the Watergate conspiracy. A lawyer by training, Dean had begun to review his law books and realized that he had committed obstruction of justice in his role as Watergate middleman. His loyalty was diminishing, as he realized that it was not being returned by the White House; that he was to be the "fall guy" if the Watergate conspiracy was discovered. Finally, Dean saw that his marriage was falling apart, the result of his continued drinking.

Still, Dean wrestled with his ethical conflict. He knew that he had two options: to tell the truth or to lie. But he dreaded the role of "squealer" or "tale teller," a role we are warned against from childhood. By the end, however, Dean felt that he had no alternatives left. The one thing he felt he could hold on to was his ability to differentiate between truth and falsehood. And the one option, he was convinced, was to take responsibility for his own actions, and come forward with the truth.

Chapter 9

COMPLIANCE OR SELF-FULFILLMENT?

The Case of Albert Speer

Michael I. Selzer

When people perform evil deeds in the name of the organization to which they belong, it is not at all because they are acting out violent and aggressive impulses of their own, but because they are prompted by the urge or the necessity to obey their superiors. In such situations, the dynamic of "I was following orders" applies to all levels of the hierarchy except the ultimate leader. The willingness of tens of thousands of people in the Third Reich to carry out deeds of terrible cruelty is accounted for by the mechanism of obedience; only Hitler's psychology requires "a different set of explanatory principles," a prominent social psychologist has argued.[1]

Someday in the future, students of the sociology of knowledge will confront the fascinating challenge of accounting for this tenet's rapid and almost unchallenged rise to the status of social science orthodoxy; presumably, they will not fail to detect its congruence with certain political ideologies that are in vogue in academic circles today. A more immediate and modest challenge faces us in the present: it is to evaluate the data and reasoning on which the construct of the primacy of the obedience mechanism rests.

In some of my work I have tried to call attention to basic flaws in the studies of Milgram and others; instances have been identified of the seeming fabrication or withholding of evidence which ought to have no place in the academic world but the presence of which here seems to reinforce the suspicion that ideological preferences have played an undue role in shaping this body of thought.[2] At the same time, I have attempted to examine data which seem to have more immediate relevance to the construct under question than some of the better known social psychological laboratory experiments with which they are associated: in particular, psychological test data obtained from leading Nazi war criminals as well as from low-ranking Nazis have been examined. These indicate, almost uniformly, the presence of unusually intense aggressive and destructive drives in Nazis, and have led me to infer that in committing the crimes they did, the Nazis, transpose contrary to the obedience hypothesis, were acting out these and related drives. Historical forces and other circumstances (including orders from authoritative sources) have functioned to legitimize the acting out of these drives, but could not have the effect they had unless the individuals concerned had a strong predisposition to engaging in violent behavior.[3] An opportunity arose for me to gain additional perspective on this question by interviewing the late Albert Speer, Hitler's friend, architect, and minister of war production, and one of the major Nazi war criminals convicted in the Nuremberg trials (he was sentenced to, and served, 20 years' imprisonment).

At the time of this interview Speer was seventy-three years old. He showed no signs of mental deterioration and lived in the abundant comfort made possible by the sales of his two volumes of memoirs. Speer had publicly acknowledged his guilt and remorse for his past career. He spoke out frequently to condemn neo-Nazi movements and to warn against the unscrupulous use of the science of technology, of which he regarded his own crimes as a foremost example.

What was Speer's understanding of the penitent's role he assumed, and how deep was his commitment to it? What psychological adjustments did he have to undergo to make possible his metamorphosis, and what kind of a person did he become as a result of them? A special circumstance lends peculiar fascination to these questions.

In 1945, G. M. Gilbert, a prison psychologist at Nuremberg, administered the Rorschach (inkblot) test to Speer. When Florence Miale and I analyzed the results we discovered a vivid but dispiriting portrait of Speer's personality. We were struck above all by his severe emotional impoverishment—an extraordinary emptiness of being—and by the ego-inflating grandiosity with which he sought to compensate for it. We found that his intellectual and social pretensions, although of great importance to him, rested on flimsy foundations and provided him with no real security or identity. We doubted his capacity to experience feelings. We also doubted his capacity to form attachments and to attain any genuine awareness of himself or his environment; his displays of emotion seemed to us phony and inappropriate. Under the circumstances, it appears to us that Speer's attachment to the Nazi party and its leaders must have been shallow and self-serving, and that his later posture as social sage and penitent was probably no less so.[4] Speer's postwar change of heart, however, was accepted as authentic by many people. It won him the friendship of prominent intellectuals (including a number of Jews) and such accolades as Oxford historian Hugh Trevor-Roper's description of him as a morally and intellectually superior man.

What is more, the validity of Speer's Rorschach responses, as well as our interpretation of them, have been called into question. Speer claimed later that he had deliberately misled Gilbert by giving "silly" and "mocking" responses to the blots. He explained that he had not wanted to take the Rorschach, but felt that his refusal to do so might create problems for him with the prison administration. He also said that he likes practical jokes and enjoyed pulling Gilbert's leg; and that bashfulness had prevented him from mentioning the sexual things "that you are supposed to see" in some of the blots.

While taking the test Speer had remarked to Gilbert, "I can't visualize very well." This is perhaps a surprising comment for an architect to make, and Speer subsequently insisted that he could, in fact, visualize very well. Nevertheless, Gilbert accepted Speer's remark as true and, as a result, thought that Speer's responses were "probably invalid" as a projection of his personality.

I was impressed by these objections, of course, but I did not consider them conclusive. On the contrary, there is a quite distinctive flavor to Speer's Rorschach responses. If he had contrived them, it seemed to me, they were *his* contrivances and as such, a reflection of his personality. And it also seemed to me that Gilbert may have been rather gullible in accepting Speer's comment that he could not visualize very well—a claim which I thought could just as well be understood as a con-artist's attempt to explain away what he may have felt was a poor performance. (Speer did not respond to 3 of the 10 Rorschach cards, and mentioned that he found 2 further ones very difficult.)

I was as hesitant, under these circumstances, about dismissing the claims of Speer's champions that his feelings of guilt and remorse were authentic, as I was about rejecting the evidence of his Rorschach which challenges those claims. A wider question also remained unresolved: Was Speer a "Nazi by circumstance," as he claimed—a man who fell in line with the Third Reich because of external pressures on him—or was he a "Nazi by personality," a man whose psychological structure predisposed him to embrace the forces which were unleashed by Adolf Hitler?

The quality of Speer's repentance could provide an understanding of the answer to this question. In approaching Speer, I was mindful of one possibility which could resolve the apparent contradiction between what the Rorschach seemed to reveal about him and his friends' defense of him. In that Rorschach, Florence Miale and I had discovered a residual and erratically manifested ability to take responsibility for his own shortcomings. Later, the publication of Speer's prison diary indicated that he was also capable of occasional, involuntary flashes of acute insight into himself. Paradoxically, these qualities did not seem to be a source of self-knowledge for Speer. I guessed that in part he was merely victimized by them, and that for the rest he dismissed them without very much effort.[5] I had thought it improbable that these qualities could have a therapeutic function for Speer, let alone that they could cause significant changes in his personality. Reports of the "new" Speer, however, suggested that I may have minimized these qualities and underestimated Speer's capacity to enlarge them and to grow with them.

Although Speer had read our analysis of his Rorschach, he at once agreed to meet with me. The only condition he set was that I render his remarks into "perfect English" when quoting them for publication. I thought that this demand, made in all seriousness and without a trace of humor, suggested a degree of vanity and vulnerability quite surprising for a man of his age (in fact, Speer spoke English rather well); and, since there is no such thing as "perfect English," that it also indicated a trite and unimaginative perfectionism. However, I said that I would try my best, and the quotations here reflect my effort to do so. At Speer's suggestion we met at a small hotel in Munich which he recommended as "clean and cheap" in case I needed a place to stay while in town.

Speer's manner toward me fluctuated greatly, and in a seemingly arbitrary way, throughout the conversation. At times he seemed almost pathetically eager to assure me he was answering my questions as fully as he could. He tried to show his solicitude by telling me that he had not extended his hand when we met out of respect for my doubts as to whether I would want to shake it. At one point he tried to have me say that I had not sought him out for professional reasons connected with my research but for other reasons. He did not specify these but I got the distinct impression that he thought—and hoped—that I wanted to establish some kind of friendship with him! Yet on other occasions Speer was tactless and overbearing, and never more so than when he interrupted a question to point out proudly that when he was my age he had just become a minister in Hitler's government. These odd fluctuations suggest that Speer did not have very much of a sense of who he really was. He gave the impression of a man who is endlessly trying out new (and often quite inappropriate) postures in a limp sort of effort to establish his own identity.

It proved all too easy to discover the former archcriminal in the social sage and penitent of his last years. To begin with, Speer recast the discredited defense used by most of his colleagues at the Nuremberg trial ("it was all Hitler's fault; we were only following orders") into what he thought of as psychological terms. The Third Reich, he explained, came into being only because of Hitler's uncanny power to "mesmerize" people. "By sheer mental force," Speer told me, "Hitler was able to convince people to follow him and to lose their own sense of reason." Thus, it was not he who attached himself to Hitler but rather, Hitler who had, in Speer's words, "a big hold on me by his means."

In response to my question, Speer acknowledged that only people who were predisposed to nazism could have allowed themselves to be mesmerized by Hitler. But when I asked him what he thought (at the time of the interview) had bound him to Hitler he could only say, "It was this gift which worked on me. It was magic!" Thus, apparently, while Hitler's other followers were predisposed to accept his leadership, Speer himself was merely a victim of Hitler's "magic."

This was not the only instance when Speer dissociated himself from his comments about Nazis in general. Near the time I interviewed him, he told me, he had seen Joachim Fest's controversial documentary movie about the Third Reich. "It was unbelievable," Speer said, referring to Hitler, "that this man could have had such influence because he did not look at all impresssive. And yet there they were, all those fanatical people around him!" Speer, evidently, did not recognize that he too was one of "those fanatical people."

Except when writing books or giving interviews, Speer told me, he did not think very much about the Third Reich and never had any spontaneous memories or thoughts about it. "The whole thing is far away from me now," he explained. "It is not much on my mind because it has been neutralized for me." The trite rationalization he offered was that Hitler's suicide severed his attachment to nazism—apparently because Hitler's magic spell over him was thereby broken.

In his later years, such regrets as Speer had for the past seemed trivial, egotistical, and almost incredibly callow. I asked him to tell me some of the ways in which he was glad he had changed, both in his dealings with himself and with others. He said that he was glad that he was no longer conceited, and also relieved not to hold an important post any longer. "Normally," he said, "people try to get some advantages out of their friends, but friendship means sticking by someone when he is Mr. Nobody again and has had bad luck."

Apparently, Speer attributed the reverses in his life to "bad luck." His remark that he was no longer conceited is, as we will see, open to question; and as of course is his rather dismal view of what friendship "normally" entails. But more noteworthy is the fact that neither part of his reply suggests the presence of any real insight into the defects of his personality when he was younger— or any indication that those defects were later corrected.

In an effort to further probe Speer's regrets about the past I asked him what he would choose if, as in the fairy tale, he could have three wishes. "I would like to undo something of the past," he began promisingly enough, but then went on to explain:

> I don't understand myself nowadays, my reactions to Hitler when he humiliated me, for instance, by summoning me back all the way from the South of France when there was no reason to do so. He would play around with me as though I were nothing, and I don't understand why I did not react to that and step down.

He thought for a while before coming up with his second wish: "Of course, that I had reacted to all the signs which were visible that some evil things were going on."

Even when he was making a big effort, as in this interview, to produce the "correct" answer, Speer was able to express his regrets about the past only in brief, limp, and self-referential remarks. His regrets did not acknowledge the sufferings undergone by millions of people at the hands of the Third Reich, and seemed to imply little more than upset over the price he, Speer, had to pay for his role as a leading Nazi. His most vivid and accessible regret about the past, though, is expressed in the perverse "wish" he came up with first: that he hadn't let Hitler kick him around!

Speer's sense of himself before his death allows little room for any recognition that he once was a leading Nazi. "Are you often recognized in public?" I asked him. "Strangely enough," he replied, apparently with genuine bafflement, "older people shy away from me. But in general people are very decent to me. Sometimes they ask for my autograph, but normally they just nod their heads." I asked whether he thought he was regarded on such occasions as a convicted war ciminal or as a former leader of

Germany. "Well," he said "I think what impresses people most is that I succeeded in getting through those 20 years of imprisonment in Spandau. 'You did a good job, you look so well after 20 years! That's what impresses people about me more than anything else!"

The extent to which Speer dealt with his Nazi past by simply cutting himself off from it became even more apparent when I asked him for three answers to the question, "Who are you?" He smiled pleasurably when he first heard the question, as though gratified by this invitation to egotistical indulgence, and answered it without a moment's pause for reflection:

> First of all, I am proud of myself because three times I have succeeded in doing something really good in very different fields. To begin with, my architectural work is not at all bad. Philip Johnson, for instance, thinks so, and I heard recently that even Mies van der Rohe, the architect I most admire, doesn't dislike my work, which was quite something.
> Then, and very much to my astonishment, I showed abilities as a technocrat and administrator beyond what people trained in these fields could show. And finally, again to my surprise, I wrote two books.
> And I am proud of all this because it is a unique thing that somebody is successful in three different fields.
> I am also proud of the fact that I could survive 20 years in Spandau and emerge from prison absolutely sane and healthy, and that I am in some ways feeling younger than people of my age. I am proud of that.

He fell silent. "Is there anything else you would say to describe yourself?" I asked, reminding him that I had wanted three answers to the question.

> "No," he replied at length. "I suppose this is all." He seemed to want to find a third answer, though, as if to oblige me by obeying the rules of the game. Finally, he said, "You could say I am proud of my children, of course, that they are succeeding. But that is not as important as the other two."

This astonishing self-portrait, it scarcely needs to be said, does not bear out the view of Speer as the penitent ex-Nazi leader.

It reveals, rather, a man who perceived himself in terms of his accomplishments alone—my question, after all, was not "What are you proud of?" but "Who are you?"—and who has succeeded almost totally in overlooking the setting of unprecedented brutality of which he was a part. His pride in his achievements as an administrator allowed no room for any acknowledgment of the terrible conditions in which he forced hundreds of thousands of slave laborers to work in the Reich's armaments factories.

Just as effortlessly, Speer de-Nazified his architectural designs. He said they were created "for the history of architecture," as ingenious a euphemism as one is likely to find for buildings constructed by the Thousand-Year Reich. When pushed a bit, he acknowledged their brutal qualities:

> In part these buildings presume many of the things which happened later—the war, the annihilation of the Jews, the killing of people. This cruelty is in some ways expressed in some of the buildings, which try to force their will on others. It was Hitler's will to overwhelm other people.

The cruelty is there, in other words: or, as Speer more deftly puts it, "is in some ways expressed in some of them." But the responsibility for this he assigned, by clear implication, to Hitler: "It was Hitler's will. . . ." Speer's claim to have won the approval of major architects calls for comment. Mies, of course, is dead; but it seems incredible that he would have had a good word to say for Speer's designs. Philip Johnson told me that he does not admire Speer's work and has never expressed appreciation for it.

Speer had mentioned Mies as the architect he most admired. When I asked him what he particularly liked about Mies' work, he referred to the Barcelona pavillion:

> What struck me most was that this was the first approach to the modern style with refined means. The Bauhaus had puritanical aims, they didn't refine anything, and their steel construction just showed as steel construction. Mies, on the other hand, is an aesthete, and he made his buildings with marble, and with chrome bands, and the windows—everything was excellent.

Speer's level of aesthetic criticism ("marble, and with chrome bands, and the windows") was what one might expect from a Saudi oil millionaire rather than from a man who had designed buildings for the history of architecture. Speer, however, remained convinced of the enduring value of his architectural achievements. One of his most bizarre contributions to Nazi architecture had been a "theory of ruin value." Classical ruins, he had noted on a trip to Italy, looked grand; and while he was happy to design buildings that would last 1,000 years, after the trip he became concerned about how they would look when they finally collapsed into ruins. He therefore proposed to Hitler that henceforth the Third Reich's buildings should be designed in such a way that they would look imposing even in ruin. Hitler was much taken with the idea and ordered it implemented.

Because this "theory" is such a vivid expression of the twin Nazi passions of grandiosity and necrophilia, I asked Speer whether he still thought it was a good idea. He said that he did. He had brought along with him to the interview a portfolio of his architectural drawings—pageproofs from a book that was soon to be published. Pointing to these, he wistfully remarked how certain details would survive in ruin, and how grand they would then look. And then he added: "How do you think Mies' buildings will look when they are ruined? A pile of rusted metal, that's all they'll be!"

While telling me about Hitler's power to mesmerize others, Speer had remarked parenthetically that he knew that was "no excuse." He added nothing to this remark, however, and since the whole thrust of his explanation was to deny his own responsibility for the role he had played in the Third Reich, this disclaimer sounded merely as if it were being recited by rote. Another question, however, provided me with a more substantial impression of Speer's moral reasoning.

I had asked him to imagine what his feelings might be about interviewing Albert Speer, if, like me, he had been the son of Jewish refugees from Germany. He had a ready answer to this. "You could have a good conscience," he assured me, " because I am acquainted with so many Jewish people who are accepting me, and we often have tea together and get along very well. So you shouldn't have a bad conscience."

A person's conscience, it seems, should be dictated by other people. If others do not feel guilty about something, why should I? And by clear implication: if others condemn something, who am I not to do so? I do not think any remark Speer made during the course of our conversation evoked more hauntingly the shadows of Nazi Germany than this one.

I had asked Speer the question about interviewing him because I thought it might reveal something about his capacity for empathic thinking. It seems notable that he could not phrase his reply in the first person, which was what my question had invited him to do. After I told him that I did not have a bad conscience about speaking to him he went on to say:

> I understand that you have to overcome some inner hesitation, or some inner wall, to come and sit down with me at a table. You are right to have this inner wall because of what happened to your family and what happened to you. That gives you the right not only to see this wall but to say, "What shall I do with it?," to say, "I don't want to see his face, I don't want to have any word with him."

Unlike in the first half of his reply, Speer made an effort to be empathic and eventually managed to paraphrase in the first person what he supposed might be my feelings about speaking with him. He was able to recognize that I might feel some loathing for him. Nevertheless, even in this setting his egotism managed to surface—as it were, on my behalf—and it did so in a most inappropriate setting. If he were me, he would have that inner wall about speaking to Albert Speer because of what had happened *to me and my family* during the Nazi period. The possibility that I might have these feelings out of revulsion for what the Nazis represented and the terrible calamities they inflicted on millions of people evidently escaped his attention. If my family had gone unscathed, I would have no grounds for loathing the Nazis.

Speer was quite anxious to have me believe that his attachment to the Third Reich had been "neutralized" for him the moment he learned of Hitler's suicide. I found this altogether plausible. Throughout our conversation he had shown little by way of emotion, except where his own egotistical gratifications were concerned. He did not *feel* guilt, but only spoke of it. This was a man, it seemed to me, who could neutralize anything because his feelings about almost everything were neutral. He could cut himself off from the past because the ties which had bound him to it then had always been tenuous. The moment Hitler was out of sight, he would have become, for Speer, out of mind, too.

A series of simple questions amplified this view of him as lacking, to a startling degree, a capacity for experiencing emotions. To the first question, "What do you enjoy?," he gave a conventional enough reply, which was, however, delivered in such a flat tone as to make it seem a rote response. He said that he enjoyed his grandchildren—"of course"—going for hikes in the mountains, and looking at nature. He added that he also enjoyed solitude—a legacy, he explained, from his prison experience.

He seemed quite thrown by my next question, however: "What do you admire?" He thought about that for a long time and finally said, "I have not so much admiration, I must say. Obviously - and strangely enough - I don't admire very much." He could not even remember the admiration he had professed a short while earlier for Mies van der Rohe.

When I asked him what frightened him, he answered, "The world situation, of course." By this, he explained, he meant the way that technology was progressing. He had warned of its danger long before Herbert Marcuse had, he told me, but he did not know how they could be averted. "I don't know any way out," he said. "I think the world is going to pieces."

I asked him what his feelings about this were. Did he, perhaps, feel depressed by his foreknowledge of the world's demise? "No," he replied, "I am not a type who is easily depressed.... I believe in destiny, that destiny is in some ways God's will... and I am not so egotistical as to believe that this world is something which is so important to the whole universe."

Even his belief that the world is doomed, then, seemed unable to move Speer to any kind of emotional expression beyond gratification that he perceived the dangers of technology before Marcuse. In place of affect he offered only tritely "philosophizing" remarks about destiny.

Speer told me he was sensitive to the charge that he was an

opportunist, though he said he can understand why it was made: "'Is Speer for real?' some people ask. 'His answers are too perfect, they fit in too well with our line.'" "Of course that kind of comment hurts me." He defended himself against these suspicions in a characteristically heavy handed fashion:

> After 20 years in prison I was, from a legal point of view, a free man, and I could have told everybody not to bother me. But it is quite obvious that I don't feel that with those 20 years everything is now cleared. I try to compensate by warning about the Neo-Nazis, which is not without danger, and I am glad about this since nobody can say it is opportunism because, as you may believe, I get very harsh letters.

This, and indeed almost all Speer's remarks, seem very far removed from being "too perfect." Speer emerged from this interview as a man of remarkable moral and emotional shallowness. He seemed to understand the bad luck which befell him after the war as a result of the magical power which Hitler had exercised over him, rather than as a punishment for deeds for which he himself was responsible. To him, the theory of Hitler's magic seemed proven by the fact that he lost all feelings of being connected to the Third Reich the moment he learned of Hitler's suicide. He failed to recognize in his sudden disenchantment with nazism the flimsiness of the emotional ties which bound him to Hitler and which, indeed, probably characterize all his attachments.

Speer was not activated by any authentic moral anguish but merely by the pretense of remorse which—in part because of the crudity of his moral reasoning—he believed was genuine. He regreted the past primarily because of the misfortunes which it brought him. He found in it the one sensation that could give him genuine satisfaction—pride in his accomplishments. For the rest, he coped with the monumental crimes of his past simply by ignoring them.

His pride in his accomplishments was well served by his success in "neutralizing," as he put it, his ties to Hitler and the Third Reich. It was this pride, I suspect, which also prompted him to play the role of penitent to which he was committed before his death. He himself seemed to have recognized and then, characteristically, to have dismissed this insight when he wrote in his prison diary, in a reflection of his confession of guilt at the Nuremberg trial, "It seems to me that . . . I am only maneuvering myself into the old position of leadership—wanting to be first even as a penitent."

His level of intellectual functioning in this role as penitent was so low, however, that he was unable to answer questions in a fashion consistent with his pretensions, or even with an elementary sense of tact. Certainly, he failed to do so in the replies he gave to me. In part, I suspect this was because he was so self-absorbed that he could not even mobilize his opportunism to reach more than a superficial understanding of what made other people tick. And I suspect that part of the reason for this, in turn, was that his understanding and experiencing of himself were too limited to help him in reaching an understanding of others.

Not every aspect of our analysis of Speer's 1945 Rorschach was borne out by this interview, and given the relatively short time (two hours) that Speer made available to me, that is only to be expected. Enough *did* emerge, however, to confirm the basic features of the personality that Florence Miale and I had discerned in the Rorschach. We overstated, I believe, only the extent of Speer's ability to assume some measure of responsibility for his own shortcomings: and even so, we had rated that ability as rather low. His capacity for occasional and involuntary flashes of insight into himself seems, as we had initially believed, incapable of providing the basis for authentic growth; indeed, that capacity was suggested only on one occasion during the interview.

In the prison diary, Speer had commented on how "monotonous and empty" the buildings he had designed for Hitler came to be to him. Reminding him of this, I asked whether he thought his buildings were in any sense a metaphor of his own personality. The question agitated him and he replied, "Well now, don't take entries in a diary as a definite opinion! I don't condemn my children, they are a part of me and I don't want to say that they are demented!".

Of course Speer did not want to say that his buildings were demented. But then, I had not asked him to say that, and in fact I had not used that term or anything close to it. It would seem, though, that close to his unconscious mind, and fairly accessible to it, Speer experienced himself as a somewhat demented man.

A person's earliest memory often reflects the course of his life and the structure of his personality. Speer's earliest memory offered an astonishingly apt metaphor of a man whose barren childhood (he told me that he was neither punished nor shown affection by his parents) helped fashion a dessicated personality and who, in a compensatory quest for liveliness, plumeted his life on a giddy, sensational, and most unnatural course:

> In 1911 when I was six, there was a long drought. We lived in Mannheim, but we had a summer house in Heidelberg—my father was very well off—and we were there. The house had a lawn which was dried brown because of the drought. The slope of the lawn was very steep and we sleighed down it, which was a sensational thing to do in the summer.

It was this quest, rather than Hitler's allegedly irresistible will, which made Speer a Nazi. He was able to recognize some of this himself. Ruminating in his Spandau prison cell in 1949 he wrote, "Since Nuremberg I have convinced myself of this concept of Hitler as the great seducer. But was he really that? Did he lead me away from myself.... Might it be more accurate to say that he actually led me to myself?" And in January 1964, he wondered whether Hitler really was "the great destructive force in my life." It seemed to him, rather, that he owed to Hitler the "vitality, dynamism and imagination" which he had experienced during the great days of the Third Reich.

Footnotes

1. Stanley Milgram, *Obedience to Authority* (New York, 1974), pp. 129–30. 205; cf. p. 5ff.
2. Hannah Arendt, *Eichmann in Jerusalem* (New York, 1964), p. 26, argues, in defense of her claim that Eichmann's personality was a "normal" one, that "half a dozen psychiatrists" had examined Eichmann and "certified him as 'normal'." In fact, only one psychiatrist,

I. S. Kulcsar, had examined Eichmann, and he considered Eichmann to be a highly deviant personality. For his part, Milgram has been less than forthright in dealing with control studies of his subjects which indicate a correlation between their behavior and their performance on, e.g., Kohlberg's moral development scale. Cf. Florence R. Miale and Michael Selzer, *The Nuremberg Mind* (New York, 1975), p. 12.

3. Principally in *The Nuremberg Mind,* op.cit., and "The Murderous Mind: A First Look at the Psychological Drawings of Adolf Eichmann," *New York Times Magazine,* November 27, 1977.

4. *Nuremberg Mind,* op.cit., pp. 254–267.

5. "I feel strangely moved by the idea that the most successful architectural creation of my life is a chimera", Albert Speer, *Spandau, The Secret Diaries* (New York: Macmillan, 1976), p. 428. See also references in my review of this book "Albert Speer, The Great Time-Server?", *The Nation,* March 22, 1976, pp. 45–46.

Chapter 10

THE GUYANA INCIDENT

Some Group Dynamic Considerations

Hugo J. Zee

Whereas much has been written about James Warren Jones' leadership role in bringing about the Jonestown, Guyana, tragedy, relatively little has been said about the active participation by his followers in this event. All that occurred in Guyana could not have happened without the active cooperation of Jones' followers. Who were these people? What were they like? How did they contribute to the tragedy? Little has been documented about individual members since 60 percent of the bodies were never claimed by anyone, and the government's effort to identify the bodies was initially delayed, resulting in one-fourth never being identified (Wooden, 1980). Many were apparently in a state of unresolved separation from their families, and the impression is that a sizable number of them were people who were disillusioned with themselves and with society. More than half of Jones' followers were in a transitional phase of life, concerned with belonging and with the identity struggles that accompany such a phase: more than 25 percent were over sixty years old, and a similar percentage were under the age of consent. While professing to be interracial, the core group was primarily white, while the membership at large was black.

Margaret Thaler Singer (1978), who studied cults, found that "About one-third are very psychologically distressed people. The other two-thirds are relatively average people, but in a period of depression, gloom, being at loose ends" (p. 27). Galanter (1980) reports a similarly high percentage (39 percent) in his study of membership in a religious sect. No doubt among the one-third who were "very psychologically distressed" were a large number of individuals suffering from borderline personality disorder—lonesome people who have a marked degree of identity confusion, who are prone to see their difficulties as emanating from outside themselves, and who rely heavily on the pleasure principle in their dealings with reality. For them, the People's Temple provided meaning by offering multiple outlets for their poorly integrated needs within the framework of working toward a vague utopian goal. The coercive means employed by Jones fit with their primitive internalized object relations: they could idealize their leader who would see to it that their aggression would be directed toward the "bad" world outside, would be vented in sadomasochistic purification rituals within the group, or would be applied to the cause. No longer did they need to feel confused; by mere submission they could feel needed. Dialogue was used more for discharge and for rationalizing a skewed view of events than for thoughtful reflection and problem solving; inconsistencies were explained away with platitudes, denial, or projection. As the group became more isolated from the surrounding world, its sense of uniqueness provided a major counterbalance to the life of emptiness and boredom that group members had experienced before. The development of stable interpersonal bonds, so difficult for individuals with borderline personalities to maintain, was discouraged in favor of more fluid bonds to the group at large, permitting unstable object relationships which cause less acute anxiety. Jones' regressive cult employed many of the coping devices used by borderline individuals—splitting, denial, primitive idealization, devaluation, projection, projective identification—devices that hinder further development, akin to Bion's (1961) basic assumption groups. Indeed, such individuals would have what Bion calls valency, i.e., a capacity for instantaneous joining in with others in sharing and acting on a basic assumption.

This one-third of the People's Temple membership could have provided the "critical mass" that maintained the group's pathological momentum. It is not known how many "very psychologically distressed" cult members were also members of the "planning committee" and the "angels," Jones' most loyal followers. However, since a narcissistic person such as Jones (Zee, 1980) often relates to others as part objects, and because a narcissistic person's choice of close associates tends to be based on such aspects as appearances, momentary needs, or attributes that reflect well on himself, Jones most likely was a poor judge of character, and thus surrounded himself with people whose commitments and values were shallow or one-sided.

Indeed, a second level of leadership, which could have been a stabilizing force and which could have assumed leadership in times of crisis, was not allowed to emerge from among the members. In fact, some who did emerge as leaders soon found themselves in disfavor. As a result, the group became extremely dependent on Jones, who eagerly reciprocated because of his own need for idealization. Hope in future leaders was discouraged; beyond Jones there was to be no hope. Narcissistic leaders such as Jones characteristically curry favor with the underprivileged with whom they sense a common bond and from whom they experience no threat. However, those who rise up from the ranks are seen as rivals and soon find themselves undercut.

The more "average" cult members may have been swept into the People's Temple at a time when they were depressed, and thus vulnerable to the cult's "love bombing" recruiting efforts and various pressure tactics such as praise for solidarity and ostracism for doubting. But when did these "average" members begin to feel they had reached the point of no return? Was it after being converted by the high-pressure appeals? Was it after making major sacrifices of money, belongings, and property to the cult? Was it after severing ties with close friends and family? Was if after giving up their children, after moving to Guyana, or after turning over their passports? Or was it after engaging in some sexual or aggressive taboos? For many, even as physically and financially depleted and as enraged and guilt ridden as they were, leaving the cult to start a new life seemed too painful a reality to face.

Freud (1921) described the impulsive and unreflective behavior of crowds in which individuals easily achieve a sense of closeness with one another by projecting their ego ideals onto the leader, resulting in their mutual identification with him. Turquet (1975) describes how in large unstructured groups or crowds, face-to-face contact is poor, the feedback an individual receives from his communications is almost nonexistent, self-assertions are attacked, and the person's sense of significance or impact is markedly reduced. In addition, in large groups traditional roles and bonds (of marriage, family, friends, neighbors, vocation) have less chance to manifest themselves and easily are disrupted. Having thus lost their moorings, individuals suffer severe identity diffusion and fear the eruption of primitive aggression. Feeling helpless, individuals may either withdraw and experience ostracism or may search for a commonality with others. Indeed, the crowd will eagerly seek unity through homogenization of its members and will accept (become a missionary of) simplisitic generalizations or cliches as absolute truth, while the idealization of the leader preserves a sense of identity via mutual, group-side identification. The individual's helplessness dissolves in the pleasure of his dependence upon an idealized leader—everyone becomes a missionary for the now unassailable ideas.

With the leader thus idealized, the members are freed from moral constraints and from the need to be critical and responsible, setting the stage for a more maladaptive, self-consuming regressive group process. Critical superego functioning, especially its discerning, evaluating, reality-testing functions, are sacrificed in favor of more personalized primitive, sadomasochistic, denouncing, and idealizing superego forerunners. A fanatic attitude now may emerge, one in which reality is replaced by a spellbinding idea (Kernberg, 1980).

Such defense mechanisms as splitting and projective identification become more prevalent (Bion, 1961; Kernberg, 1975). As the followers feel relieved of responsibility, more primitive wishes and needs may emerge, which encourage the leader to further his own ends. Thus, the leadership is subjected to considerable projective identification not only of superego elements, as Freud suggested, but also of primitive object relationships and superego forerunners. The sense of mutual identification existing between group members and their leader may or may not be conscious; that is, after attributing a disavowed aspect of the self to the leader, the member maintains an unconscious relationship so he can vicariously experience that which he repudiates in himself. Often what appears to come from the leader is in actuality an expression, via projective identification, of the group's suppressed wishes. The leader may even become an "automaton" of the group. Such collusion between the leader and his group is common. For example, Jones' favored status within his cult went well beyond the functional needs of his position. He got choice foods, enjoyed special fineries, had mistresses, dwelled in air conditioned comfort, lived in the best quarters, was beyond criticism—all in sharp contrast to his followers' life style. The leader's enjoyment of a special status has been observed with such regularity among cults that it cannot simply be ascribed to the leader's narcissism, but must represent a collusion that meets a number of members' needs, e.g., to gain favor, to atone for guilt, vicarious pleasure. Likewise, the tendency to lay sole blame for the mass suicide on Jones, as if he were a mass murderer, should be seriously questioned. In Bion's (1961) terms, Jones became the basic assumption leader of primitive group behavior par excellence. He responded to their dependency pleas by offering love and faith as well as forgiveness and punishment; he became their fight-flight leader who identified and mobilized them against their "enemy"; and by giving them hope of delivery from despair and fear, however folly the terms, he became their pairing leader.

An extreme example of the fanatic attitude is found in the so-called "white-night" rituals—the ultimate loyalty test in which all members of the cult, children and adults, were to drink in sacramental fashion an allegedly poisonous drink in a weird parody of the communion rite. Jones would eventually tell them that this was merely a test of loyalty and that the drink would not kill them—but not until he had watched their agony which was sometimes augmented by some contrived displays of screams, convulsions, or cowardice. These ceremonies had their first beginnings in the early 1970's when they were still in San Francisco, but became more frequent and elaborate in the year and a half they were in Guyana (Kilauff & Javers, 1978).

The abject submission by the members to this ritual represented a bribe for some kind of magic gesture (acceptance, forgiveness, healing, security, a favor, a blessing) from their leader; while to Jones it gave vent to his sadistic tendencies in the service of controlling his now projected, vengeance-seeking superego. Later, their sense of purpose and belonging was enhanced by rituals more of a fight-flight variety, i.e., his followers were called on an emergency basis because some vaguely described "enemy" was closing in on them. Drinking the quasi-poisonous liquid now was a pledge of their willingness to die for their socialistic cause. Finally, death was seen as a delivery from unfair persecution. The white-night ritual now became the "white knight," the deliverer—death would not be final, but could be a bridge to "the other side," to the good object. By now, reality was no longer being served, an ideology had taken its place.

Freud (1921) saw in the idealization of the leader an enactment of the "myth of the hero," where the youngest son kills the father, thus becoming the idealized hero of the oppressed siblings, who identify with his deed and share in celebrating the patricide without having to acknowledge their guilt. However, in the idealization of the hero is a remnant of the idealization of the Oedipal father, whose feared reprisal must be appeased and whose blessing must be sought. But in a severely regressed and closed group, such as the People's Temple, where reinstatement of the vanquished father is deficient because of extreme envy, any potential challenger—real or imagined, person or thing—is feared not as a justice-seeking father, which would cause severe neurotic anxiety requiring atonement, but rather as a more destructive, arbitrary, unforgiving enemy, resulting in annihilatory psychotic anxiety. The members of the People's Temple, terrified by such things as an inquiry into their faith-healing practices and a documentary magazine article about their sect, reacted by suppressing disagreement, instituting loyalty rituals, and projecting the "danger" onto either suspected members or the outside. This regressed group attempted to mollify or fight their enemy by offering bribes and votes; they then took flight to Guyana; and finally, lacking the reparative faith to restore its damaged objects, the group resorted to suicide. Survival seemed at stake. Now lower-level paranoid-schizoid defenses (projection, projective identification, splitting, idealization, and devaluation) prevailed over higher-level defensive operations (repression, reaction formation, sublimation, etc.).

To a point, Jones fit Freud's image of the hero well (Kilauff & Javers, 1978). Jones, who had rejected his own father, had his followers call him "Father," and he adopted an assortment of orphaned children to enhance this image. In addition, he became the champion of the oppressed against racial prejudice, the Ku Klux Klan, poverty, capitalism, and vaguely described official authorities. To broaden his sphere of influence (but also to placate persecutory anxiety), Jones used his followers to help elect politicians and used their money to make donations to liberal causes. His followers were not only the immediate beneficiaries of his apparent good deeds, but they also shared in the public honors Jones received in the group's name. However, after political, religious, and community leaders paid their respects by visiting the People's Temple, Jones often entertained his congregation by mocking these dignitaries, thus shifting his followers' feelings of being honored by these Oedipal figures to feelings of triumph over them. Instead of feeling atoned, Jones and his followers became partners in the devaluation process and they undermined the good that came from superego supports. Thus was vented a latent but powerful envious rage against superego values and the people who stood for them—an envy which in part had been aggravated by the severe deprivation and alienation many had suffered. On the other hand, their idealized group seemed to offer immediate gratification, but such idealization was rendered shrill since it was not tempered by reality—external reality was simply devalued.

Since their own leadership lacked the stamina and resilience to contain and work out such rage among themselves, it was instead deflected outside the group where, unfortunately, it had less chance to be met and tested out. As the group closed itself off from the external world, reality as a corrective force on fantasy was not adequately engaged. Instead, the external world became a target for their projected distortions and began to appear more as a life-threatening enemy. As the cult became a closed system, psychotic phenomena began to flourish and became the order of the day.

Functioning at such an archaic, paranoid-schizoid level, it is not surprising to read of the cult members turning over their personal belongings to the Temple, thereby removing any doubt of loyalty and the consequence that might bring; that corrupt healing practices were blindly accepted as magic or rationalized as a means to their end; that inquiries and dialogue turned into interrogations and terrifying purification events; that they became participants in severe and arbitrary punishments for behavior that was loosely interpreted as lustful, perverted, lazy, or treacherous to the cause. Parents abdicated their role with their children and turned them over to the cult to be cared for, educated, and chastised. Parents even condoned brutal forms of punishment for rather typical childish offenses, such as submerging them in a dark well; or applying electrodes to shock them; or frightening them with snakes; and beating them with "the board of education"—until they had pleaded sufficiently and gratefully to "Father" for mercy. When the sect moved to Guyana, the children were among the first to go, much to the surprise of the parents who were caught off guard (Wooden, 1981).

The extent and persistence of this regressive sequence (most regressive large group phenomena are transitory) make one pause, for it is not easily explained. "You can fool some people all the time; all people some of the time; but you can't fool all people all the time." Most of the People's Temple's dubious practices existed long before their move to Guyana in the summer of 1977, when there was ample opportunity to get an outsider's perspective or to join a less extreme congregation. Even though some members defected and expressed alarm, by and large the group stayed intact then, of its own volition. Membership was more by persuasion than by coercion (which became a factor after a considerable investment into the group had been made). The situation brings to mind Goffman's (1961) "total institution" or the techniques described in brainwashing, i.e., the isolation from the outside world; making the members totally dependent on the central authority which controls privileges, uses threats or physical abuse, removes features of self-identification; and spending endless time and effort in rationalizing and demonstrating acceptance of the ideology, while discouraging deviance, privacy, outside interests. But the participants of the People's Temple were at the outset not unwilling captives—not until the last year and a half were alternative options closed to them. Why were they willing participants to such an extent?

One possible reason is that this group was composed of a large number of chronically alienated people. This impression is dramatically conveyed by the fact that so many of the bodies remained unclaimed by friends or relatives, and that so many followers were in a transitional phase of life—two-thirds making up the very young or the very old. Recent studies of converts to cults (see Ungerleider & Wellisch, 1979; Galanter, 1980; Shaver, Lenauer, & Sadd, 1980) reflect such alienation as compared to nonconverts in terms of weaker ties to outsiders, hostile feelings towards parents and authorities, a lonelier childhood. Like Singer (1978), a significantly high percentage of emotional disorders was reported—heavy substance abuse particularly being mentioned.

An additional source of alienation falls in the area of sociology. Recent technological breakthroughs have caused enormous shifts in established concepts and values. They have affected the very foundations of society, i.e., religion, the expectations of attainment of ideals, the family, sexual identity and role, right and wrong and justice, attitudes about the worth of life, property, tradition, and nature, the concept of evil, and so forth. As such values and concepts have become more relative, those who are deficient in them, i.e., poorly internalized object relations, suffer even more alienation due to the lack of unambigious superego nutriments with which to interact.

For such a population, the cult may offer a special relationship akin to Winnicott's (1953) transitional phenomenon in which one's intrapsychic wishes are blended with the external reality, creating a more personal, familiar, though illusionary intermediate experience. Such a transitional experience in which one establishes an "as if" sense of familiarity with the surroundings is a ubiquitous phenomenon in well-adapted people of all ages. However, for the more alienated person it becomes a much more rigid mode of relating, and the shifting between a subjectively imbued reality and objectivity is more difficult.

Winnicott (1953) describes the transitional phenomenon as follows:

> It is assumed that the task of reality acceptance is never completed, that no human being is free from the strain of relating inner and outer reality and that relief from this strain is provided by an intermediate area of experience which is not challenged (arts, religion, etc.). This intermediate area is in direct continuity with the play area of the small child who is "lost" in play.

Horton, Lowry, and Coppolillo (1974) further elaborate:

> The ability to personalize and to make an external object internally meaningful—is a developmental milestone. It takes its origin, in part, from the time a child is able to imbue a toy or other concrete object with the life he feels stirring inside of himself.... With further growth and development the object itself becomes less important in that almost any object or institution can be taken to a greater or lesser degree into the transitional area of experience.

One may assume that chronically alienated people in particular have difficulties in relating their inner and outer reality and that relief from this strain could be provided by the kind of intermediate experiences which a cult might offer. The People's Temple cult actively invited and evoked personalized relationships, thus restoring and reinforcing the illusion of intimate familiarity—the cult as the new family offering a father and mother of archetypal proportions, a fellowship of "brothers" and "sisters," an outlook on life of childlike simplicity, and providing a never-ending supply of supports—a home base—that makes one feel cared for, and so forth. Unlike more integrated and well-adapted individuals who use this mode of relating only transitionally, the chronically alienated person has a constant need, is fixated to such an illusionary mode of relating lest he become anxious, enraged, and even chaotically impulsive. Modell (1976) describes such behavior for borderline patients in the therapeutic relationship. When such a soothing relationship is challenged by the inevitable frustrations of psychotherapy, parameters may be called for as the treatment may become chaotic due to the patient's erratic, impulsive, and ragelike behavior. Although borderline patients have great difficulty shifting between the "intermediate mode" and external reality, they are not unique in this and people will vary in the degree of rigidity.

A narcissistic leader such as Jones (Zee, 1980) is particularly drawn to such a group of alienated individuals. Having suffered from excessive empathic failure and feeling exploited, he feels a common bond with the "downtrodden" and can tune in and play into their wish for a savior. His cynicism and extreme envy have stood in the way of his superego development, leaving him with excessive grandiosity. Kernberg (1975) states that the narcissist suffers from a pathological fusion of the real self, the ideal self, and the ideal object, i.e., there is a blurring of ego and superego functions. As a result, the narcissist is less apt to strive towards the ideal as he experiences himself to be (fused with) the ideal. In that respect, his grandiose fantasy will thrive on the applause, the idealization, and the submission the group is willing to give for fulfilling their role for them.

The cult as the "new family" can only have its maximum effect if the family of origin, always a barrier against excessive group influences, is broken down. This fits well with Freud's concept of the group's myth of the patricidal hero. In the same paper he added the following footnote:

> Two people coming together for the purpose of sexual satisfaction, in so far as they seek for solitude, are making a demonstration against the herd instinct, the group feeling. The more they are in love, the more completely they suffice for each other. Their rejection of the group's influence is expressed in the shape of a sense of shame. Feelings of jealously of the most extreme violence are summoned up in order to protect the choice of a sexual object from being encroached upon by a group tie. It is only when the affectionate, that is, personal factor of a love relation gives place entirely to the sensual one, that it is possible for two people to have sexual intercourse in the presence of others or for there to be simultaneous sexual acts in a group, as occurs at an orgy. But at that point a regression has taken place to an early stage in sexual relations, at which being in love as yet played no part and all sexual objects were judged to be of

equal value, somewhat in the sense of Bernard Shaw's malicious aphorism to the effect that being in love means greatly exaggerating the difference between one woman and another. (p. 140)

In the People's Temple cult marital bonds were actively discouraged Jones appointed a marriage committee that attempted to regulate courtship, marriage, and intercourse. Couples were told to change partners. Extramarital liaisons were ecouraged. The living quarters discouraged privacy. Children were to call their parents by their first names; only Jones and his wife were to be called father and mother. Family members were encouraged to spy on one another. In many of his 6-hour sermons, Jones dwelled on sex. He forced others to concede his heterosexual supremacy and insisted that all cult members confess their homosexuality. As the group's influence grew, mature personal relationships not only were destroyed but were replaced with the kind of primitive, part-object, poorly differentiated, polymorphous, impersonal relationships more characteristic of psychotic patients.

The mass suicide in Guyana may never be fully explained, but a number of features stand out. Foremost is the baffling influence of group dynamics on the cult members' reality testing, yet history is replete with examples of how the wish for concurrence with others replaces the ability to think critically. The well-known Milgram experiments (Meyer, 1974) indicated that people would willingly and actively participate, on behalf of a vaguely known authority, in a procedure that seemingly threatened someone else's life. Janis' (1974) examples of "groupthink" at high governmental levels serve as another reminder of our vulnerability to concurring, even if that means sacrificing our unique insights. It could be said that one's ability to make a creative impact and to keep a sense of efficacy, especially in groups where envy can be strong, takes considerable courage—it may for many be preferable to concur rather than be real and alone. Reality testing does require a capacity for grieving and tolerating the painful awareness of the shortcomings of their ideology. But the cult had long since abandoned work towards developing such a capacity of self-awareness.

References

Bion, W. R. *Experiences in group and other papers.* New York: Basic Books, 1961.

Freud, S. (1921). *Group psychology and the analysis of the ego.* Standard Edition 1955, *18*: 69–143.

Galanter, M. Psychological induction into the large group: Findings from a modern religious sect. *American Journal of Psychiatry,* 1980, *137* (12): 1574–79.

Goffman, E. *Asylums. Essays on the social situation of mental patients and other inmates.* Chicago: Aldine Publishing Co., 1961.

Horton, P. W., Lowry, J. W., & Coppolillo, H. P. Personality disorder and transitional relatedness. *Archives of General Psychiatry,* 1974, *30* (5):618–27.

Janis, I. Groupthink. In R. A. Miner (Ed.), *Annual editions: Readings in psychology.* Guilford, Conn.: Dushkin Publishing Group, 1974, 283–288.

Kernberg, O. F. *Borderline conditions and pathological narcissism.* New York: Jason Aronson, 1975.

———. *Internal world and external reality.* New York: Jason Aronson, 1980.

Kilauff, M., & Javers, R. *The suicide cult: The inside story of the People's Temple Sect and the massacre in Guyana.* New York: Bantam Books, 1978.

Meyer, P. If Hitler asked you to electrocute a stranger, would you? Probably. In R. A. Miner (Ed.), *Annual editions: Readings in psychology.* Guilford, Conn.: Dushkin Publishing Group, 1974, 273–279.

Modell, A. H. The holding environment and the therapeutic action of psychoanalysis. *Journal of the American Psychoanalytic Association.* *24*: 285–308, 1976.

Singer, M. T. Quoted in Why people join. Time Magazine 112, *23*: 27, 1978.

Shaver, P., Lenauer, M., & Sadd, S. Religiousness, conversion, and subjective well-being: The "healthy minded" religion of modern American woman. *American Journal of Psychiatry,* 1980, *137* (12): 1563–68.

Turquet, P. Threats to identity in the large group. In L. Kreeger (Ed.), *The large group: Dynamics and therapy,* London: Constable, 1975, 87–144.

Ungerleider, J. T., & Wellisch, D. K. Coercive persuasion (brainwashing), religious cults, and deprogramming. *American Journal of Psychiatry,* 1979, *136* (3): 279–282.

Winnicott, D. W. Transitional objects and transitional phenomena, *International Journal of Psychoanalysis,* 1953, *34*: 89–97.

Wooden, K. *The children of Jonestown.* McGraw-Hill, New York, 1980.

Zee, H. J. The Guyana incident—Some psychoanalytic considerations. *Bulletin of the Menninger Clinic,* 1980, *44*, (4): 345–363.

EPILOGUE

Max Rosenbaum

In a recent study, two Swedish scholars reported on their study of a cooperative village founded in 1968 by a yogi leader in an inland region of California. They concluded that the "... psychological reason for staying on may be that the commune provides a psychosocial environment that allows for a continued inward search at the same time that it offers prescriptions and a set of interrelated ideological beliefs that can be put to practice in daily life . . ." (Rosen & Nordquist, 1980). There is apparently a synthesis of religion and psychotherapy in what these people are looking for—a search which many people are engaged in. This search has been noted by other writers. (Berger, 1970, Cox, 1977, Rigby, 1974, Robbins, et al., 1978). This search for inner peace *may* be the answer as to why people comply. The following is from the *New York Times*, January 10, 1981:

DAUGHTER OF A JONESTOWN VICTIM IS FOLLOWER OF INDIA CULT LEADER
  Los Angeles, Jan. 10 (UPI)—The 28-year-old daughter of Representative Leo J. Ryan, the California Democrat who was killed in Jonestown, Guyana, two years ago by members

of the People's Temple cult, has become a devoted follower of India's most controversial cult leader. But the Congressman's daughter, Shannon Jo Ryan, was quoted as saying in a Los Angeles Times article published recently that she saw no irony in her allegiance to Bhagwan Sheree Rajneesh, at whose retreat in Poona, India, she had been living.

REFERENCES

Berger, P. *A rumor of angels.* New York: Doubleday, 1970.
Cox, H. *Turning East.* New York: Simon and Schuster, 1977.
New York Times, *Daughter of a Jonestown victim is follower of India cult leader.* January 10, 1981.
Rigby, A. *Alternative realities.* London: Routledge & Kegan Paul, 1974.
———*Communes in Britain.* London: Routledge & Kegan Paul, 1974.
Robbins, T., Anthony, D., & Richardson, J. T. Theory and research on today's "new religions." *Sociological Analysis*, 1978, *39*: 95–122.
Rosen, A-S., & Nordquist, T. A. Ego developmental level and values in a yogic community. *Journal of Personality and Social Psychology*, 1980, *39*: 1152–1160.

NAME INDEX

Abse, D. W., 156
Addey, D., 195
Agnew, Spiro T., 206
Ajzen, I., 66
Alexander, F. G., 196
Allen, V. L., 162
Allport, G. W., 132
Amalrik, Andrea, 82
Applebaum, S. A., 143
Arendt, Hannah, 12, 13, 14, 15, 33, 35, 36, 40, 227
Aristotle, 45, 46, 47
Aronfreed, J., 133
Asch, Solomon, 44, 45
Aubin, N., 163, 170, 176

Back, Kurt, 18
Baker, G., 108
Balint, M., 102
Bally, G., 101
Barker, E. C. H., 174
Barnes, R. D., 18
Barnett, S. A., 96
Baroja, J. C., 112, 165
Barthes, Roland, 59
Basaglia, E., 99
Baskin, W., 177
Battegay, Raymond, 18

Becker, E., 16
Becker, H. S., 187
Bellah, R. N., 108, 109
Benedetti, G., 94
Berger, P., 243
de Bergerac, C., 167
Berne, Eric L., 39
Bettelheim, Bruno, 80
Bhagwan Sheree Rajneesh, 244
Biddis, M. D., 154
Biderman, A. D., 174
Biddle, B. J., 162
Bion, W. R., 230, 232, 233
Blumer, H., 70
Bodin, J., 157
Boguet, H., 150, 157
Borkin, Joseph, 16
Bourguignon, Erika, 113
Boyd, J. W., 195, 196
Boyer, P., 176, 197
Brattle, T., 151
Braun, Joseph, 13
Brehm, J. W., 68
Brown, P., 157
Breuer, J., 155
Buber, Martin, 140
Buhrich, N., 156
Burr, G. L., 164

246 NAME INDEX

Calef, R., 165, 175
Calley, Lt. William, 21
Calvin, John, 188
Campbell, J., 54
Cartwright, F. F., 154
Catherinet, F. M., 150, 152
Caufield, Jack, 207, 208
Caulfield, E., 155
Cesbron, H., 155
Charcot, J. M., 155, 157, 181, 182
Charpentier, J., 96
Chodoff, P., 156
Chotiner, Murray, 207
Christian, J. J., 96
Clive, J., 58
Cohen, A. R., 68
Cohn, N., 56, 185
Colson, Charles, 208
Comstock, C., 134
Considine, D. M., 138
Cooley, Charles, 39
Coppolillo, H. P., 238
Coutler, J., 161, 184
Cox, H., 243
Cox, R. H., 117
Crawford, T. J., 65
Crespi, I., 66
Curran, C. E., 41
Cutten, G. B., 184

Dean, John, 206–212
Delay, J., 99
Demos, J., 155, 158, 159, 160
Deniker, P., 99
Dicks, H. V., 184
Diethelm, O., 181
Dietrich, SS General Josef, 15
Dillenberger, John, 108, 109
Dubreuil, D., 195
Dukor, B., 91
Durkheim, E., 81, 99

Eibl-Eibesfeldt, I., 86
Eichmann, Adolph, 16, 21, 33, 34, 35, 36, 227–228
Einstein, Albert, 43
Elias, Norbert, 74
Ellenberger, H., 112, 182, 198
Erlichman, John, 207, 208, 211
Esquirol, J. E. D., 157, 180

Fenichel, O., 156
Fest, Joachim, 218

Festinger, L., 67
Fishbein, M., 66
Ford, Henry, 12
Frank, J., 69
Franks, C., 160
Fromm, Eric, 42, 95, 96
Freud, Sigmund, 20, 37, 40, 42, 87, 89, 99, 108, 155, 158, 232, 239

Gaar, Georgius, 181
Gaster, T. H., 195
Gergen, K. J., 19
Gilbert, G. M., 215
Glanvill, J., 152, 170
Glock, C. Y., 108, 114, 124
Grinker, R. R., 143
Galanter, M., 230
Glazer, M. W., 143
Goffman, E., 162, 236
Golding, P., 195
Gottlieb, J., 162, 166, 175, 195
Grandier, Urban, 176
Guazzo, F. M., 151, 152
Guillain, C. J. M., 182
Guthrie, W. K., 60
Guze, S. B., 156

Haldeman, Robert, 208, 209, 210, 211
Hall, J. R., 185, 186
Hall, M., 197
Hammarskjöld, D., 144
Hamon, J., 99
Hansen, C., 155, 184
Häring, Bernard, 141
Harlow, H. S., 94
Harlow, M. K., 94
Harris, B., 18
Harris, V. A., 183
Harsnett, Samuel, 162, 163, 167, 170, 172, 173, 174, 179, 180, 196
Harvey, D. J., 19
Harvey, J. H., 18, 19
Hawthorne, Nathaniel, 68
Hearst, Patricia, 154
Heider, F., 20
Henle, M., 43, 44
Henry, G. W., 155, 196
Heschel, Rabbi A. J., 139
Hess, Rudolph, 17
Hess, W. R., 96
Hewitt, E. C., 184

NAME INDEX 247

Hilgard, E. R., 163
Hill, D. G., 125
Himmler, Henrich, 15
Hinson, E. G., 184
Hitler, Adolf, 13, 14, 15, 17, 26, 35, 37, 38, 41, 42, 213–228
Hoekema, A. A., 184
Hood, W., 19
Holcombe, W. H., 197
Hole, C., 169
Horton, P. W., 238
Hurd, G., 118
Hutchinson, T., 162, 167
Huxley, A., 164, 177

Ibsen, Henrik, 81
Ignatius of Loyola, 56
Irving, David, 15

Jacoby, G. W., 157
Janet, P., 155, 156, 157, 181, 197
Janis, I., 240
Jackson, D. D., 88
Jacobson, Edith, 132
James, William, 44
Javers, R., 186, 233
Johnson, D. P., 185, 186
Johnson, M. P., 65
Johnson, Philip, 220, 221
Jones, E. E., 71, 183, 196
Jones, Reverend Jim, 13, 17, 21, 26, 41, 101, 185
Jorden, E., 155
Joyce, James, 59
Jung, Carl, 37, 38, 102

Kanouse, D. E., 71
Kant, Immanuel, 80, 89
Kelly, H. A., 71, 157, 177, 178, 195, 196
Kelman, H. C., 21, 27, 51, 52, 63
Keniston, Kenneth, 123
Kernberg, O. F., 143, 232
Kilauff, M., 233
Kilduff, M., 186
Kilham, W., 29, 30
King, R. G., 30
Kluckhohn, Clyde, 110
Knapp, Elizabeth, 166, 175, 176
Kocher, P. H., 196
Kogon, E., 184
Kohlberg, L., 133, 228
Kohler, Wolfgang, 43, 44

Kohut, Heinz, 85, 87, 100
Kramer, H., 150, 154, 157
Krohn, A., 155, 156
Kroll, J., 196
Kulcsar, I. S., 228

Lang, Daniel, 14, 15
LaPiere, R. T., 64
Law, T. G., 168, 179
Lawrence, L. H., 21, 27
Lawson, D., 151, 165
Lazarus, A., 69
Lea, H. C., 150
Lenin, 202
Leone, M. P., 108
Leventhal, H., 108
Lewis, I. M., 170
Lewin, Kurt, 43, 47
Lewis, Sinclair, 116
Lhermitte, J., 164
Liddy, Gordon, 209
Lingeman, R., 115
Llamas, R., 118
Lowry, J. W., 238
Lyons, H., 156

Mackay, C., 47
Mandrou, R., 157, 168
Mancuso, J. C., 184
Mann, L., 29, 30
Manson, J. C., 184
Mantell, D. M., 29
Marcuse, Herbert, 224
Marie, P., 155
Marty, Martin, 111
Martyr, Justin, 178
Martines, L., 168
Marx, Karl, 202
Masters, Edgar Lee, 116
Masterson, J. F., 143
Mather, C. A., 153, 170, 180
McCasland, S. V., 150, 195
McGuire, W., 19
Mead, George Herbert, 20, 39
Meher Baba, 121, 124
Mersky, H., 156
Merton, R. K., 81, 99
Meyer, P., 240
Miale, Florence, 215, 216, 226, 228
Michalis, S., 163, 164, 170, 180
Milgram, Stanley, 18, 19, 20, 28, 29, 30, 31–34, 36, 40, 41, 45, 71, 83, 100, 214, 240
Mill, John Stuart, 25, 46, 202

248 NAME INDEX

Milosz, C., 52, 53, 68
Mischel, W., 160
Mitchell, John, 210
Mixon, D., 18
Modell, A. H., 238
Monod, Jacques, 90, 91
More, G. A., 153
Moreno, Jacob L., 39, 55
Mother Samuel, 151
Murray, M., 56

Nauman, E., 150, 165
Neaman, Judith, 113, 154
Needleman, J., 108
Neugebauer, R., 196
Nietzsche, 38
Nisbett, R., 71, 183, 187
Nissenbaum, S., 170, 197
Nixon, Richard, 206–212
Nordquist, T. A., 243
Notenstein, W. A., 169, 179

Oates, W. E., 184
O'Connor, N., 160
Oesterreich, T. K., 150, 152, 157, 159, 162, 167, 177, 178, 198
O'Faolain, J., 168
Orne, M., 19
Orwell, George, 11, 12, 59

Pande, S. K., 112
Pattison, E. M., 13, 114, 118, 119, 120, 131, 132
Perry, Ralph B., 43, 44
Piaget, Jean, 97
Pickett, R., 157
Podhoretz, N., 74
Portman, A., 104
Pruyser, P., 131

Radtke, H. L., 195
Rahner, K., 141
Richardson, J. T., 185, 186, 187
Richer, P., 155
Richter, A., 154
Rieff, Philip, 110
Riesman, D., 78
Rigby, A., 244
Roback, A. A., 155, 157
Robbins, R. H., 150, 159, 169, 177, 181
Robbins, T., 244
Roberts, A., 171

Robespiere, 202
Roof, W. C., 115
Rosen, A. S., 243
Rosen, B., 157
Ross, J. M., 132
Ross, L., 183, 187, 196
Rotenstreich, Nathan, 36, 37
Rubenstein, R. L., 184, 187
Rule, Margaret, 175, 176
Russell, D. S., 195
Ryan, Congressman Leo, 13, 186, 243–44
Ryan, Shannon Jo, 243–44

Samarin, W. J., 184
Sanford, N., 134
Sarbin, T. R., 162, 184
Satre, J. P., 100, 109, 111
Schein, E. H., 174
Schneier, I., 174
Schuman, H., 65
Selenick, S. T., 196
Selzer, Michael, 15, 228
Shakespeare, William, 55, 60
Shanab, M. E., 29
Shaver, K. G., 20
Shaw, Bernard, 240
Shelly, P. B., 25
Sheridan, C. L., 30
Sherif, C., 19
Sherif, M., 19
Shrycock, R. H., 167
Singer, Margaret Thaler, 230
Skinner, B. F., 45, 69, 70
Slaater, E., 156
Slavson, S. R., 84
Smith, W. D., 195
Smith-Rosenberg, C., 181, 198
Socrates, 60
Spanos, N. P., 18, 157, 162, 166, 175, 184
Speer, Albert, 213–227
Spitz, Rene, 94
Sprenger, James, 150, 154, 157
Stagg, F., 184
Stamm, H. J., 195
Stark, R., 114
Stekel, Wilhelm, 139
Strommen, M., 131
Summers, M., 150
Szasz, Thomas, 39, 40, 99

Talmon, Jacob L., 36, 64
Temkin, O., 195, 196

NAME INDEX

Thewlis, J., 138
Thomas, E. J., 162
Thomas, K., 159, 161, 171, 179
Thompson, R., 155
Throckmorton, Robert, 151
Tillyard, E. M. W., 161
Toner, P. J., 195
Tourney, G., 181
Trevor-Roper, Hugh, 215
Trilling, Lionel, 54
Turner, R. H., 162

Upham, C. D., 165, 176

Vallins, S., 71
van der Rohe, Mies, 220, 221, 222, 224
Veith, I., 155, 157, 183
von Mises, 202

Wallace, E. R., 108
Walsh, John, 160, 161
Walsh, Maurice, 17

Watson, D. L., 57
Wiener, B., 71
Werble, B., 143
Wesley, John, 57
White, J., 19
White, L., 60
Wieman, Regina W., 129
Wilkins, K., 181
Willard, S. A., 166, 175
Wilson, E., 195
Winnicott, D. W., 237
Wolpe, J., 69
Wooden, K., 229, 235
Woods, W., 168
Woodland, W. E., 164, 165
Wuthnow, R., 108

Yahya, K. A., 29

Zaretsky, I. I., 108
Zee, Hugo J., 18, 231
Zilboorg, G., 155, 196
Zimmerman, C. C., 126

SUBJECT INDEX

Age of colonialism, 58
Age of reason, 57–58
Agentic behavior, 31–32
Agentic state, 31, 32, 36, 40
Aggression and freedom, restriction of, 95–96
Alienation, People's Temple and, 237, 238–239
American Civil Liberties Union, 203
American Psychiatric Association, 203
American Psychological Association *Code of Ethics on Experimental Research*, 29
Amnesia, spontaneous, 152
"Anomia", 81
Antipsychiatry, 99
Anxiety, 32–33
Association, 20
Auschwitz, 27
Authority, compliance and power, theories about, 12–13
Authority vs. autonomy, control of conduct, 199–205

Balance theory, 67–68
Behavior modification, 69
Behavior theory, 69–70
Beyond Freedom and Dignity, 70
The Boy of Bilson, 162
Brainwashing, 26–27, 41, 236

Brookings Institute, 208, 209
Brown vs. the Board of Education, 51

Chance and Necessity, 90
Children of God, 125
Chinese communists, techniques of persuasion, 174
Church of Satan, 122
The Civilizing Function, 74
Cognitive theory, 66–67
Cohersive persuasion, 174
Collective education, 80
Collective superego, 80
Commission, 20
Compendium Maleficarum, 150, 152, 154
Compliance
  autonomous external, 143
  chance or necessity, 90
  culural and religious, 115–117
  ethics of, 50–53
  external and internal, 138
  between freedom and compulsion, 77–104
  to a group, 81
  healthy side of, 137–147
  internal, 143
  in the laboratory, 71
  politics of, 50–53
  psychology of, 50–53
  psychotherapy and, 72

SUBJECT INDEX

and religion, 107–134
or self-fulfillment?
the case of Albert Speer, 213–217
in service of fidelity and love, 143–44
in service of priorities and creativity, 145–46
and sex differences, 30
and sincerity, 50–74
social-psychological theories, 64–71
Compulsion (*see* Compliance? Between Freedom and Compulsion, 74–104)
Compulsion and freedom, 86
Compulsion and school systems, 93
Conduct, control of, 199–205
Conformity vs. compliance, 50–74
Conscience, 90
Control of conduct: authority vs. autonomy, 199–205
Control of expression, 58
Contracts vs. commands, 204
Counteranthropomorphism, 30
Creativity, compliance in service of, 145–46
Creativity and security, 101–102
Criminal Law Bulletin, 199
Criminal responsibility, 20
Cross-cultural studies, 29
Cults, religious, 120–126
Cultural compliance and religion, 115–117
Cultural evolutionism, 108
Cultural variation in demonic roles, 164
Cybernetic model, 31

Dachau, 27
Dean, John, summary of remarks, 206–212
Defense mechanism, 232, 234–235
Demonic possession: a social psychological analysis, 149–88
characteristics of, 149–153
convulsions, 150–51
increased intelligence, clairvoyance, and amnesia, 151–153
involuntariness, 153–54
other transcendent phenomena, 153
disease, from possession to, 181

exorcism (*see* Exorcism)
history, 195–96
hysteria, from possession to, 18–83
implications, 183–88
oral fixation, 158–60
as propoganda device, 180
psychiatric formulations and socially defined reality, 160–62
psychiatric interpretations, 154–61
social functions of, 175–183
exorcism and religious proselytizing, 177–80
witchcraft accusation, 175–77
social psychological interpretation, 162–82
cultural variation, 164
socialization into the demonic role, 162–75
witchcraft, 157–58
women, 198
Des Malades Mentales, 180
Developmental stages of responsibility, 20
Dissonance theory, 68–69
Divine Light Mission, 121
Don Quixote, 54–55

Education, freedom and compulsion in, 92
Education system, 84
Ego, 87, 133
"Ego morality", 132
Egocentric network, 118
Eichmann in Jerusalem, 33, 227
Escape from Freedom, 42
Essays on Contemporary Events, 38
Ethics, politics, and the psychology of compliance, 50–53
Evolutionary theories, 30–31
The Examination of John Walsh, 161
Existentialism, 109–110, 143
and the religious cult, 122
Exorcism, 164, 167
Jewish, 167, 196
as a propoganda device, 180
public, 170–72
and religious proselytizing, 177–80
Experiments, sequential nature of, 33
Expression, control of, 58
external compliance, autonomous, 143

Extrinsic and intrinsic institution, 139–41
"Extrinsic religion", 132

Family coalitions with the supernatural, 128
Family conflict as a projection of religious conflict, 130–31
Family of God, 125
The Family Lives its Religion, 129
Family, and religious compliance, 126–30
Fidelity and love, compliance in service of, 143–44
The Fight with the Shadow, 38
The Flies, 100
Ford Motor Company, 12
Forseeability, 20
Freedom and aggression, restriction of, 95–96
Freedom and compulsion, 74–104
in education, 92
Freedom in games, 97
Freedom of the mentally ill patient, 99
Freedom by reason and conscious, 89

General Theory of Value, 43
Germans Remember, 14
Gestalt psychology, 43
Ghost Dance cult, 27
Goethe's *Faust*, 38
Group behavior, 96
Group dynamic considerations, Guyana incident, 229–40
Group dynamics, cult members and, 240
"Group psychopathology", 184
"Groupthink", 240
Guilt, 27
Guyana, 13, 17, 26, 101, 107, 138, 184, 186, 229–44
Guyana incident, some group dynamic considerations, 229–41

Handsome Lake cult, 27
Hare Krishna, 121
Healthy side of compliance, 137–47
"Hillside Strangler", 184
Hitler's War, 15
Holocaust, 17, 36, 138
Homer's Thersites, 55

Hypnosis, 41
Hypophysealadrenocortical reactions, 96
Hysteria, 38
and demonic possession, 180–83

Identification, mutual, 232–233
I. G. Farben, 16, 17
Individual, religious compliance and, 131–34
Inner peace, search for, 243
Intention, 20
Internal compliance, 143
Internal Revenue Service, 207
Internalization, 52
Intimate psychological network, 118–119
"Intrinsic religion", 132
Iran, 83, 146

Jewish demonology, 195–96
Jewish exorcism, 167
Jonestown, 107, 184, 185–88, 229–40
and the apocalyptic world view, 185–86
Jordanian experiments, 29
Judaism, 140
Justification, 20

Ketman, 52–53
Kibbutz education, 80

Language of sincerity, 58–59
Law, human responsibility towards, 91
Leader, idealization of, 232–234
Legal responsibility, 20
Lever, 82–84
Liability, 20
Los Angeles Times, 244
Love and fidelity, compliance in service of, 43–44

Main Street, 116
Manson "family", 101
A Manual of Exorcism, 152, 164, 167
Mass psychosis, 38
Mayo Clinic, 17
Mechanism of compliance, 52
Mechanism of identification, 52
Messianic leaders, 26–27
Moral behavior, 133

Moral capacity, 133
Moral ego functions, 133
Moral liability, 20
The Most Strange and Admirable Discovery of the Three Witches of Warboys, 151, 153, 154
Motility, outside of inner motion, 94
My Lai, 21, 45
The Myth of Mental Illness, 39
Narcissism, 80
Nazi Germany, 14, 15, 16, 17, 18, 33–38, 42–45, 82, 213–218
Negligence, 20
Networks, 118
Neurophysiological conditions, dependence on, 88
New York Times, 243
New York Times Magazine, 228
Nineteen Eighty-Four, 11, 12, 59
Norms, conflict of, 77
The Nuremberg Mind, 228
Nuremberg trials, 214, 215, 217, 227

Obedience, 25, 28, 29, 30, 100
  Albert Speer and, 213–228
Obedience to authority, 30
On Liberty, 25
Oral fixation, demonic possession and, 158–160

Paranoid-schizoid defenses, 234
Past, influence of, 88
Patricidal hero, 239
Pattison Psychological Inventory, 119
Pentagon Papers, 208
People's Temple, 27, 185–88, 229–40, 243–44
Persuasion, 63
Persuasion theory, 65–67
Phaidon, 60
Physiological dysfunction, social role formation and, 197
The Place of Value in a World of Facts, 43
Plato's *Dialogues*, 60
Politics of compliance, 50–63
Portrait of the Artist as a Young Man, 59
Possession (*see* Demonic possession)
Power, control of conduct, 202–204
Propaganda devices, demonic possession and exorcism as, 180

Protecting group, 85
Psychiatric interpretation of demonic possession, 154–61
Psychoanalysis, point of view of, 87
Psychology of compliance, 50–53
Psychotherapy and compliance, 72
Psychotropic drugs, 99

"Queen Mab", 25

Realms of Value, 43
Reciprocal aggression, 96
Regulation of social relations, principles of, 204–205
Relationships, elements of, 119
Religion and compliance, 107–134
  cultural compliance, 115–117
  definition of religion, 114
  the family and, 126–130
  historical perspectives, 107–113
  and the individual, 131–134
  and social network compliance, 118–125
Religion, dimensions of, 114
Religious conflict, as projection of family conflict, 130
Religious Systems and Psychotherapy, 117
Religious youth cults, 120–126
  alternative to family, 122

Self-experience in groups, 84
Self-fulfillment of compliance, case of Albert Speer, 213–227
Sex difference and compliance, 30
Sincerity
  compliance and conformity in age of, 50–53
  and individualism, 53–55
  language of, 58–59
  religion and politics of, 55–58
Situational etiquette, 33
Social control, 61
Social ego, 16
Social functions of demonic possession, 175–86
Social network, 118
Social network compliance, religion and, 118–125
Social psychological analysis of demonic possession, 149–88
Social relations, principles for regulation of, 204–205

Social psychological interpretation of demonic possession, 162–82
Social-psychological theories, 64–71
Social role formulation, and physiological dysfunction, 197
Socialization onto the demonic role, 162–75
Socially defined reality, 160
"Son of Sam", 184
Sophism, 60
Space restriction, 96–97
Spandau prison, 227
Speer, Albert, case of, 213–228
  Albert Speer, the Great Time Server?, 228
  Spandau, the Secret Diaries, 228
Spoon River Anthology, 116
Suggestion, 42
Superego, 79–80, 132, 232, 235, 237
Supernaturalism, 112
Symbolic interaction, person perception and, 70

Theosphy, 122
Therapeutic state, 203, 204
Third Reich (*see* Nazi Germany)
The Thought and Character of William James, 44

Thought control, 26–27
"Total institution", 236
Totalitarian democracy, 64
Transference, 42
Transitional phenomenon, 237–38
Treatise on Politics, 45

Unhealthy compliance, basis for, 142
United States Department of Justice, 203

Vietnam, 13, 21
Vietnam Cao Movement, 27

Wannsee Conference, 34, 35
Watergate, 206–212
Witchcraft, accusations and possession, 175–77
Witchcraft, demonic possession and, 157–58
Women, demonic possession and, 198
Wotan, 37, 38

Yad Vashem, 36
Youth cults, 120–126